# CASANOVA
# LUXURIA

## MATT FRACTION
## GABRIEL BÁ

**colors by Cris Peter**
**letters by Dustin Harbin**

**CASANOVA VOL. 1: LUXURIA.** Contains material originally published in magazine form as CASANOVA #1-7 and CASANOVA: LUXURIA #1-4. First printing 2011. ISBN# 978-0-7851-4862-3. Published by MARVEL WORLDWIDE, INC., a subsidiary of MARVEL ENTERTAINMENT, LLC. OFFICE OF PUBLICATION: 135 West 50th Street, New York, NY 10020. Copyright © 2006, 2007, 2010, and 2011 MILKFED CRIMINAL MASTERMINDS, INC. All rights reserved. $14.99 per copy in the U.S. and $16.99 in Canada (GST #R127032852); Canadian Agreement #40668537. "Casanova" and all characters featured herein and the distinctive names and likenesses thereof, and all related indicia are trademarks of MILKFED CRIMINAL MASTERMINDS, INC. No similarity between any of the names, characters, persons, and/or institutions in this magazine with those of any living or dead person or institution is intended, and any such similarity that may exist is purely coincidental. ICON and the Icon logo are trademarks of Marvel Characters, Inc. **Printed in the USA. Manufactured between 12/10/10 and 12/29/10 by QUAD/GRAPHICS, DUBUQUE, IA, USA.**

Representation: Law Offices of Harris M. Miller II, P.C.

10 9 8 7 6 5 4 3 2 1

ICON Edition

| | |
|---|---|
| Editor | Alejandro Arbona |
| Senior Editor | Stephen Wacker |
| Collection Editor | Jennifer Grünwald |

book design
**Gabriel Bá**

Matt Fraction:
For my friend Héctor Sebastián Casanova
who had cancer when I started writing this
and didn't when I stopped.
Life is Grand.

Gabriel Bá:
Dedicated to Laerte Coutinho,
whose images live in my head and have
inspired me throughout this series.

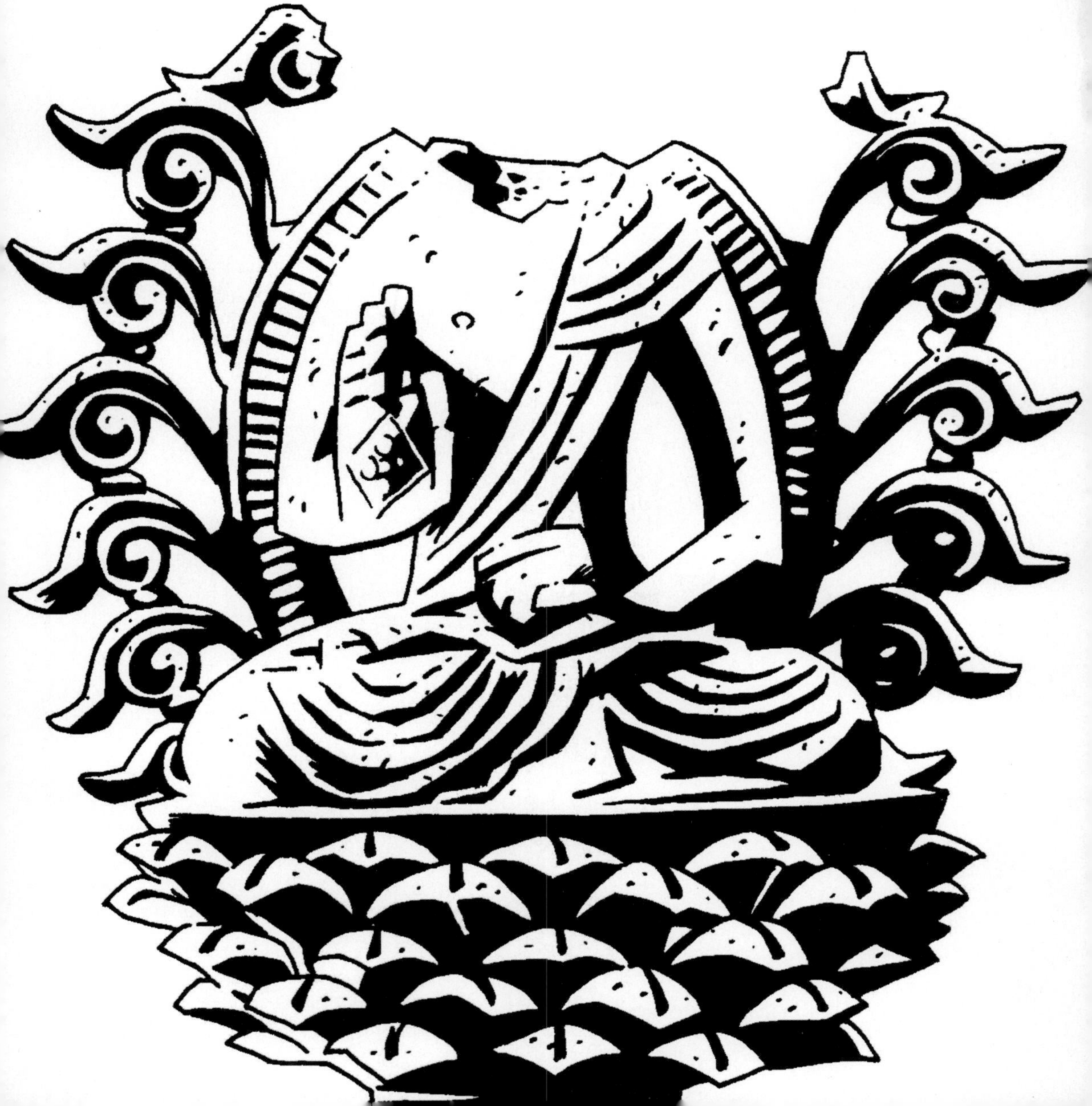

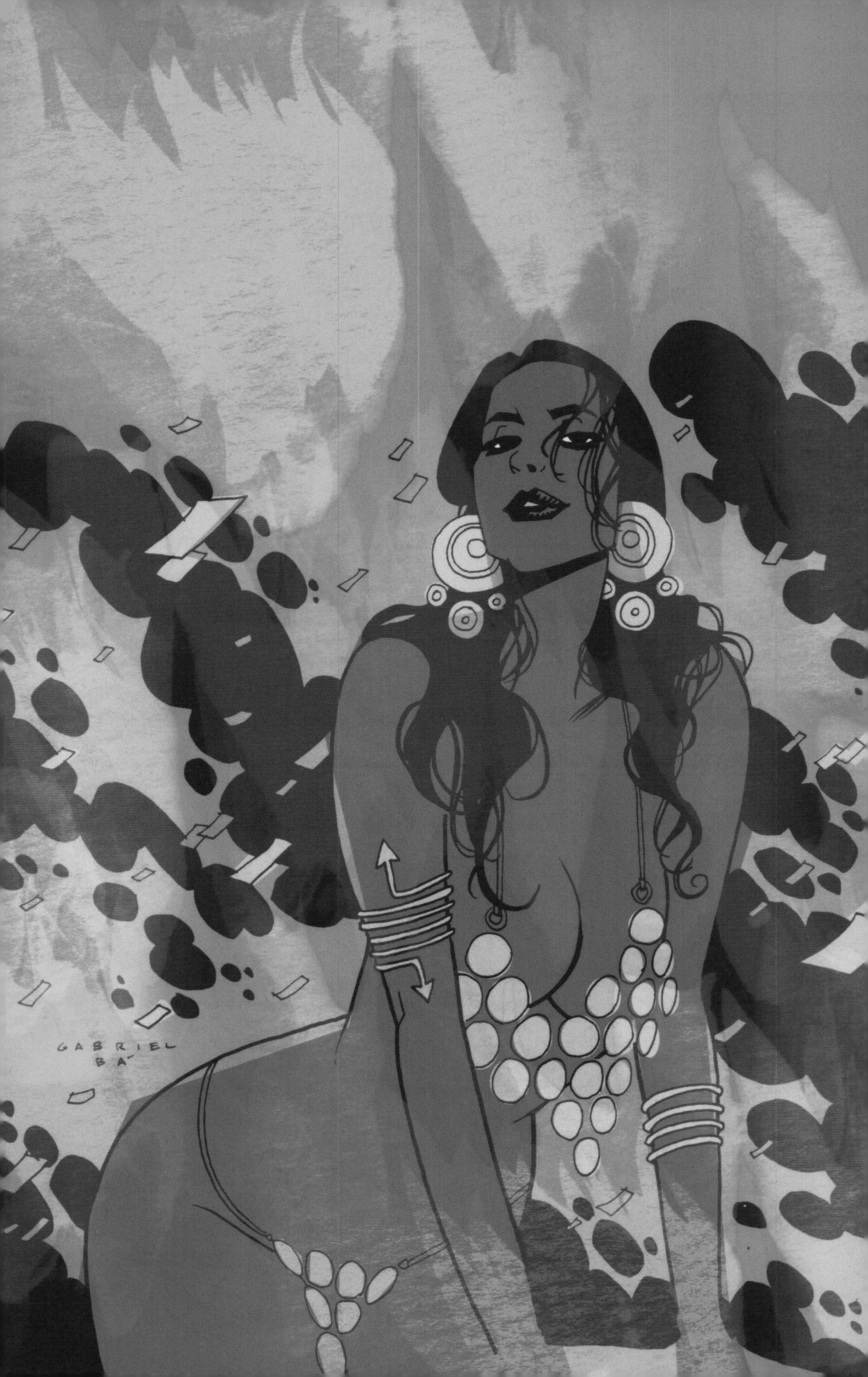
GABRIEL BÁ

"Quantum mechanics
forbids a single history."
Thomas Hertog

"... My parents... don't worry in the
least about their own insignificance;
they don't give a damn about it...
While I... I feel only
boredom and anger."
Ivan Turgenev
FATHERS AND SONS (1862)

"Boys, Girls, Men, Women!
The world is on FIRE
Serve the LORD
and You Can Have These Prizes!"
Ad on the back cover of
WEIRD SCIENCE-FANTASY #24
June 1954

# CHAPTER 1
# EXECUTION DAYS

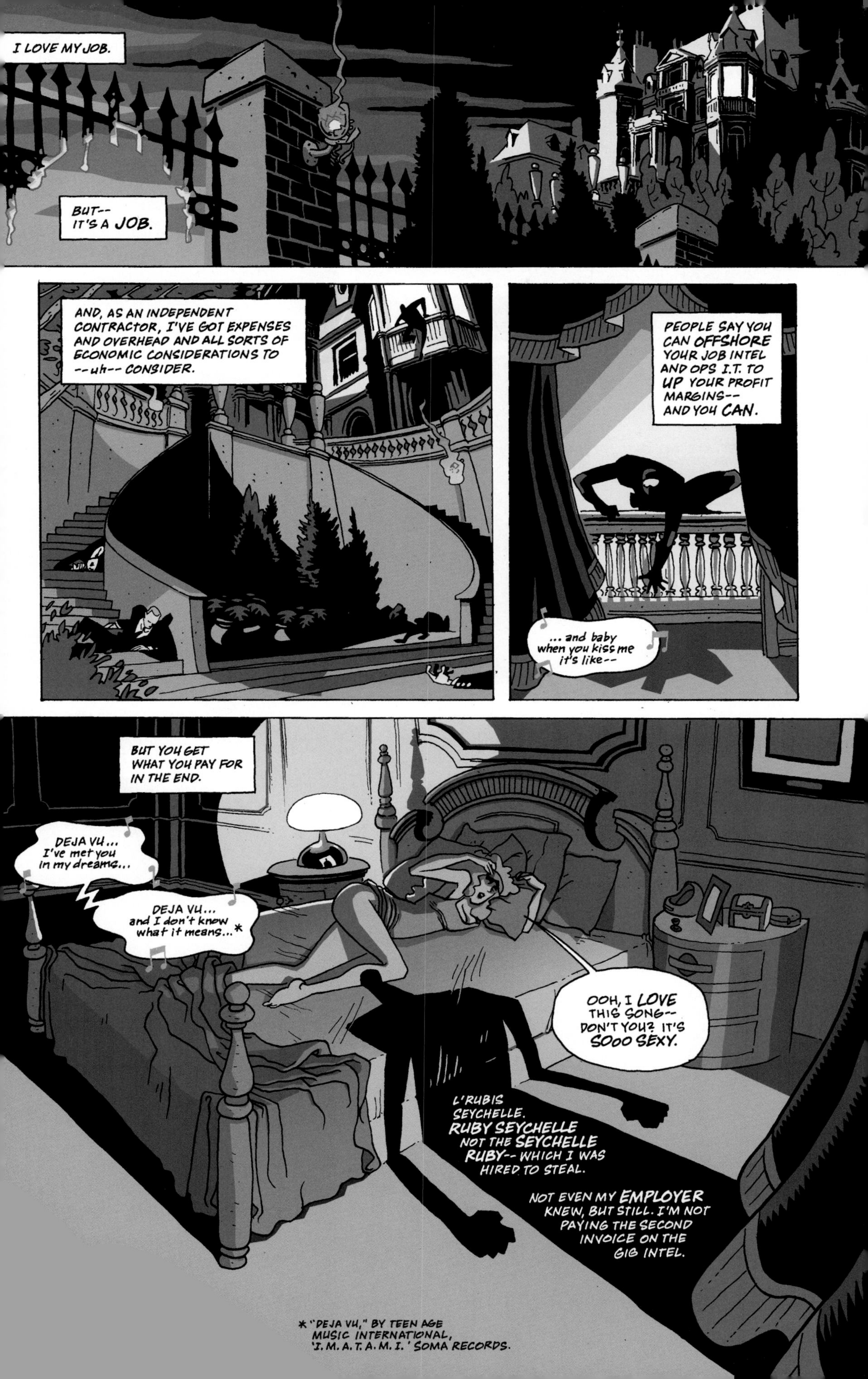

I LOVE MY JOB.
BUT-- IT'S A JOB.
AND, AS AN INDEPENDENT CONTRACTOR, I'VE GOT EXPENSES AND OVERHEAD AND ALL SORTS OF ECONOMIC CONSIDERATIONS TO --uh-- CONSIDER.
PEOPLE SAY YOU CAN OFFSHORE YOUR JOB INTEL AND OPS I.T. TO UP YOUR PROFIT MARGINS-- AND YOU CAN.
... and baby when you kiss me it's like--
BUT YOU GET WHAT YOU PAY FOR IN THE END.
DEJA VU... I've met you in my dreams...
DEJA VU... and I don't know what it means...*
OOH, I LOVE THIS SONG-- DON'T YOU? IT'S SOOO SEXY.
L'RUBIS SEYCHELLE. RUBY SEYCHELLE NOT THE SEYCHELLE RUBY-- WHICH I WAS HIRED TO STEAL.
NOT EVEN MY EMPLOYER KNEW, BUT STILL. I'M NOT PAYING THE SECOND INVOICE ON THE GIG INTEL.
* "DEJA VU," BY TEEN AGE MUSIC INTERNATIONAL, 'I.M.A.T.A.M.I.' SOMA RECORDS.

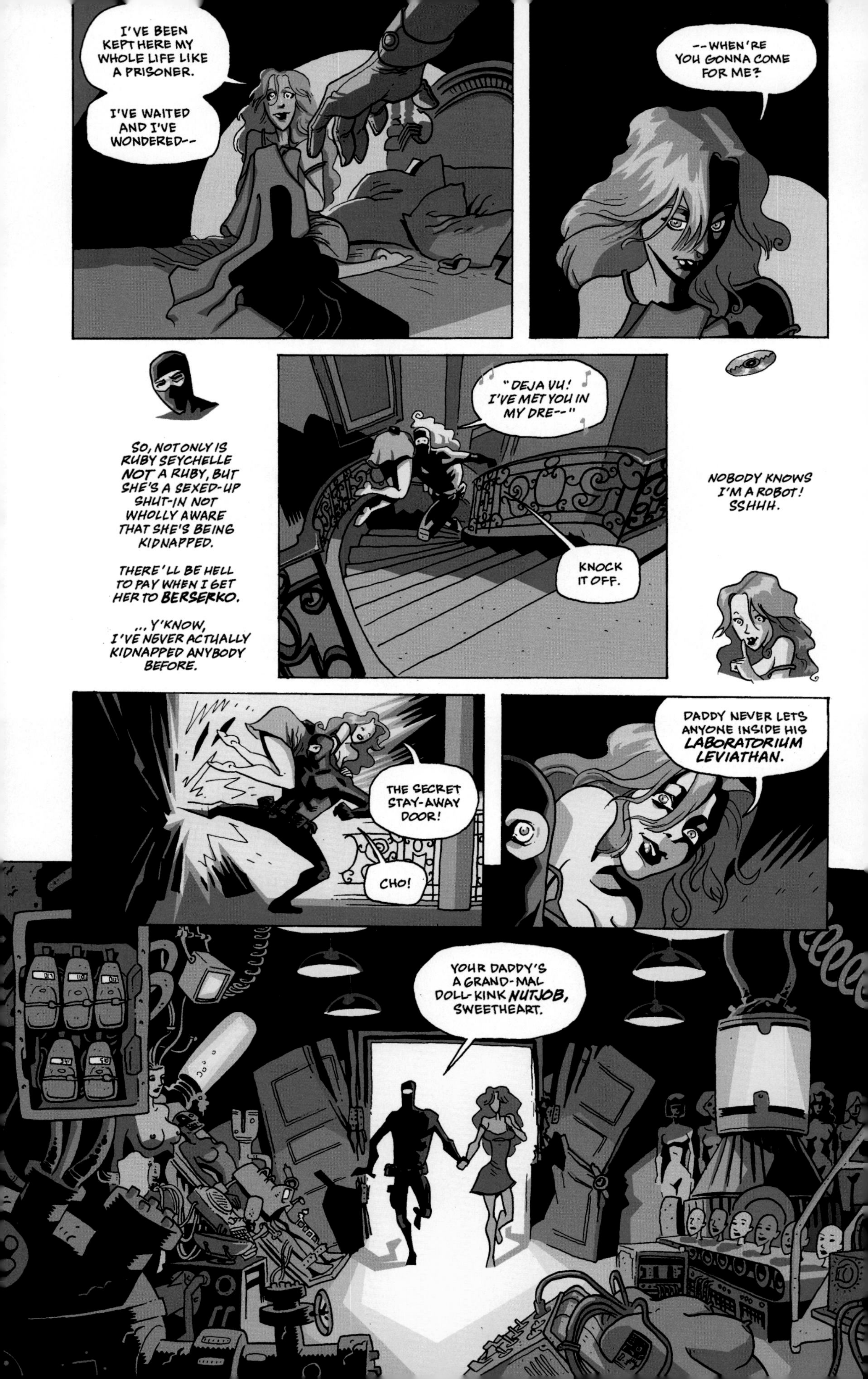
I'VE BEEN KEPT HERE MY WHOLE LIFE LIKE A PRISONER.
I'VE WAITED AND I'VE WONDERED--
--WHEN'RE YOU GONNA COME FOR ME?
SO, NOT ONLY IS RUBY SEYCHELLE NOT A RUBY, BUT SHE'S A SEXED-UP SHUT-IN NOT WHOLLY AWARE THAT SHE'S BEING KIDNAPPED.
THERE'LL BE HELL TO PAY WHEN I GET HER TO BERSERKO.
...Y'KNOW, I'VE NEVER ACTUALLY KIDNAPPED ANYBODY BEFORE.
"DEJA VU! I'VE MET YOU IN MY DRE--"
KNOCK IT OFF.
NOBODY KNOWS I'M A ROBOT! SSHHH.
THE SECRET STAY-AWAY DOOR!
CHO!
DADDY NEVER LETS ANYONE INSIDE HIS LABORATORIUM LEVIATHAN.
YOUR DADDY'S A GRAND-MAL DOLL-KINK NUTJOB, SWEETHEART.

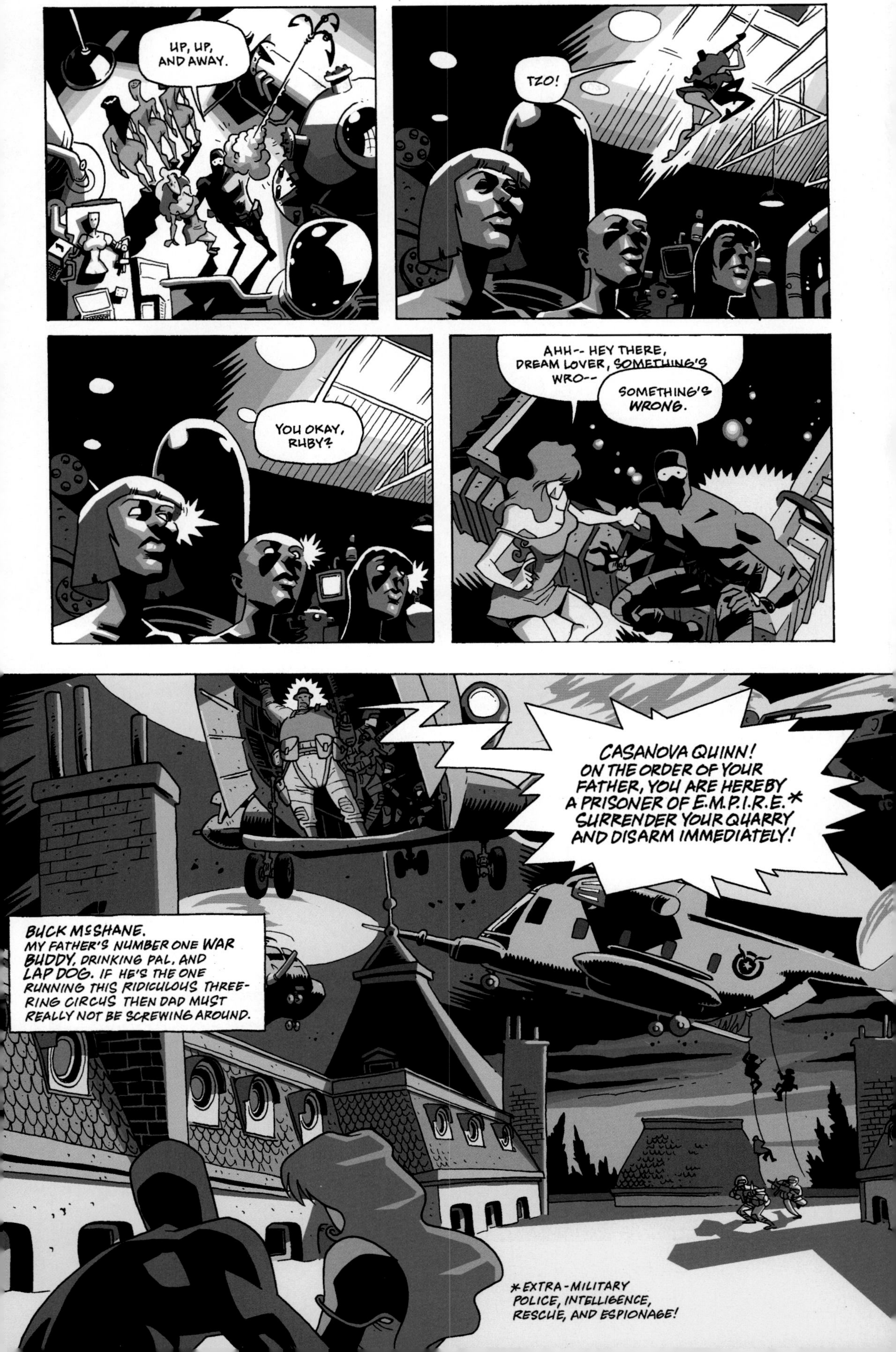
UP, UP, AND AWAY.
TZO!
YOU OKAY, RUBY?
AHH-- HEY THERE, DREAM LOVER, SOMETHING'S WRO--
SOMETHING'S WRONG.
CASANOVA QUINN! ON THE ORDER OF YOUR FATHER, YOU ARE HEREBY A PRISONER OF E.M.P.I.R.E.* SURRENDER YOUR QUARRY AND DISARM IMMEDIATELY!
BUCK McSHANE. MY FATHER'S NUMBER ONE WAR BUDDY, DRINKING PAL, AND LAP DOG. IF HE'S THE ONE RUNNING THIS RIDICULOUS THREE-RING CIRCUS THEN DAD MUST REALLY NOT BE SCREWING AROUND.
*EXTRA-MILITARY POLICE, INTELLIGENCE, RESCUE, AND ESPIONAGE!

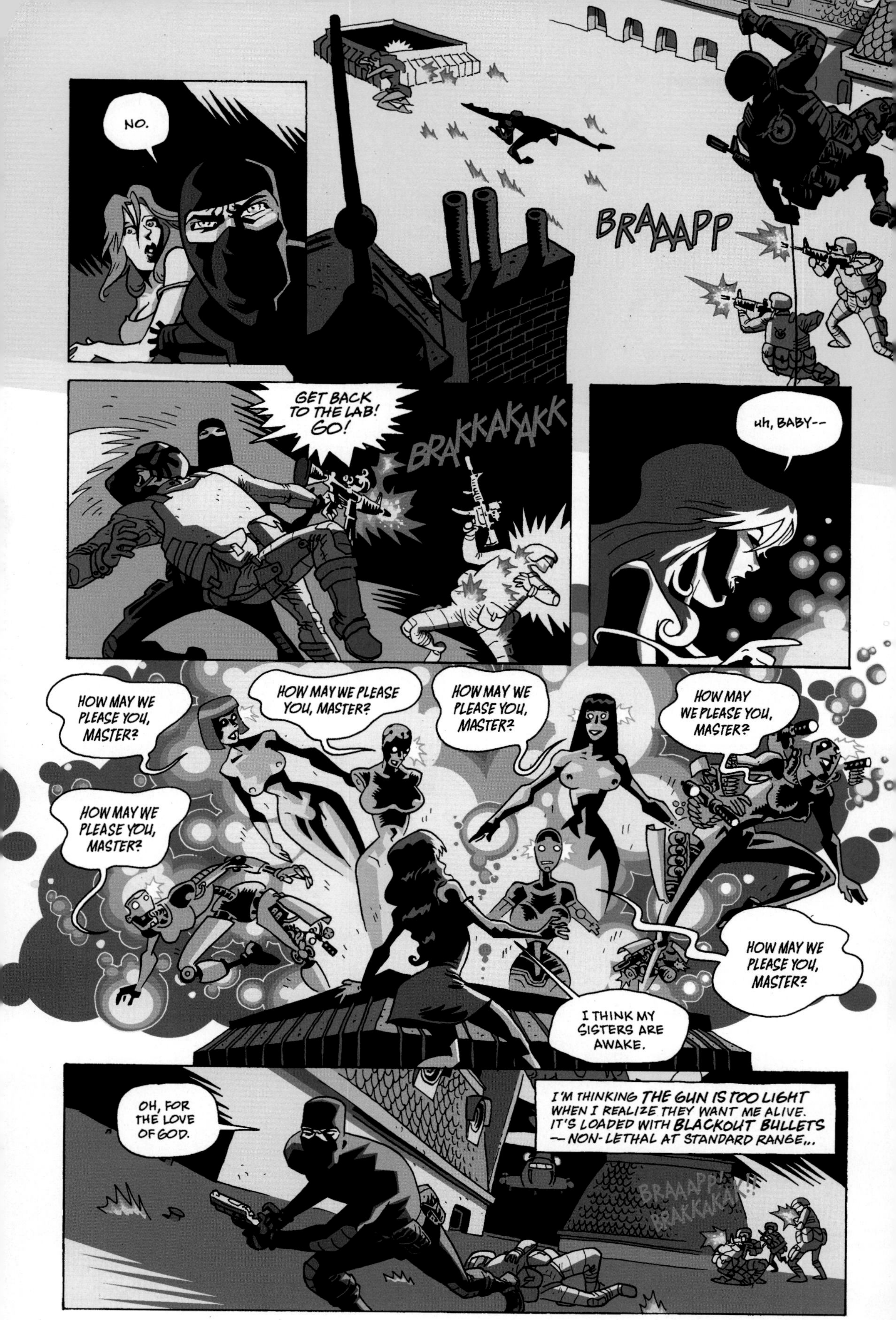
NO.
BRAAAPP
GET BACK TO THE LAB! GO!
BRAKKAKAKK
uh, BABY--
HOW MAY WE PLEASE YOU, MASTER?
HOW MAY WE PLEASE YOU, MASTER?
HOW MAY WE PLEASE YOU, MASTER?
HOW MAY WE PLEASE YOU, MASTER?
HOW MAY WE PLEASE YOU, MASTER?
HOW MAY WE PLEASE YOU, MASTER?
I THINK MY SISTERS ARE AWAKE.
OH, FOR THE LOVE OF GOD.
I'M THINKING THE GUN IS TOO LIGHT WHEN I REALIZE THEY WANT ME ALIVE. IT'S LOADED WITH BLACKOUT BULLETS -- NON-LETHAL AT STANDARD RANGE...
BRAAAPP BRAKKAKAK!!

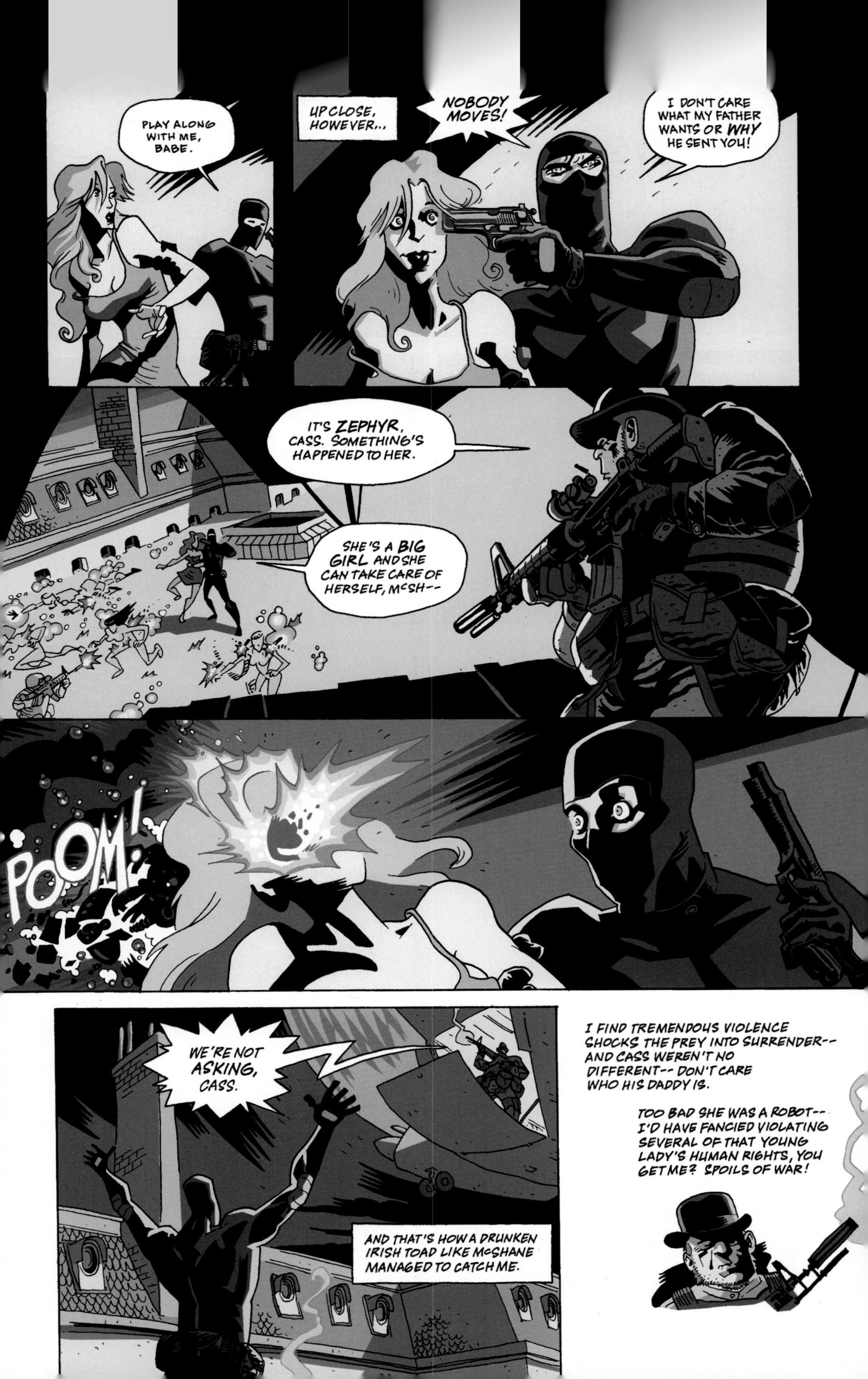
PLAY ALONG WITH ME, BABE.
UP CLOSE, HOWEVER...
NOBODY MOVES!
I DON'T CARE WHAT MY FATHER WANTS OR WHY HE SENT YOU!
IT'S ZEPHYR, CASS. SOMETHING'S HAPPENED TO HER.
SHE'S A BIG GIRL AND SHE CAN TAKE CARE OF HERSELF, McSH--
POOM!
WE'RE NOT ASKING, CASS.
AND THAT'S HOW A DRUNKEN IRISH TOAD LIKE McSHANE MANAGED TO CATCH ME.
I FIND TREMENDOUS VIOLENCE SHOCKS THE PREY INTO SURRENDER-- AND CASS WEREN'T NO DIFFERENT-- DON'T CARE WHO HIS DADDY IS.
TOO BAD SHE WAS A ROBOT-- I'D HAVE FANCIED VIOLATING SEVERAL OF THAT YOUNG LADY'S HUMAN RIGHTS, YOU GET ME? SPOILS OF WAR!

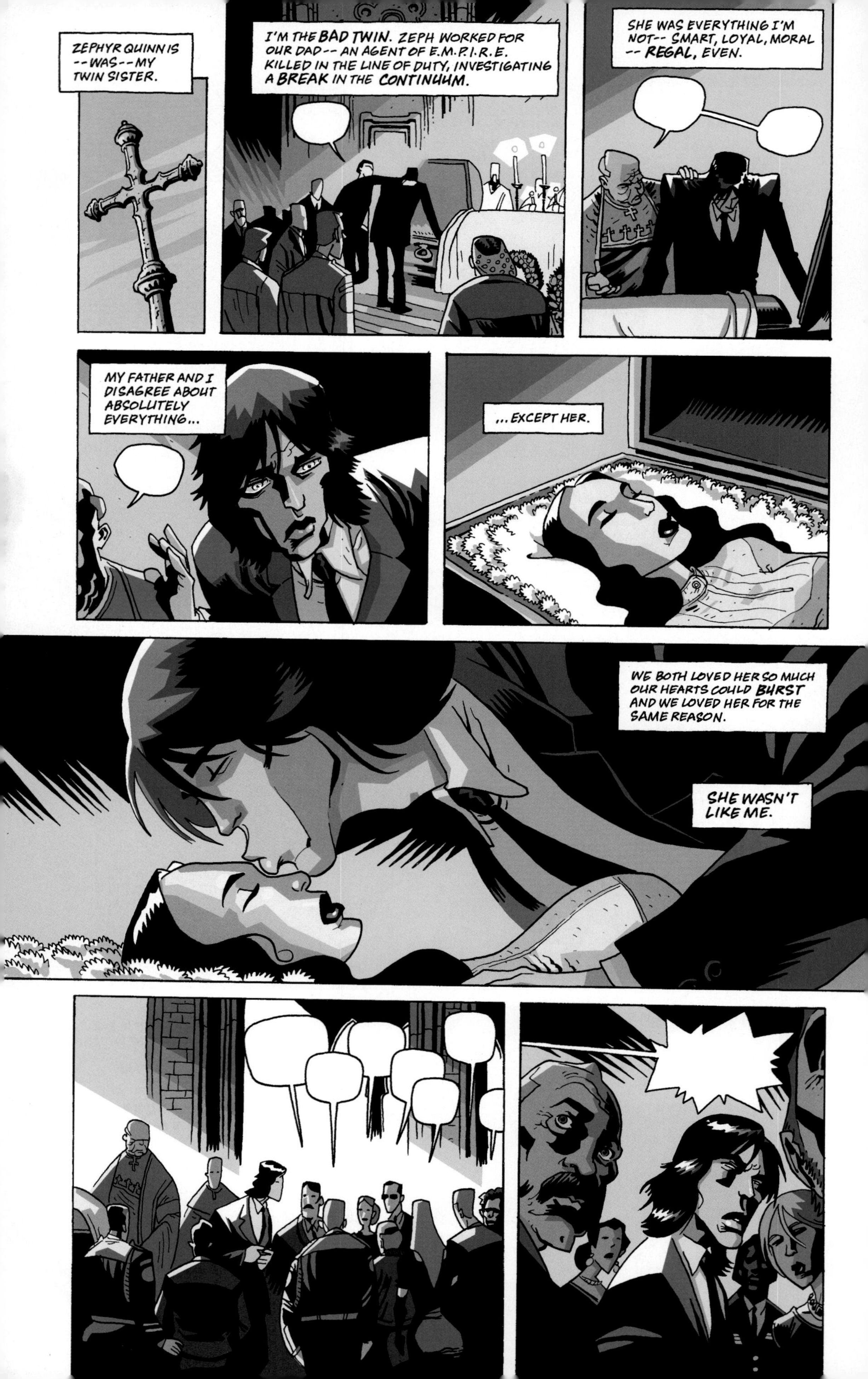
ZEPHYR QUINN IS --WAS-- MY TWIN SISTER.
I'M THE BAD TWIN. ZEPH WORKED FOR OUR DAD-- AN AGENT OF E.M.P.I.R.E. KILLED IN THE LINE OF DUTY, INVESTIGATING A BREAK IN THE CONTINUUM.
SHE WAS EVERYTHING I'M NOT-- SMART, LOYAL, MORAL -- REGAL, EVEN.
MY FATHER AND I DISAGREE ABOUT ABSOLUTELY EVERYTHING...
...EXCEPT HER.
WE BOTH LOVED HER SO MUCH OUR HEARTS COULD BURST AND WE LOVED HER FOR THE SAME REASON.
SHE WASN'T LIKE ME.

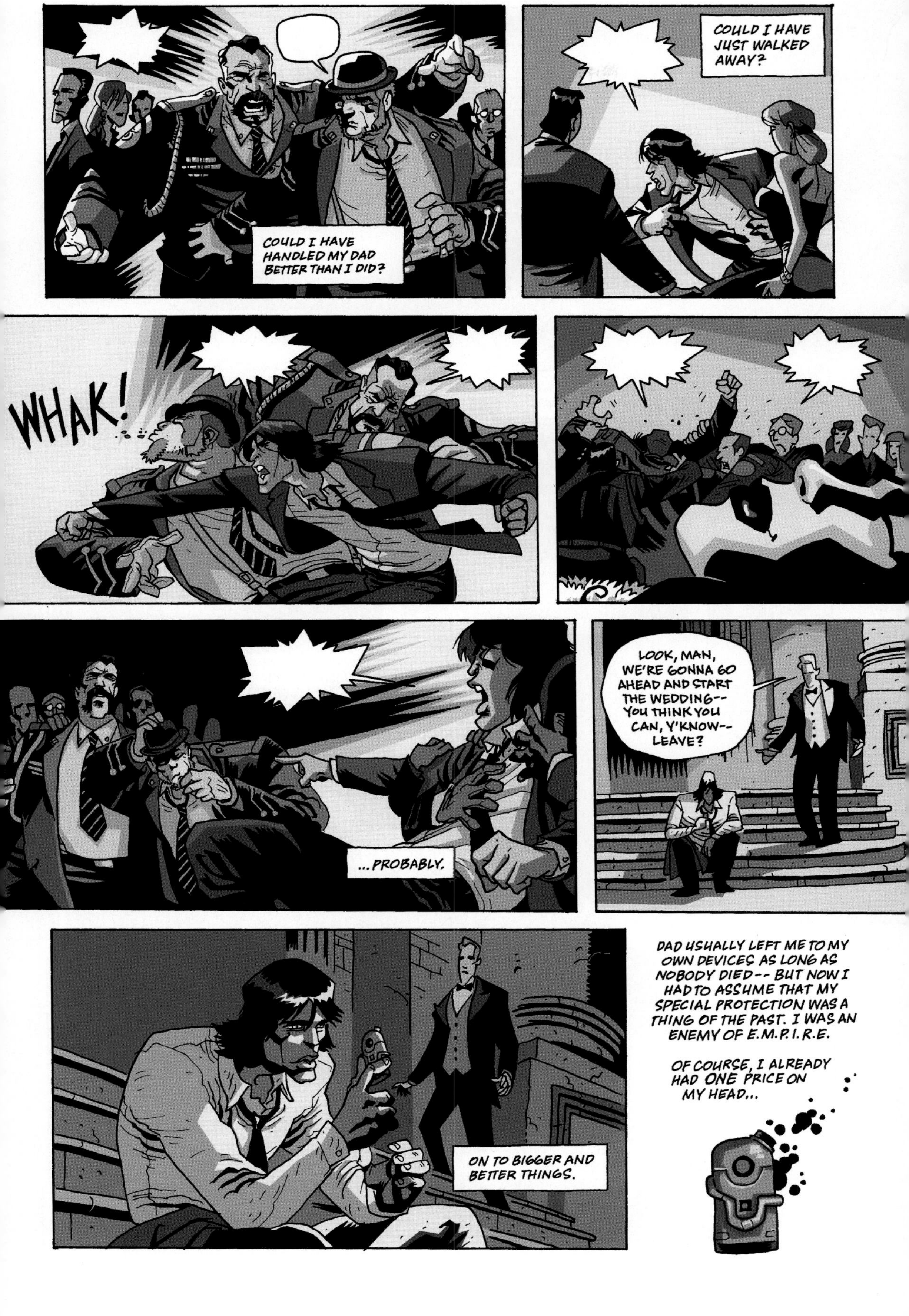
COULD I HAVE HANDLED MY DAD BETTER THAN I DID?
COULD I HAVE JUST WALKED AWAY?
WHAK!
...PROBABLY.
LOOK, MAN, WE'RE GONNA GO AHEAD AND START THE WEDDING-- YOU THINK YOU CAN, Y'KNOW-- LEAVE?
ON TO BIGGER AND BETTER THINGS.
DAD USUALLY LEFT ME TO MY OWN DEVICES AS LONG AS NOBODY DIED-- BUT NOW I HAD TO ASSUME THAT MY SPECIAL PROTECTION WAS A THING OF THE PAST. I WAS AN ENEMY OF E.M.P.I.R.E.
OF COURSE, I ALREADY HAD ONE PRICE ON MY HEAD...

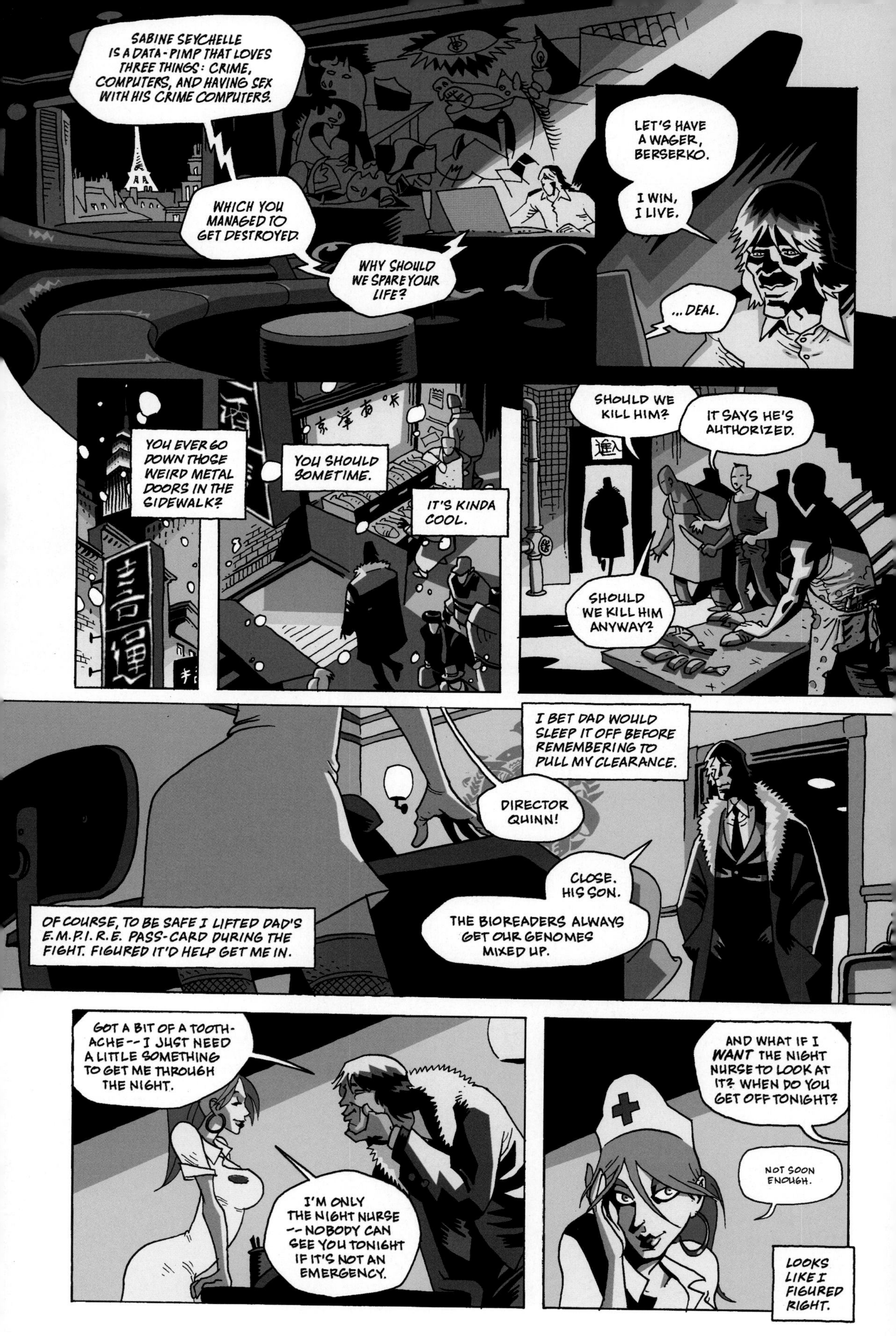
SABINE SEYCHELLE IS A DATA-PIMP THAT LOVES THREE THINGS: CRIME, COMPUTERS, AND HAVING SEX WITH HIS CRIME COMPUTERS.
WHICH YOU MANAGED TO GET DESTROYED.
WHY SHOULD WE SPARE YOUR LIFE?
LET'S HAVE A WAGER, BERSERKO.
I WIN, I LIVE.
...DEAL.
YOU EVER GO DOWN THOSE WEIRD METAL DOORS IN THE SIDEWALK?
YOU SHOULD SOMETIME.
IT'S KINDA COOL.
SHOULD WE KILL HIM?
IT SAYS HE'S AUTHORIZED.
SHOULD WE KILL HIM ANYWAY?
I BET DAD WOULD SLEEP IT OFF BEFORE REMEMBERING TO PULL MY CLEARANCE.
DIRECTOR QUINN!
CLOSE. HIS SON.
THE BIOREADERS ALWAYS GET OUR GENOMES MIXED UP.
OF COURSE, TO BE SAFE I LIFTED DAD'S E.M.P.I.R.E. PASS-CARD DURING THE FIGHT. FIGURED IT'D HELP GET ME IN.
GOT A BIT OF A TOOTH-ACHE--I JUST NEED A LITTLE SOMETHING TO GET ME THROUGH THE NIGHT.
I'M ONLY THE NIGHT NURSE--NOBODY CAN SEE YOU TONIGHT IF IT'S NOT AN EMERGENCY.
AND WHAT IF I WANT THE NIGHT NURSE TO LOOK AT IT? WHEN DO YOU GET OFF TONIGHT?
NOT SOON ENOUGH.
LOOKS LIKE I FIGURED RIGHT.

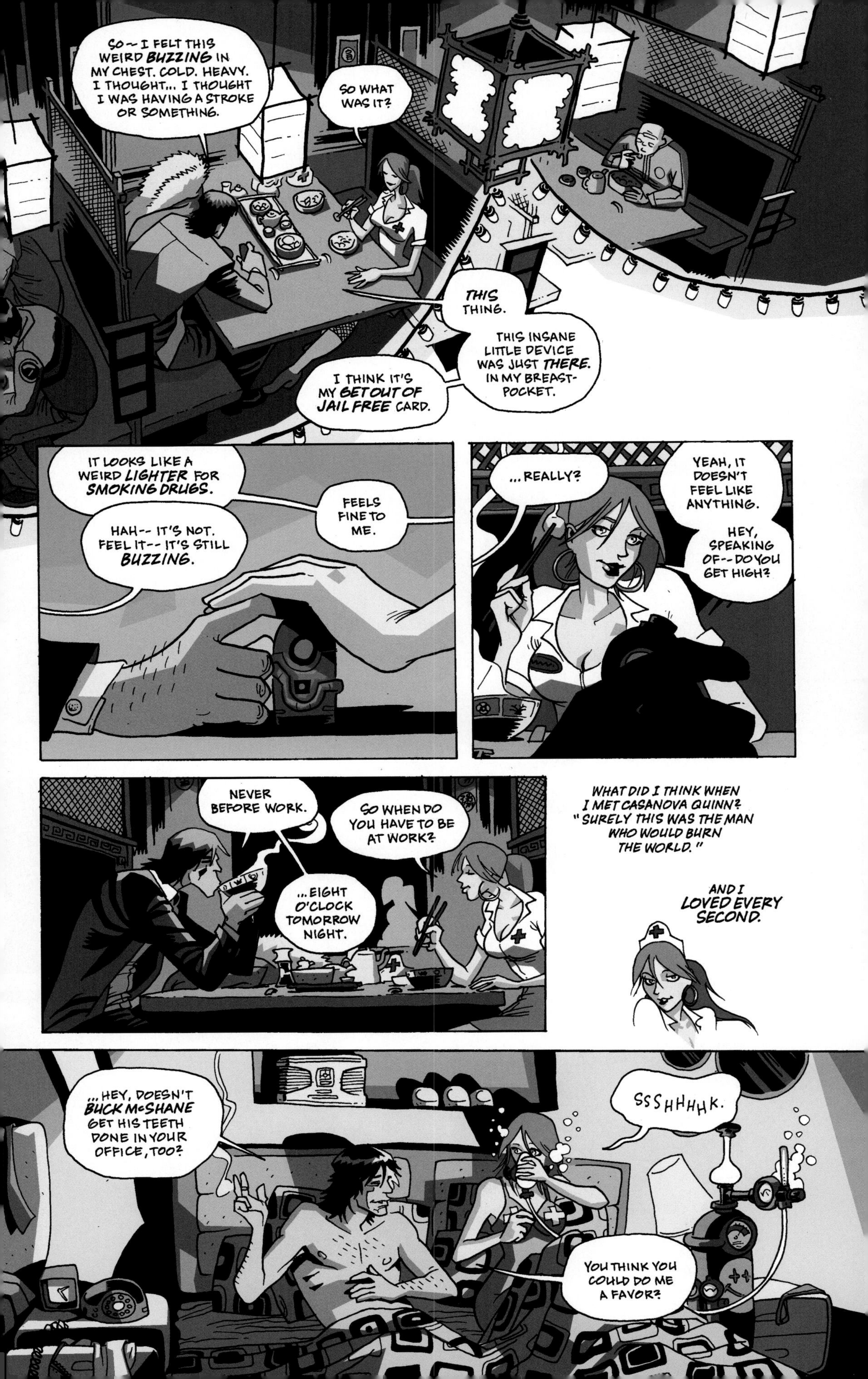

SO -- I FELT THIS WEIRD BUZZING IN MY CHEST. COLD. HEAVY. I THOUGHT... I THOUGHT I WAS HAVING A STROKE OR SOMETHING.
SO WHAT WAS IT?
THIS THING.
THIS INSANE LITTLE DEVICE WAS JUST THERE. IN MY BREAST-POCKET.
I THINK IT'S MY GET OUT OF JAIL FREE CARD.
IT LOOKS LIKE A WEIRD LIGHTER FOR SMOKING DRUGS.
FEELS FINE TO ME.
HAH-- IT'S NOT. FEEL IT-- IT'S STILL BUZZING.
...REALLY?
YEAH, IT DOESN'T FEEL LIKE ANYTHING.
HEY, SPEAKING OF--DO YOU GET HIGH?
NEVER BEFORE WORK.
SO WHEN DO YOU HAVE TO BE AT WORK?
...EIGHT O'CLOCK TOMORROW NIGHT.
WHAT DID I THINK WHEN I MET CASANOVA QUINN? "SURELY THIS WAS THE MAN WHO WOULD BURN THE WORLD."
AND I LOVED EVERY SECOND.
...HEY, DOESN'T BUCK McSHANE GET HIS TEETH DONE IN YOUR OFFICE, TOO?
SSSHHHHK.
YOU THINK YOU COULD DO ME A FAVOR?

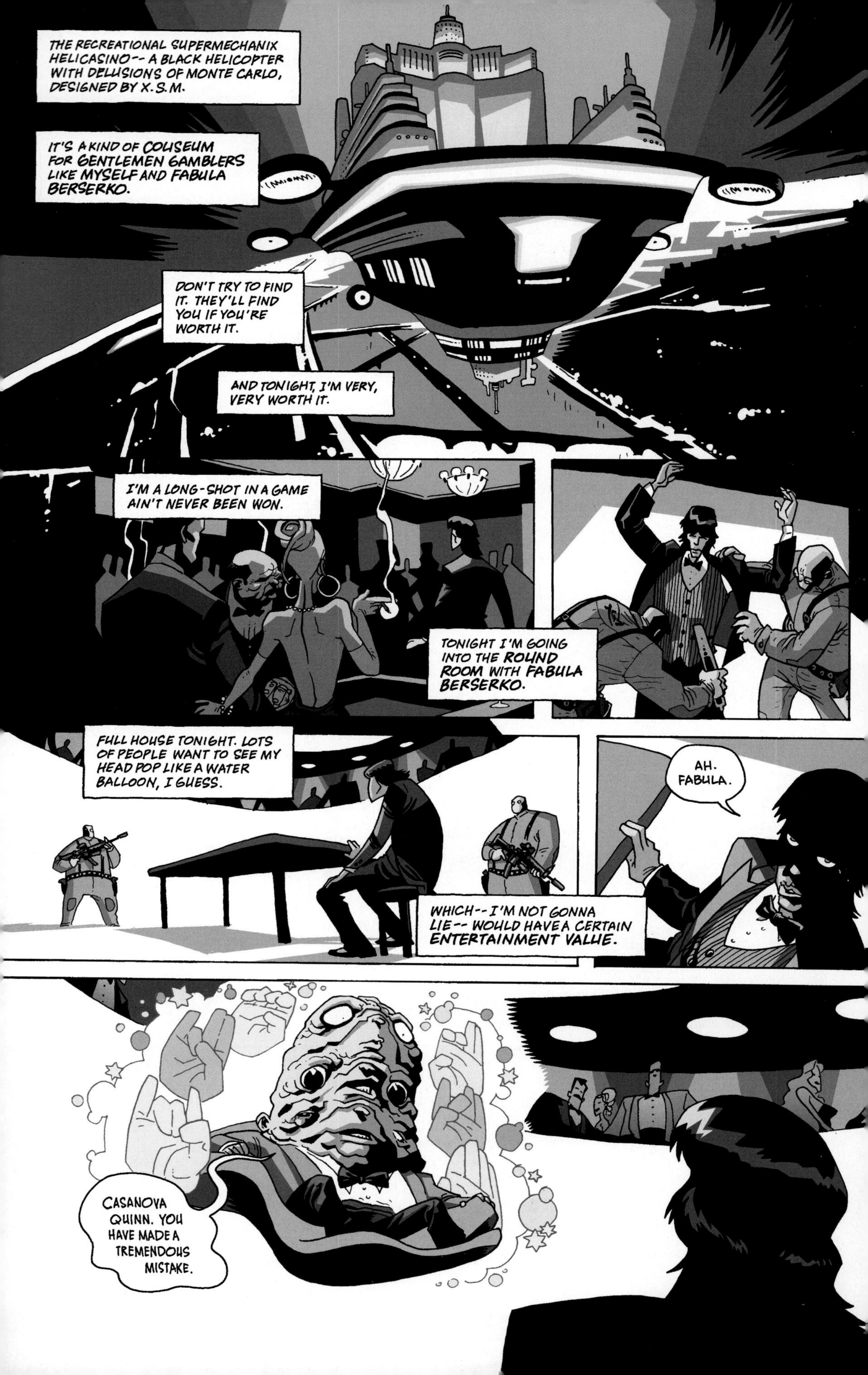
THE RECREATIONAL SUPERMECHANIX HELICASINO-- A BLACK HELICOPTER WITH DELUSIONS OF MONTE CARLO, DESIGNED BY X.S.M.
IT'S A KIND OF COLISEUM FOR GENTLEMEN GAMBLERS LIKE MYSELF AND FABULA BERSERKO.
DON'T TRY TO FIND IT. THEY'LL FIND YOU IF YOU'RE WORTH IT.
AND TONIGHT, I'M VERY, VERY WORTH IT.
I'M A LONG-SHOT IN A GAME AIN'T NEVER BEEN WON.
TONIGHT I'M GOING INTO THE ROUND ROOM WITH FABULA BERSERKO.
FULL HOUSE TONIGHT. LOTS OF PEOPLE WANT TO SEE MY HEAD POP LIKE A WATER BALLOON, I GUESS.
WHICH-- I'M NOT GONNA LIE-- WOULD HAVE A CERTAIN ENTERTAINMENT VALUE.
AH. FABULA.
CASANOVA QUINN. YOU HAVE MADE A TREMENDOUS MISTAKE.

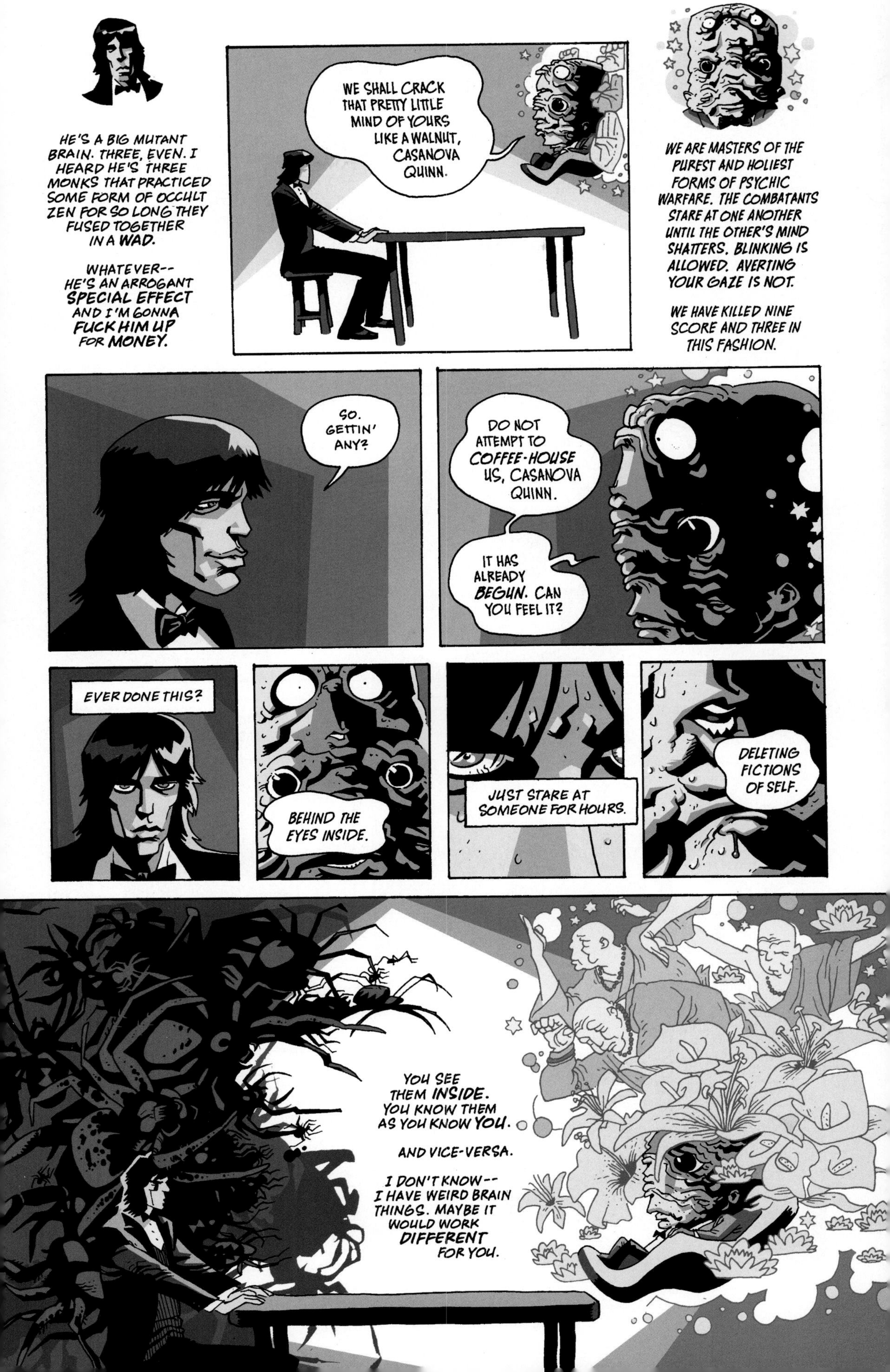
HE'S A BIG MUTANT BRAIN. THREE, EVEN. I HEARD HE'S THREE MONKS THAT PRACTICED SOME FORM OF OCCULT ZEN FOR SO LONG THEY FUSED TOGETHER IN A WAD.
WHATEVER-- HE'S AN ARROGANT SPECIAL EFFECT AND I'M GONNA FUCK HIM UP FOR MONEY.
WE SHALL CRACK THAT PRETTY LITTLE MIND OF YOURS LIKE A WALNUT, CASANOVA QUINN.
WE ARE MASTERS OF THE PUREST AND HOLIEST FORMS OF PSYCHIC WARFARE. THE COMBATANTS STARE AT ONE ANOTHER UNTIL THE OTHER'S MIND SHATTERS. BLINKING IS ALLOWED. AVERTING YOUR GAZE IS NOT.
WE HAVE KILLED NINE SCORE AND THREE IN THIS FASHION.
SO. GETTIN' ANY?
DO NOT ATTEMPT TO COFFEE-HOUSE US, CASANOVA QUINN.
IT HAS ALREADY BEGUN. CAN YOU FEEL IT?
EVER DONE THIS?
BEHIND THE EYES INSIDE.
JUST STARE AT SOMEONE FOR HOURS.
DELETING FICTIONS OF SELF.
YOU SEE THEM INSIDE. YOU KNOW THEM AS YOU KNOW YOU.
AND VICE-VERSA.
I DON'T KNOW-- I HAVE WEIRD BRAIN THINGS. MAYBE IT WOULD WORK DIFFERENT FOR YOU.

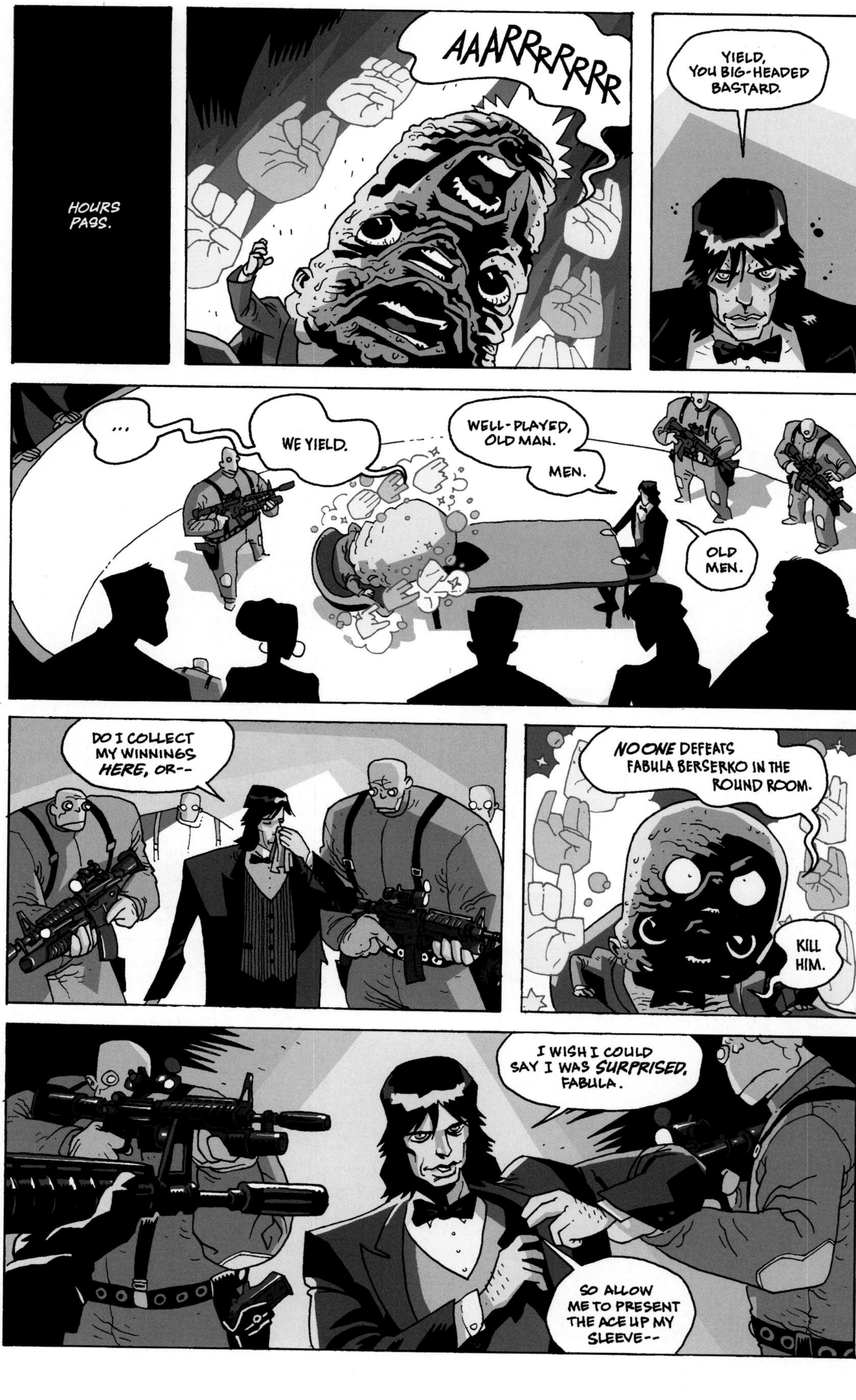
HOURS PASS.
AAARRRRRRR
YIELD, YOU BIG-HEADED BASTARD.
...
WE YIELD.
WELL-PLAYED, OLD MAN.
MEN.
OLD MEN.
DO I COLLECT MY WINNINGS HERE, OR--
NO ONE DEFEATS FABULA BERSERKO IN THE ROUND ROOM.
KILL HIM.
I WISH I COULD SAY I WAS SURPRISED, FABULA.
SO ALLOW ME TO PRESENT THE ACE UP MY SLEEVE--

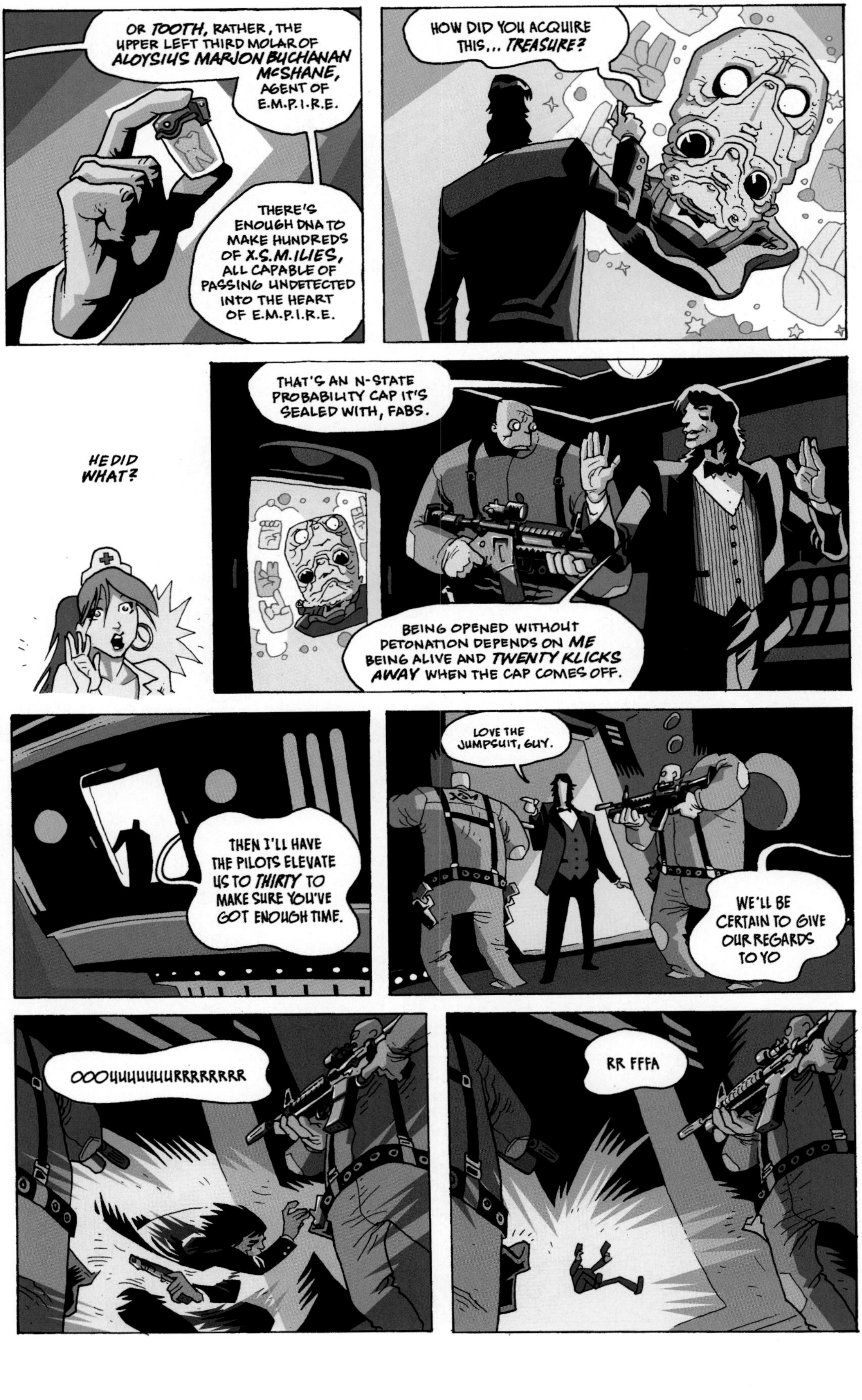
OR TOOTH, RATHER, THE UPPER LEFT THIRD MOLAR OF ALOYSIUS MARJON BUCHANAN McSHANE, AGENT OF E.M.P.I.R.E.
THERE'S ENOUGH DNA TO MAKE HUNDREDS OF X.S.M.ILIES, ALL CAPABLE OF PASSING UNDETECTED INTO THE HEART OF E.M.P.I.R.E.
HOW DID YOU ACQUIRE THIS... TREASURE?
HE DID WHAT?
THAT'S AN N-STATE PROBABILITY CAP IT'S SEALED WITH, FABS.
BEING OPENED WITHOUT DETONATION DEPENDS ON ME BEING ALIVE AND TWENTY KLICKS AWAY WHEN THE CAP COMES OFF.
THEN I'LL HAVE THE PILOTS ELEVATE US TO THIRTY TO MAKE SURE YOU'VE GOT ENOUGH TIME.
LOVE THE JUMPSUIT, GUY.
WE'LL BE CERTAIN TO GIVE OUR REGARDS TO YO
OOOUUUUUUURRRRRRRR
RR FFFA

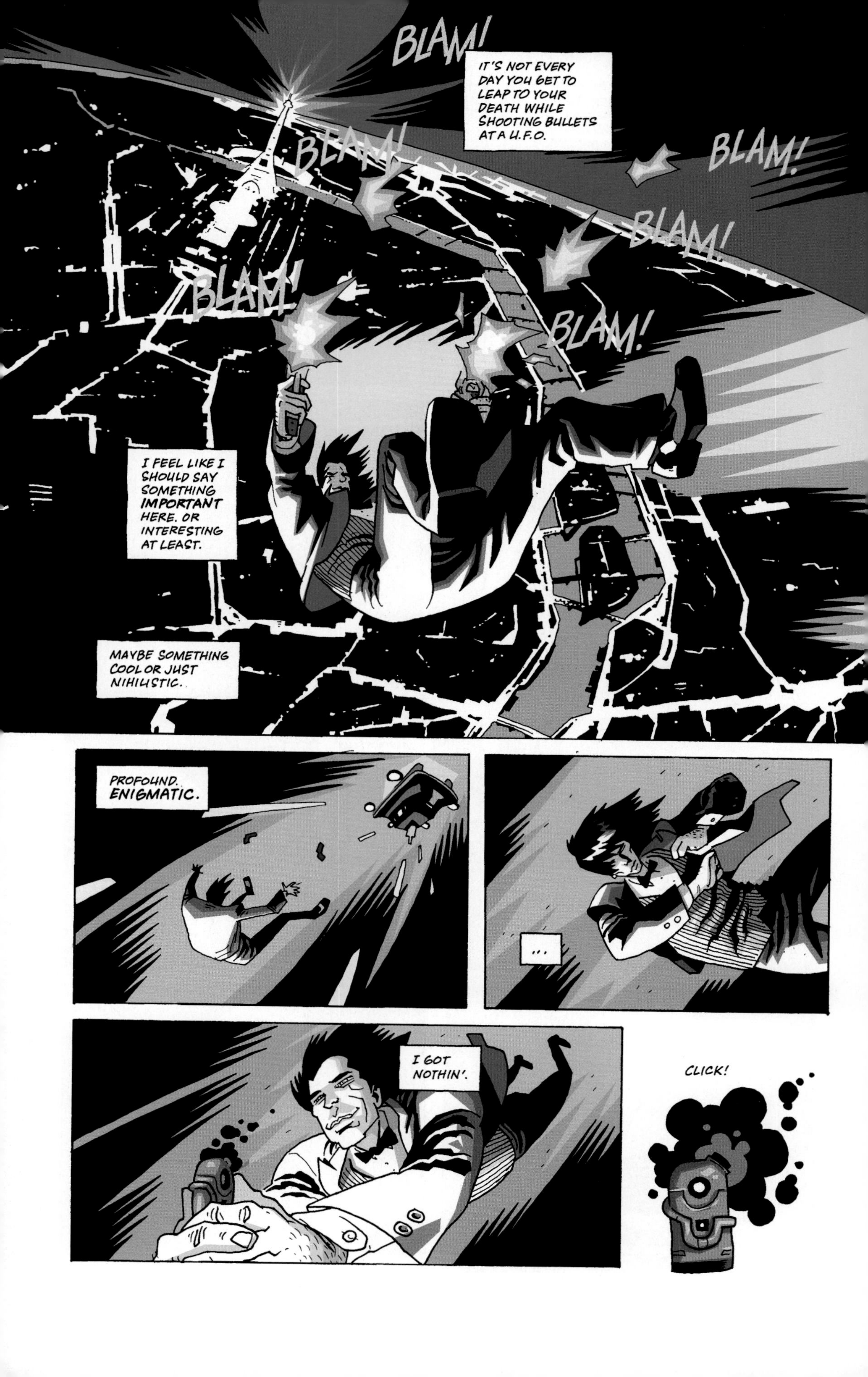
BLAM!
IT'S NOT EVERY DAY YOU GET TO LEAP TO YOUR DEATH WHILE SHOOTING BULLETS AT A U.F.O.
BLAM!
BLAM!
BLAM!
BLAM!
BLAM!
I FEEL LIKE I SHOULD SAY SOMETHING IMPORTANT HERE. OR INTERESTING AT LEAST.
MAYBE SOMETHING COOL OR JUST NIHILISTIC.
PROFOUND. ENIGMATIC.
...
I GOT NOTHIN'.
CLICK!

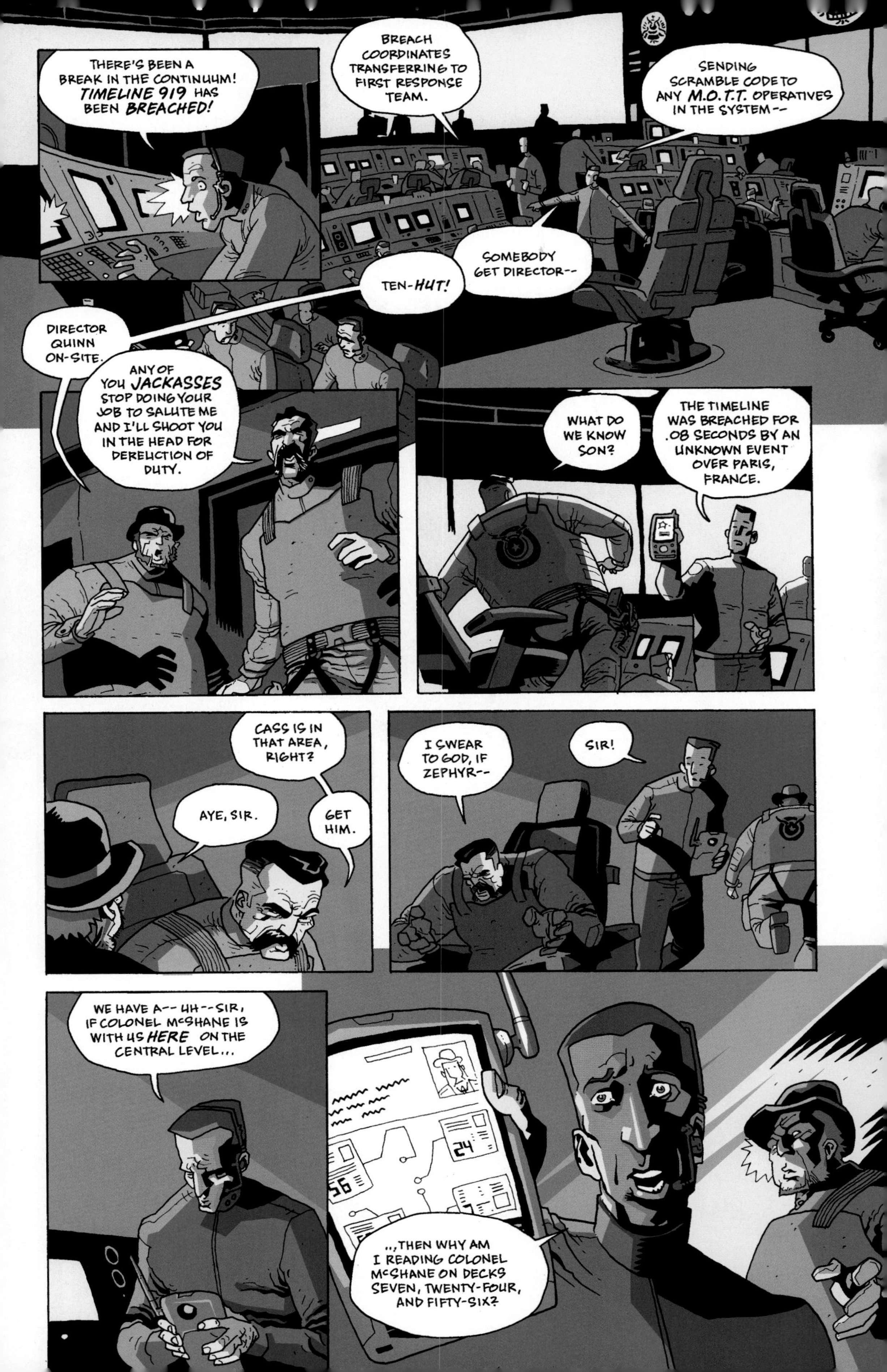
THERE'S BEEN A BREAK IN THE CONTINUUM! TIMELINE 919 HAS BEEN BREACHED!
BREACH COORDINATES TRANSFERRING TO FIRST RESPONSE TEAM.
SENDING SCRAMBLE CODE TO ANY M.O.T.T. OPERATIVES IN THE SYSTEM--
SOMEBODY GET DIRECTOR--
TEN-HUT!
DIRECTOR QUINN ON-SITE.
ANY OF YOU JACKASSES STOP DOING YOUR JOB TO SALUTE ME AND I'LL SHOOT YOU IN THE HEAD FOR DERELICTION OF DUTY.
WHAT DO WE KNOW SON?
THE TIMELINE WAS BREACHED FOR .08 SECONDS BY AN UNKNOWN EVENT OVER PARIS, FRANCE.
CASS IS IN THAT AREA, RIGHT?
AYE, SIR.
GET HIM.
I SWEAR TO GOD, IF ZEPHYR--
SIR!
WE HAVE A-- UH --SIR, IF COLONEL McSHANE IS WITH US HERE ON THE CENTRAL LEVEL...
...THEN WHY AM I READING COLONEL McSHANE ON DECKS SEVEN, TWENTY-FOUR, AND FIFTY-SIX?
24
56

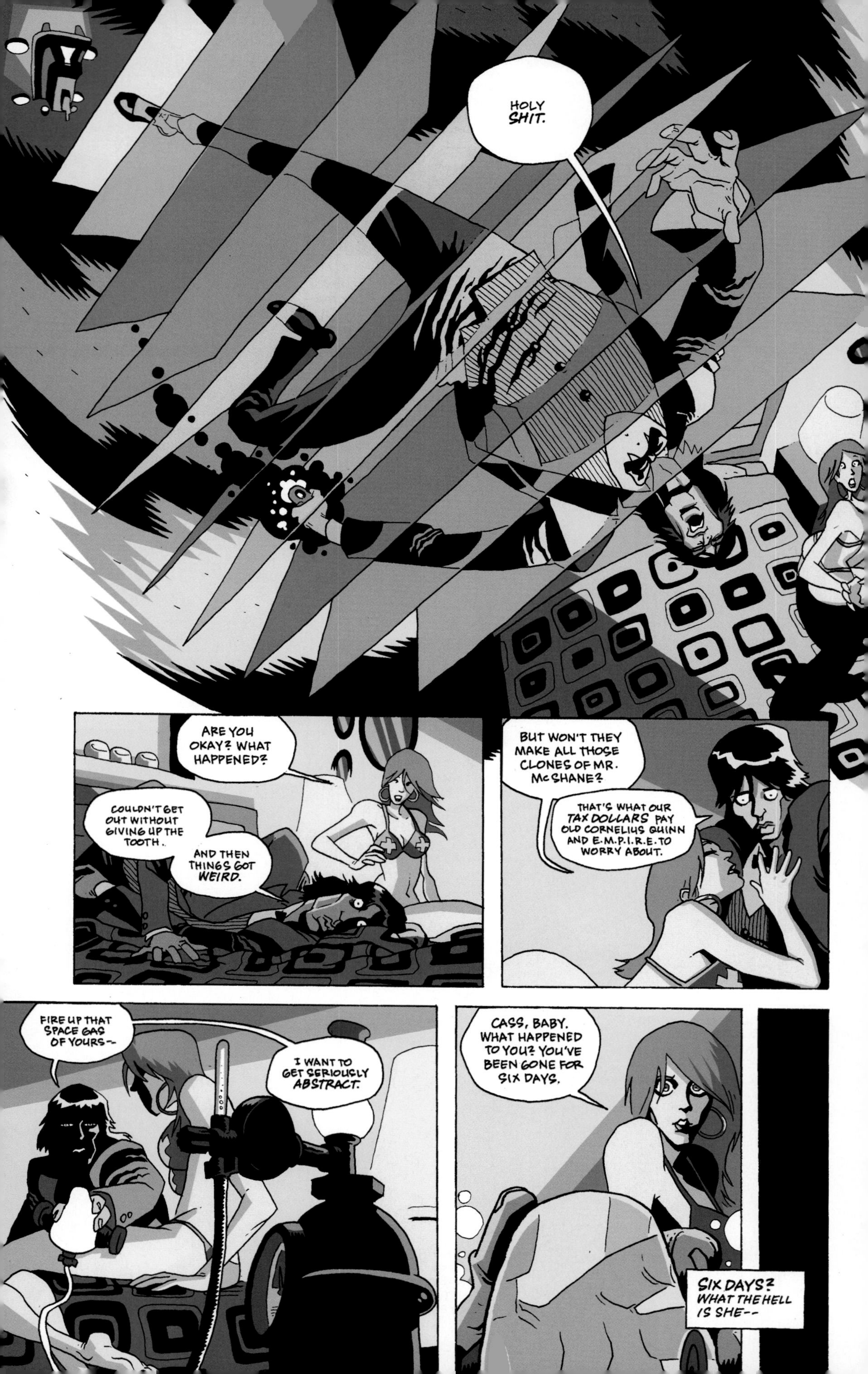
HOLY SHIT.
ARE YOU OKAY? WHAT HAPPENED?
COULDN'T GET OUT WITHOUT GIVING UP THE TOOTH.
AND THEN THINGS GOT WEIRD.
BUT WON'T THEY MAKE ALL THOSE CLONES OF MR. McSHANE?
THAT'S WHAT OUR TAX DOLLARS PAY OLD CORNELIUS QUINN AND E.M.P.I.R.E. TO WORRY ABOUT.
FIRE UP THAT SPACE GAS OF YOURS--
I WANT TO GET SERIOUSLY ABSTRACT.
CASS, BABY. WHAT HAPPENED TO YOU? YOU'VE BEEN GONE FOR SIX DAYS.
SIX DAYS? WHAT THE HELL IS SHE--

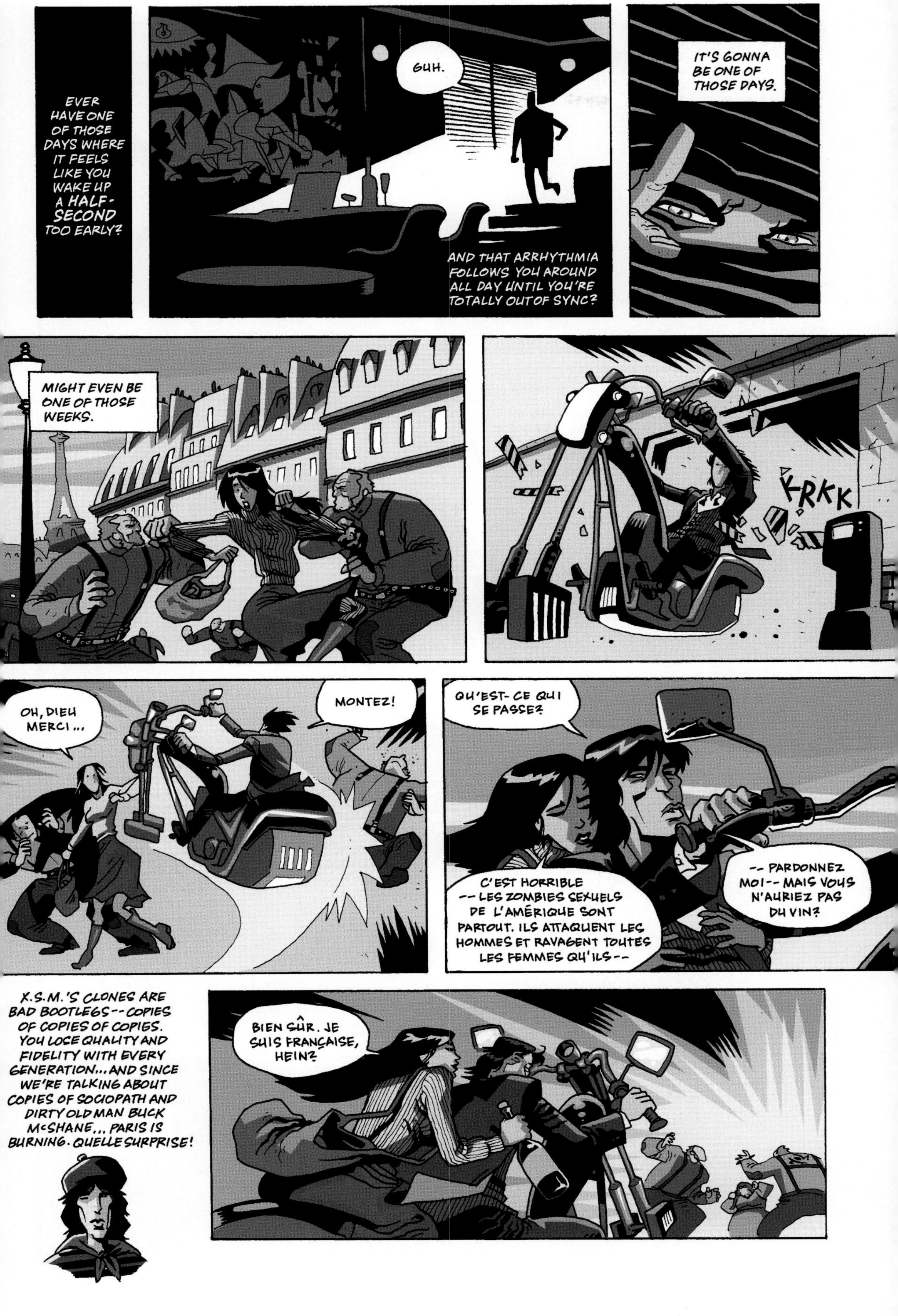

EVER HAVE ONE OF THOSE DAYS WHERE IT FEELS LIKE YOU WAKE UP A HALF-SECOND TOO EARLY?
GUH.
AND THAT ARRHYTHMIA FOLLOWS YOU AROUND ALL DAY UNTIL YOU'RE TOTALLY OUT OF SYNC?
IT'S GONNA BE ONE OF THOSE DAYS.
MIGHT EVEN BE ONE OF THOSE WEEKS.
KRKK
OH, DIEU MERCI...
MONTEZ!
QU'EST-CE QUI SE PASSE?
C'EST HORRIBLE --LES ZOMBIES SEXUELS DE L'AMÉRIQUE SONT PARTOUT. ILS ATTAQUENT LES HOMMES ET RAVAGENT TOUTES LES FEMMES QU'ILS--
--PARDONNEZ MOI--MAIS VOUS N'AURIEZ PAS DU VIN?
X.S.M.'S CLONES ARE BAD BOOTLEGS--COPIES OF COPIES OF COPIES. YOU LOSE QUALITY AND FIDELITY WITH EVERY GENERATION... AND SINCE WE'RE TALKING ABOUT COPIES OF SOCIOPATH AND DIRTY OLD MAN BUCK McSHANE... PARIS IS BURNING. QUELLE SURPRISE!
BIEN SÛR. JE SUIS FRANÇAISE, HEIN?

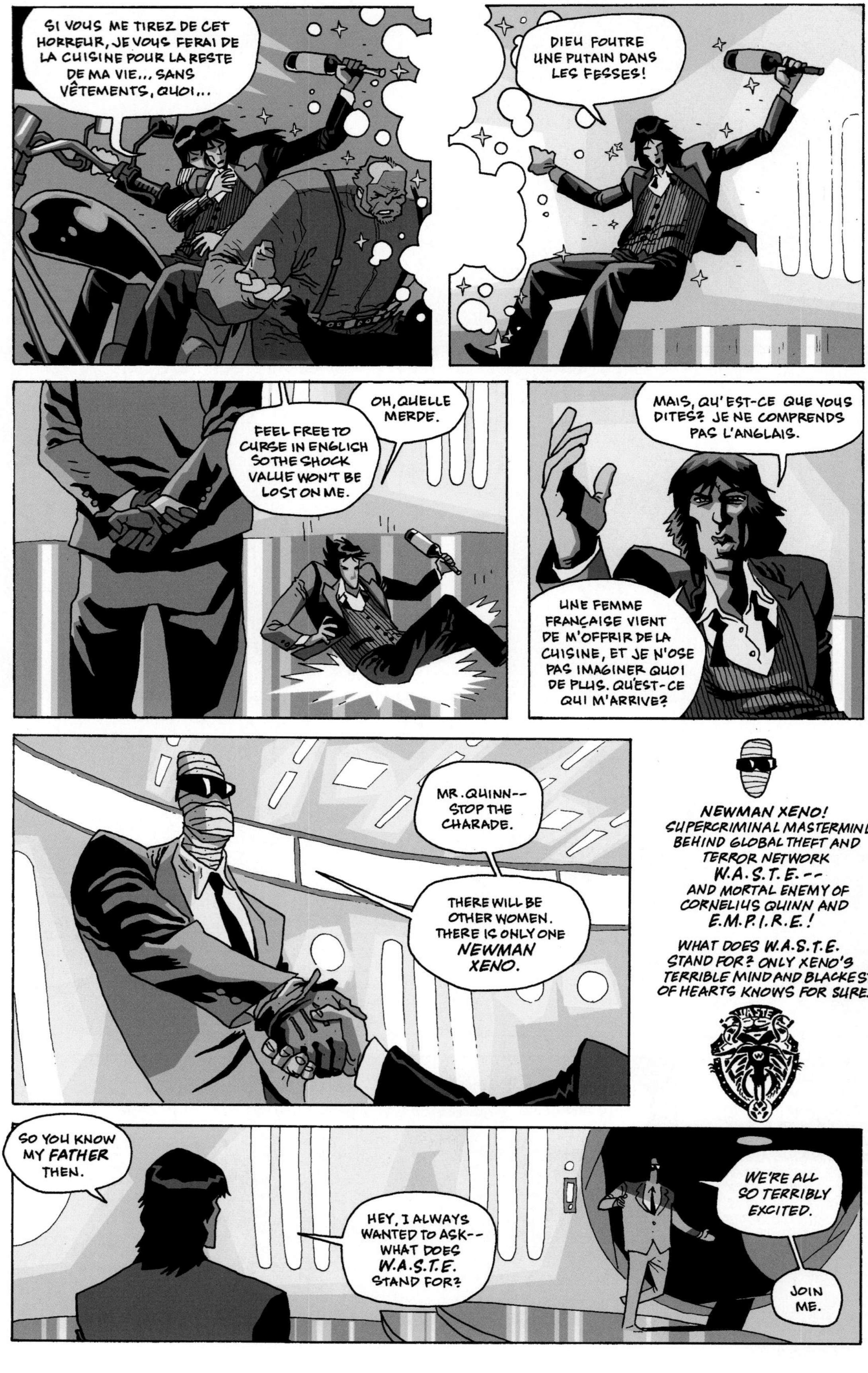
SI VOUS ME TIREZ DE CET HORREUR, JE VOUS FERAI DE LA CUISINE POUR LA RESTE DE MA VIE... SANS VÊTEMENTS, QUOI...
DIEU FOUTRE UNE PUTAIN DANS LES FESSES!
OH, QUELLE MERDE.
FEEL FREE TO CURSE IN ENGLISH SO THE SHOCK VALUE WON'T BE LOST ON ME.
MAIS, QU'EST-CE QUE VOUS DITES? JE NE COMPRENDS PAS L'ANGLAIS.
UNE FEMME FRANÇAISE VIENT DE M'OFFRIR DE LA CUISINE, ET JE N'OSE PAS IMAGINER QUOI DE PLUS. QU'EST-CE QUI M'ARRIVE?
MR. QUINN-- STOP THE CHARADE.
THERE WILL BE OTHER WOMEN. THERE IS ONLY ONE NEWMAN XENO.
NEWMAN XENO! SUPERCRIMINAL MASTERMIND BEHIND GLOBAL THEFT AND TERROR NETWORK W.A.S.T.E.-- AND MORTAL ENEMY OF CORNELIUS QUINN AND E.M.P.I.R.E.!
WHAT DOES W.A.S.T.E. STAND FOR? ONLY XENO'S TERRIBLE MIND AND BLACKEST OF HEARTS KNOWS FOR SURE...!
SO YOU KNOW MY FATHER THEN.
HEY, I ALWAYS WANTED TO ASK-- WHAT DOES W.A.S.T.E. STAND FOR?
WE'RE ALL SO TERRIBLY EXCITED.
JOIN ME.

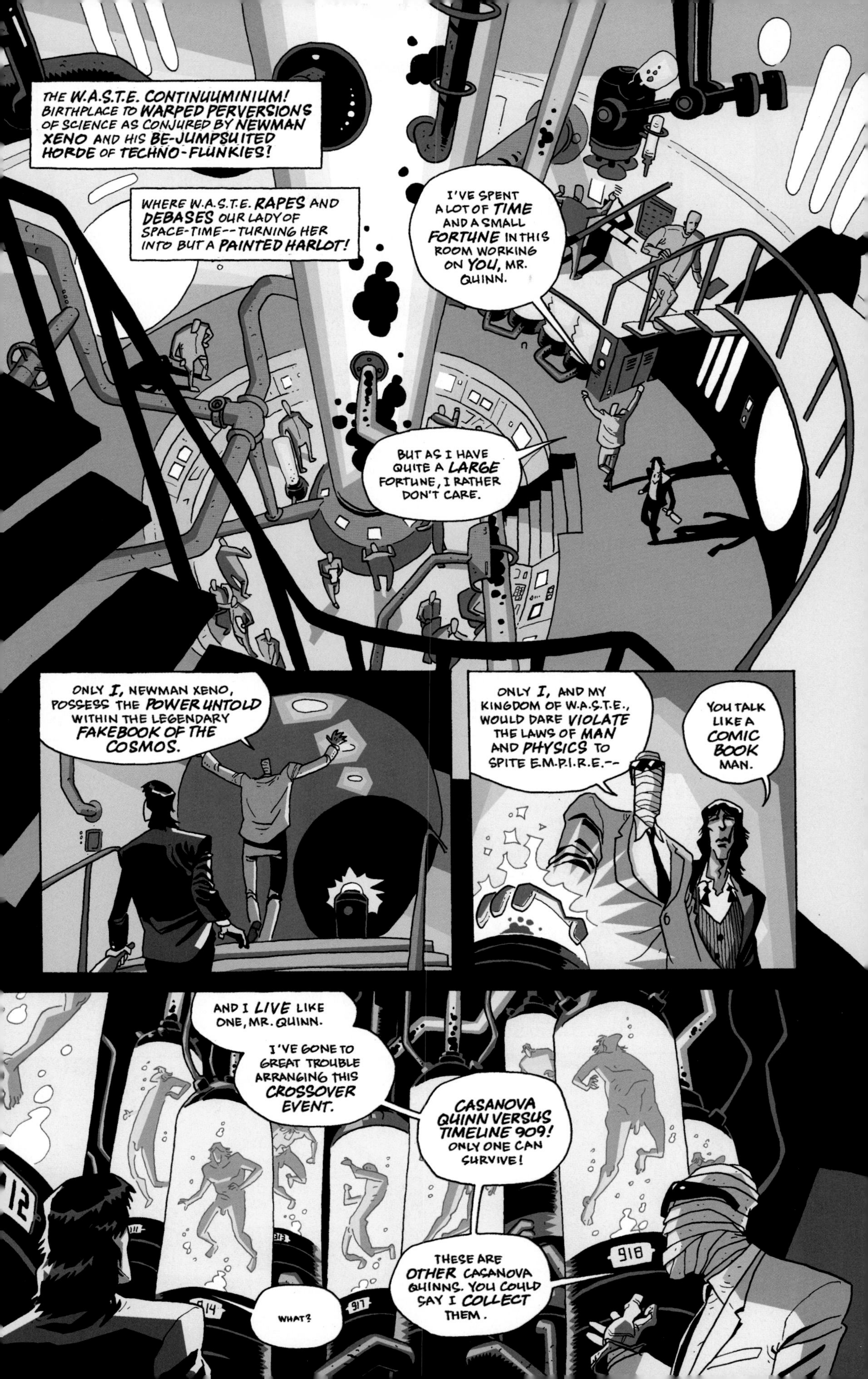
THE W.A.S.T.E. CONTINUUMINIUM! BIRTHPLACE TO WARPED PERVERSIONS OF SCIENCE AS CONJURED BY NEWMAN XENO AND HIS BE-JUMPSUITED HORDE OF TECHNO-FLUNKIES!
WHERE W.A.S.T.E. RAPES AND DEBASES OUR LADY OF SPACE-TIME--TURNING HER INTO BUT A PAINTED HARLOT!
I'VE SPENT A LOT OF TIME AND A SMALL FORTUNE IN THIS ROOM WORKING ON YOU, MR. QUINN.
BUT AS I HAVE QUITE A LARGE FORTUNE, I RATHER DON'T CARE.
ONLY I, NEWMAN XENO, POSSESS THE POWER UNTOLD WITHIN THE LEGENDARY FAKEBOOK OF THE COSMOS.
ONLY I, AND MY KINGDOM OF W.A.S.T.E., WOULD DARE VIOLATE THE LAWS OF MAN AND PHYSICS TO SPITE E.M.P.I.R.E.--
YOU TALK LIKE A COMIC BOOK MAN.
AND I LIVE LIKE ONE, MR. QUINN.
I'VE GONE TO GREAT TROUBLE ARRANGING THIS CROSSOVER EVENT.
CASANOVA QUINN VERSUS TIMELINE 909! ONLY ONE CAN SURVIVE!
THESE ARE OTHER CASANOVA QUINNS. YOU COULD SAY I COLLECT THEM.
WHAT?

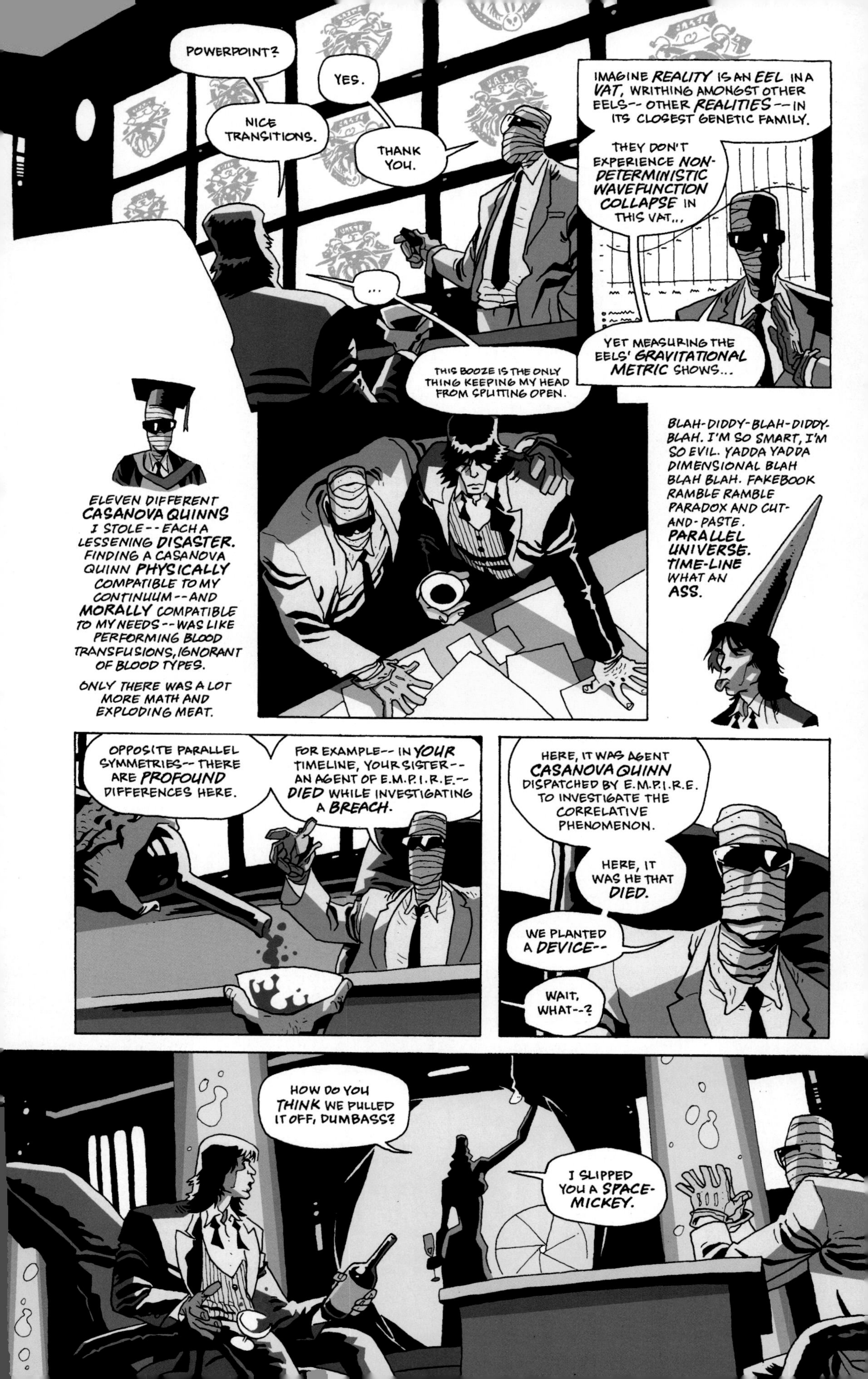
POWERPOINT?
YES.
NICE TRANSITIONS.
THANK YOU.
...
THIS BOOZE IS THE ONLY THING KEEPING MY HEAD FROM SPLITTING OPEN.
IMAGINE REALITY IS AN EEL IN A VAT, WRITHING AMONGST OTHER EELS-- OTHER REALITIES -- IN ITS CLOSEST GENETIC FAMILY.
THEY DON'T EXPERIENCE NON-DETERMINISTIC WAVEFUNCTION COLLAPSE IN THIS VAT...
YET MEASURING THE EELS' GRAVITATIONAL METRIC SHOWS...
ELEVEN DIFFERENT CASANOVA QUINNS I STOLE--EACH A LESSENING DISASTER. FINDING A CASANOVA QUINN PHYSICALLY COMPATIBLE TO MY CONTINUUM--AND MORALLY COMPATIBLE TO MY NEEDS--WAS LIKE PERFORMING BLOOD TRANSFUSIONS, IGNORANT OF BLOOD TYPES.
ONLY THERE WAS A LOT MORE MATH AND EXPLODING MEAT.
BLAH-DIDDY-BLAH-DIDDY-BLAH. I'M SO SMART, I'M SO EVIL. YADDA YADDA DIMENSIONAL BLAH BLAH BLAH. FAKEBOOK RAMBLE RAMBLE PARADOX AND CUT-AND-PASTE. PARALLEL UNIVERSE. TIME-LINE WHAT AN ASS.
OPPOSITE PARALLEL SYMMETRIES-- THERE ARE PROFOUND DIFFERENCES HERE.
FOR EXAMPLE-- IN YOUR TIMELINE, YOUR SISTER--AN AGENT OF E.M.P.I.R.E.-- DIED WHILE INVESTIGATING A BREACH.
HERE, IT WAS AGENT CASANOVA QUINN DISPATCHED BY E.M.P.I.R.E. TO INVESTIGATE THE CORRELATIVE PHENOMENON.
HERE, IT WAS HE THAT DIED.
WE PLANTED A DEVICE--
WAIT, WHAT--?
HOW DO YOU THINK WE PULLED IT OFF, DUMBASS?
I SLIPPED YOU A SPACE-MICKEY.

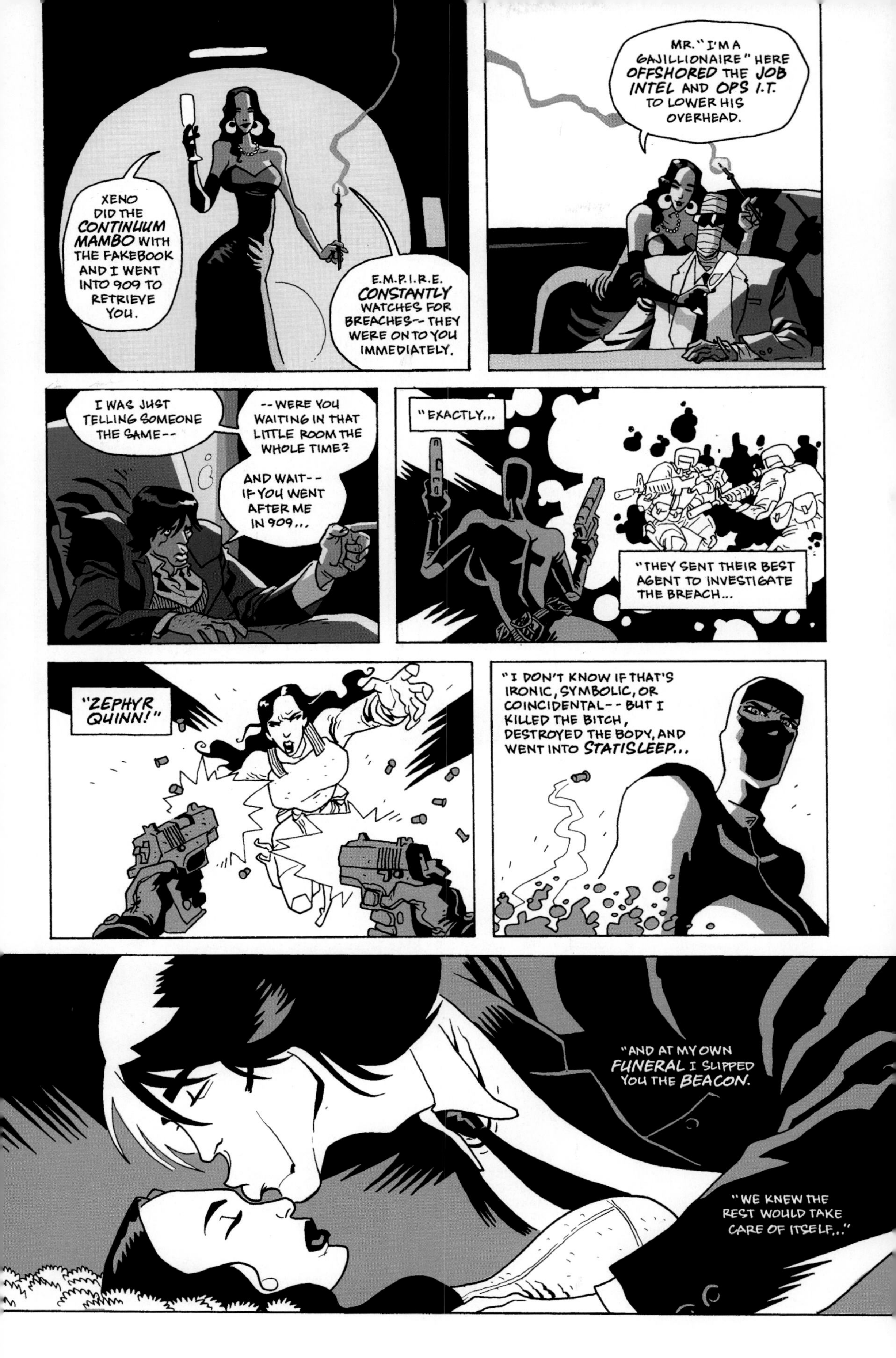
XENO DID THE CONTINUUM MAMBO WITH THE FAKEBOOK AND I WENT INTO 909 TO RETRIEVE YOU.
E.M.P.I.R.E. CONSTANTLY WATCHES FOR BREACHES-- THEY WERE ON TO YOU IMMEDIATELY.
MR. "I'M A GAJILLIONAIRE" HERE OFFSHORED THE JOB INTEL AND OPS I.T. TO LOWER HIS OVERHEAD.
I WAS JUST TELLING SOMEONE THE SAME--
--WERE YOU WAITING IN THAT LITTLE ROOM THE WHOLE TIME?
AND WAIT-- IF YOU WENT AFTER ME IN 909...
"EXACTLY...
"THEY SENT THEIR BEST AGENT TO INVESTIGATE THE BREACH...
"ZEPHYR QUINN!"
"I DON'T KNOW IF THAT'S IRONIC, SYMBOLIC, OR COINCIDENTAL-- BUT I KILLED THE BITCH, DESTROYED THE BODY, AND WENT INTO STATISLEEP...
"AND AT MY OWN FUNERAL I SLIPPED YOU THE BEACON.
"WE KNEW THE REST WOULD TAKE CARE OF ITSELF..."

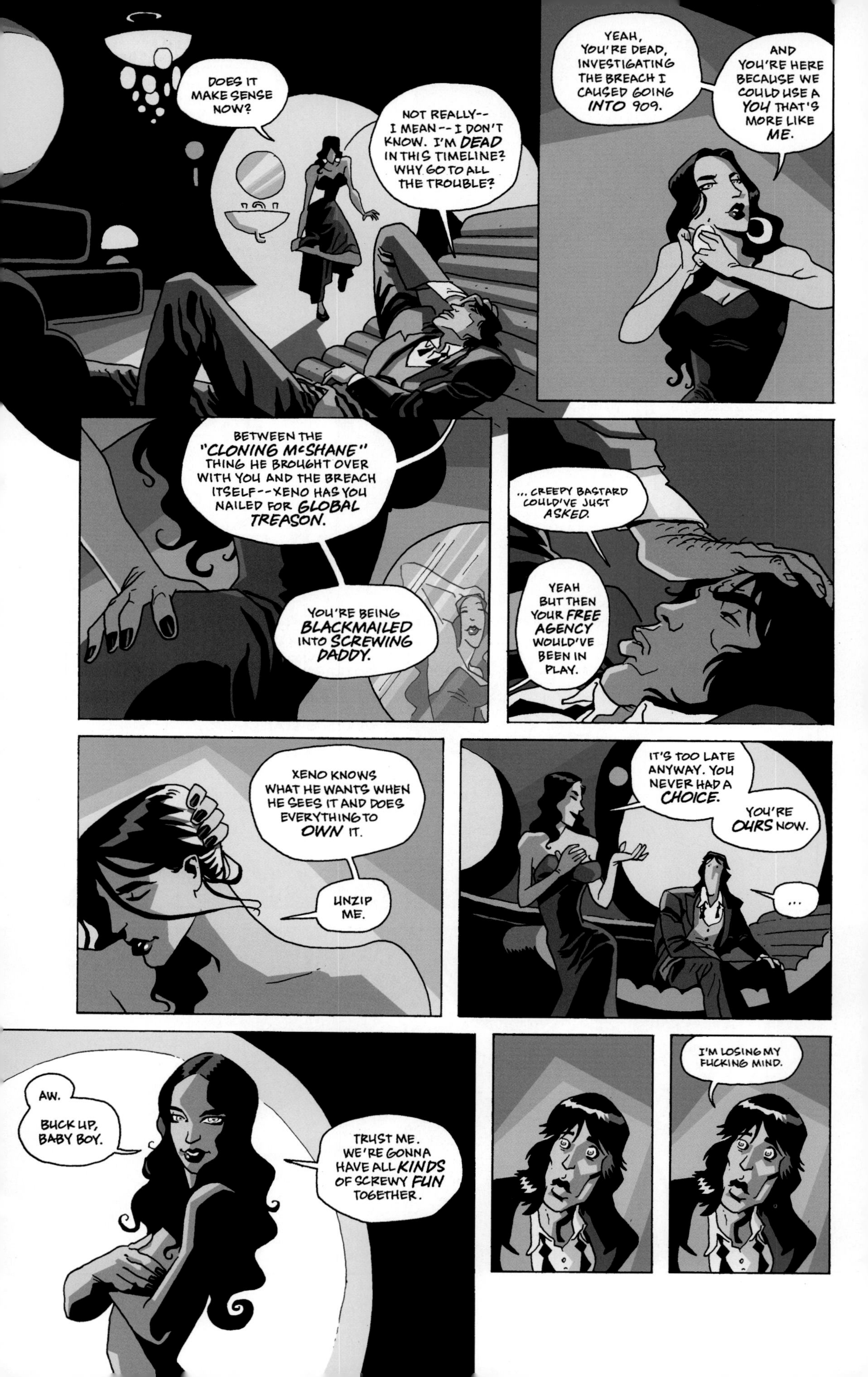
DOES IT MAKE SENSE NOW?
NOT REALLY-- I MEAN-- I DON'T KNOW. I'M DEAD IN THIS TIMELINE? WHY GO TO ALL THE TROUBLE?
YEAH, YOU'RE DEAD, INVESTIGATING THE BREACH I CAUSED GOING INTO 909.
AND YOU'RE HERE BECAUSE WE COULD USE A YOU THAT'S MORE LIKE ME.
BETWEEN THE "CLONING McSHANE" THING HE BROUGHT OVER WITH YOU AND THE BREACH ITSELF--XENO HAS YOU NAILED FOR GLOBAL TREASON.
YOU'RE BEING BLACKMAILED INTO SCREWING DADDY.
...CREEPY BASTARD COULD'VE JUST ASKED.
YEAH BUT THEN YOUR FREE AGENCY WOULD'VE BEEN IN PLAY.
XENO KNOWS WHAT HE WANTS WHEN HE SEES IT AND DOES EVERYTHING TO OWN IT.
UNZIP ME.
IT'S TOO LATE ANYWAY. YOU NEVER HAD A CHOICE.
YOU'RE OURS NOW.
...
AW.
BUCK UP, BABY BOY.
TRUST ME. WE'RE GONNA HAVE ALL KINDS OF SCREWY FUN TOGETHER.
I'M LOSING MY FUCKING MIND.

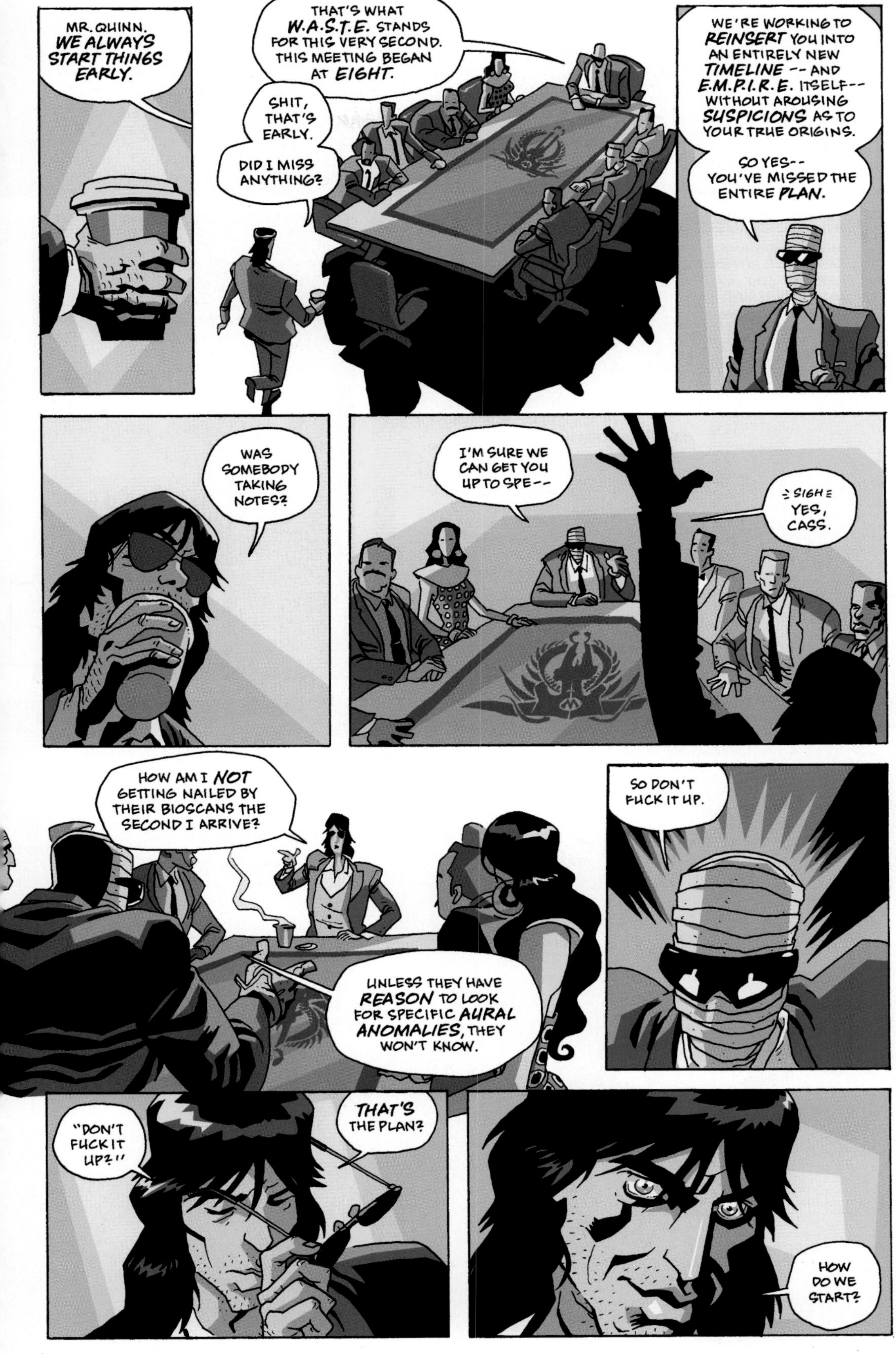
MR. QUINN. WE ALWAYS START THINGS EARLY.
THAT'S WHAT W.A.S.T.E. STANDS FOR THIS VERY SECOND. THIS MEETING BEGAN AT EIGHT.
SHIT, THAT'S EARLY.
DID I MISS ANYTHING?
WE'RE WORKING TO REINSERT YOU INTO AN ENTIRELY NEW TIMELINE -- AND E.M.P.I.R.E. ITSELF-- WITHOUT AROUSING SUSPICIONS AS TO YOUR TRUE ORIGINS.
SO YES-- YOU'VE MISSED THE ENTIRE PLAN.
WAS SOMEBODY TAKING NOTES?
I'M SURE WE CAN GET YOU UP TO SPE--
=SIGH= YES, CASS.
HOW AM I NOT GETTING NAILED BY THEIR BIOSCANS THE SECOND I ARRIVE?
UNLESS THEY HAVE REASON TO LOOK FOR SPECIFIC AURAL ANOMALIES, THEY WON'T KNOW.
SO DON'T FUCK IT UP.
"DON'T FUCK IT UP?"
THAT'S THE PLAN?
HOW DO WE START?

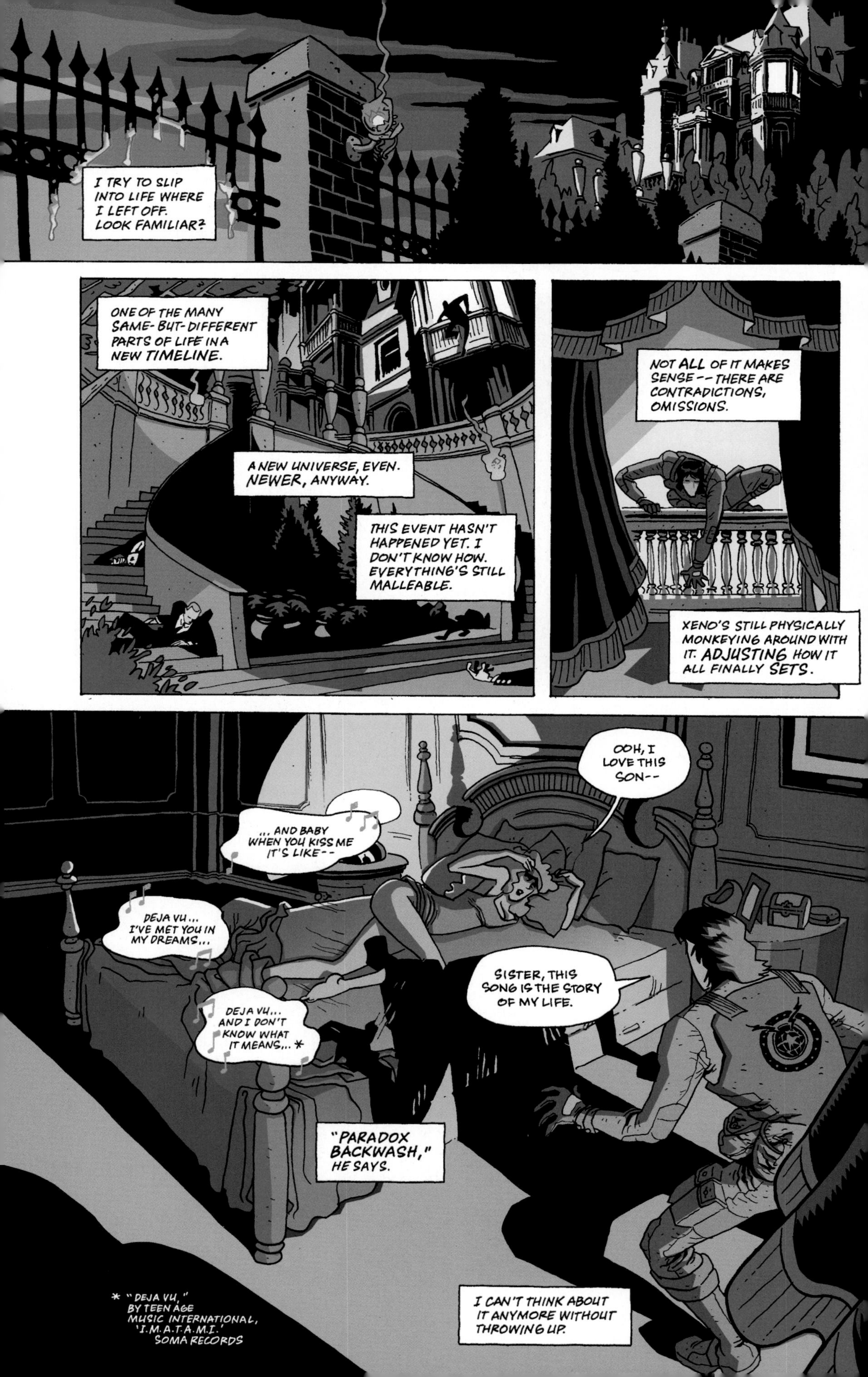
I TRY TO SLIP INTO LIFE WHERE I LEFT OFF. LOOK FAMILIAR?
ONE OF THE MANY SAME-BUT-DIFFERENT PARTS OF LIFE IN A NEW TIMELINE.
A NEW UNIVERSE, EVEN. NEWER, ANYWAY.
THIS EVENT HASN'T HAPPENED YET. I DON'T KNOW HOW. EVERYTHING'S STILL MALLEABLE.
NOT ALL OF IT MAKES SENSE--THERE ARE CONTRADICTIONS, OMISSIONS.
XENO'S STILL PHYSICALLY MONKEYING AROUND WITH IT. ADJUSTING HOW IT ALL FINALLY SETS.
OOH, I LOVE THIS SON--
...AND BABY WHEN YOU KISS ME IT'S LIKE--
DEJA VU... I'VE MET YOU IN MY DREAMS...
SISTER, THIS SONG IS THE STORY OF MY LIFE.
DEJA VU... AND I DON'T KNOW WHAT IT MEANS...*
"PARADOX BACKWASH," HE SAYS.
* "DEJA VU," BY TEEN AGE MUSIC INTERNATIONAL, 'I.M.A.T.A.M.I.' SOMA RECORDS
I CAN'T THINK ABOUT IT ANYMORE WITHOUT THROWING UP.

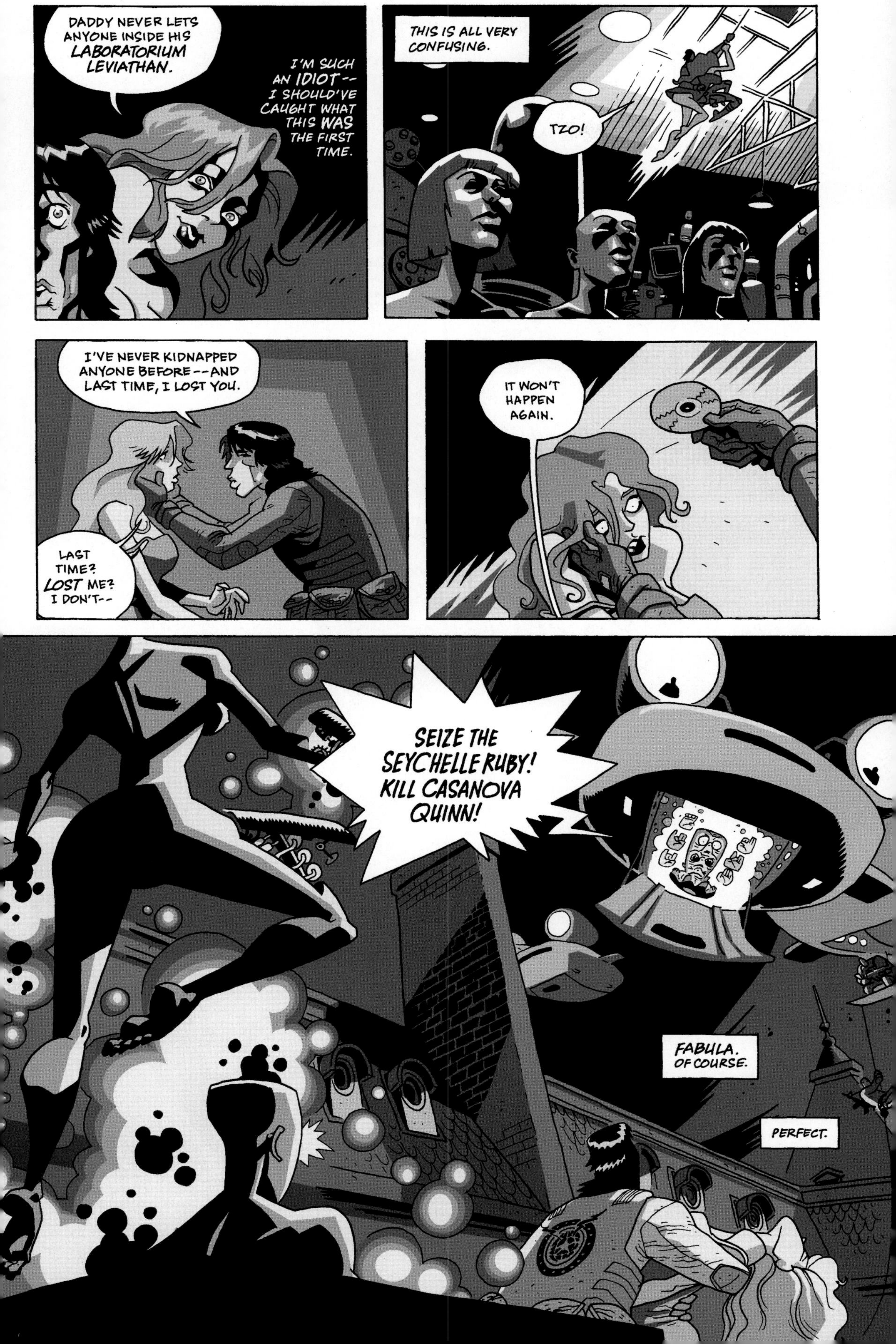
DADDY NEVER LETS ANYONE INSIDE HIS LABORATORIUM LEVIATHAN.
I'M SUCH AN IDIOT -- I SHOULD'VE CAUGHT WHAT THIS WAS THE FIRST TIME.
THIS IS ALL VERY CONFUSING.
TZO!
I'VE NEVER KIDNAPPED ANYONE BEFORE -- AND LAST TIME, I LOST YOU.
LAST TIME? LOST ME? I DON'T--
IT WON'T HAPPEN AGAIN.
SEIZE THE SEYCHELLE RUBY! KILL CASANOVA QUINN!
FABULA. OF COURSE.
PERFECT.

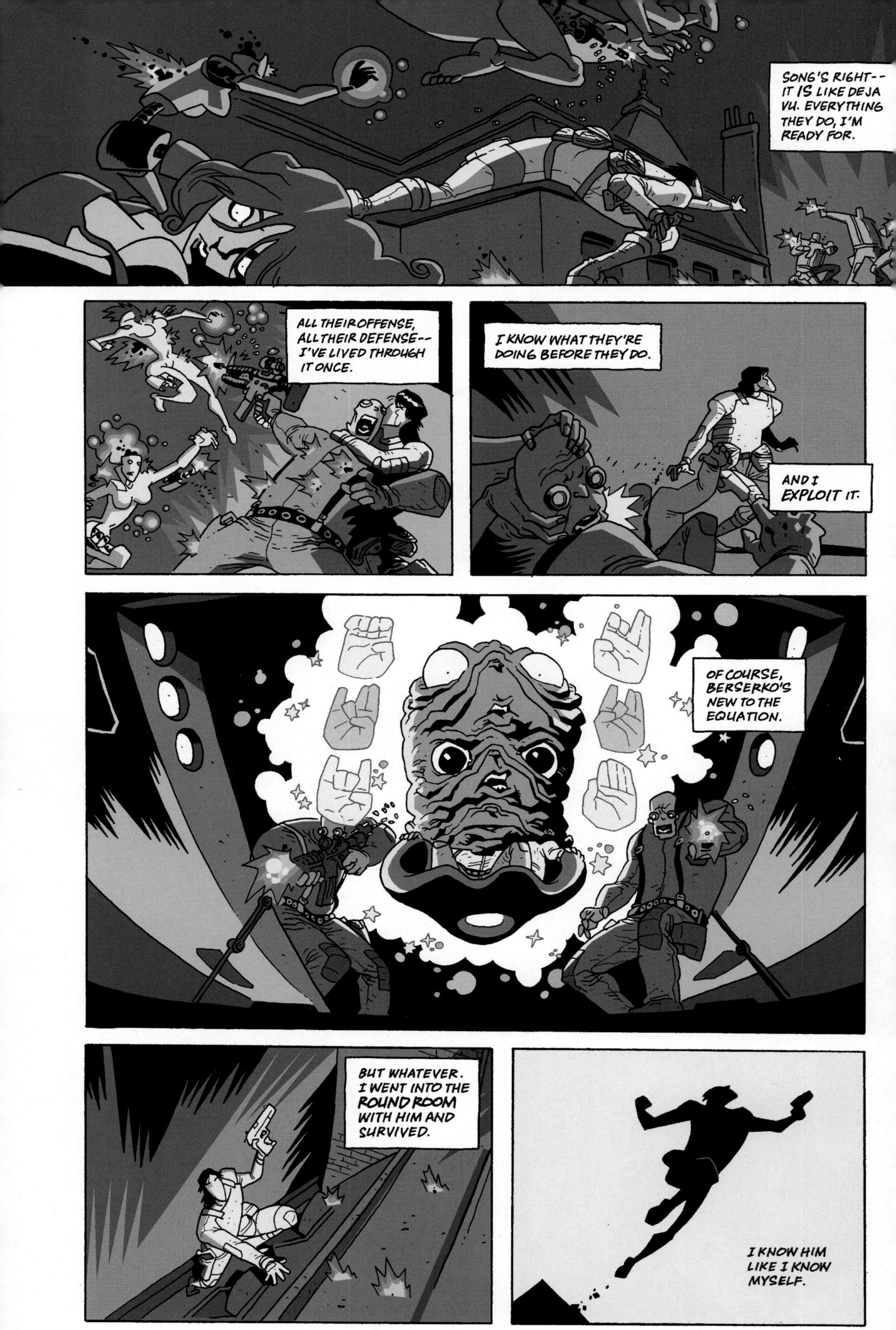
SONG'S RIGHT--
IT IS LIKE DEJA VU. EVERYTHING THEY DO, I'M READY FOR.
ALL THEIR OFFENSE, ALL THEIR DEFENSE--
I'VE LIVED THROUGH IT ONCE.
I KNOW WHAT THEY'RE DOING BEFORE THEY DO.
AND I EXPLOIT IT.
OF COURSE, BERSERKO'S NEW TO THE EQUATION.
BUT WHATEVER. I WENT INTO THE ROUND ROOM WITH HIM AND SURVIVED.
I KNOW HIM LIKE I KNOW MYSELF.

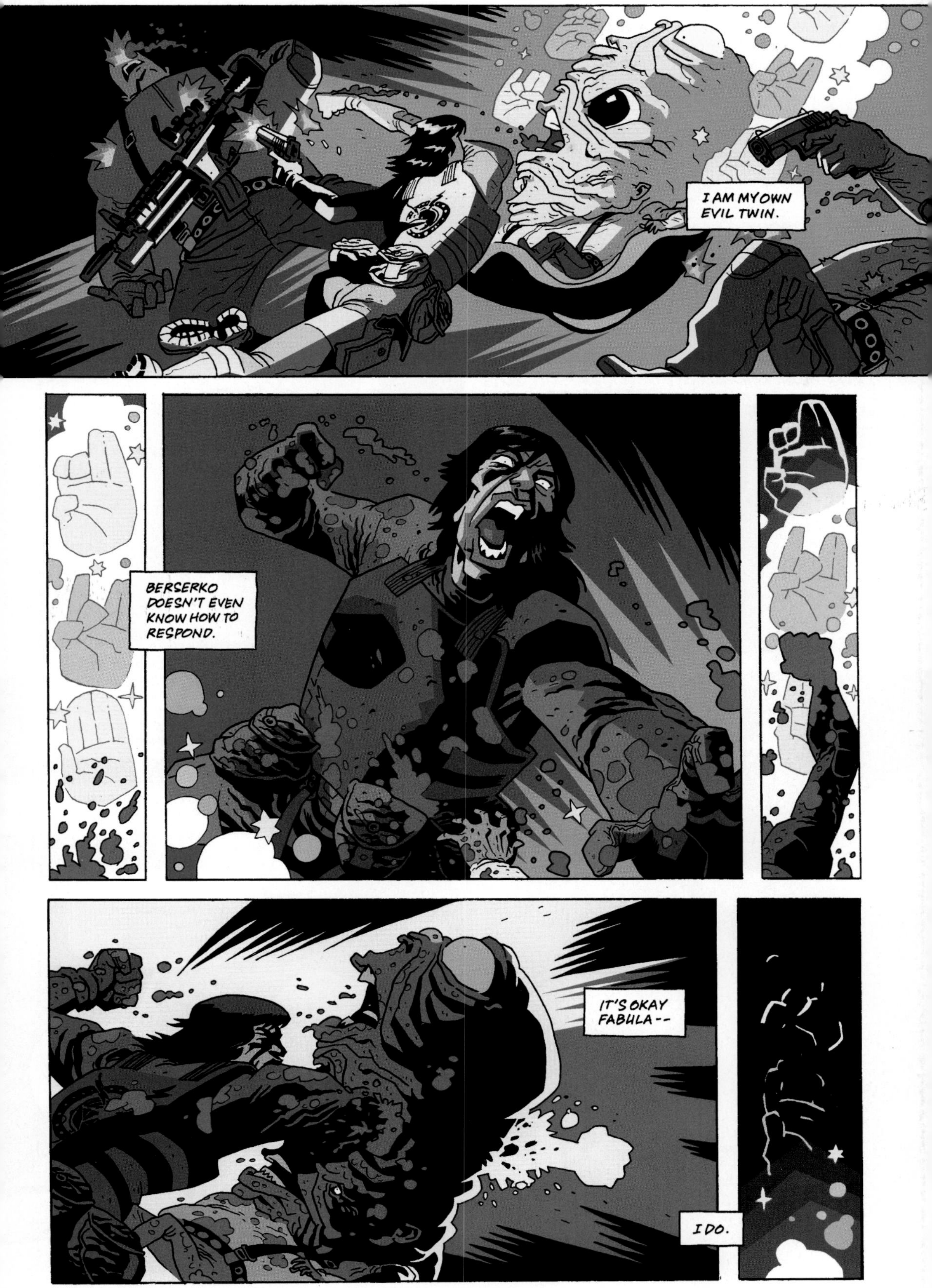
I AM MY OWN EVIL TWIN.
BERSERKO DOESN'T EVEN KNOW HOW TO RESPOND.
IT'S OKAY FABULA--
I DO.

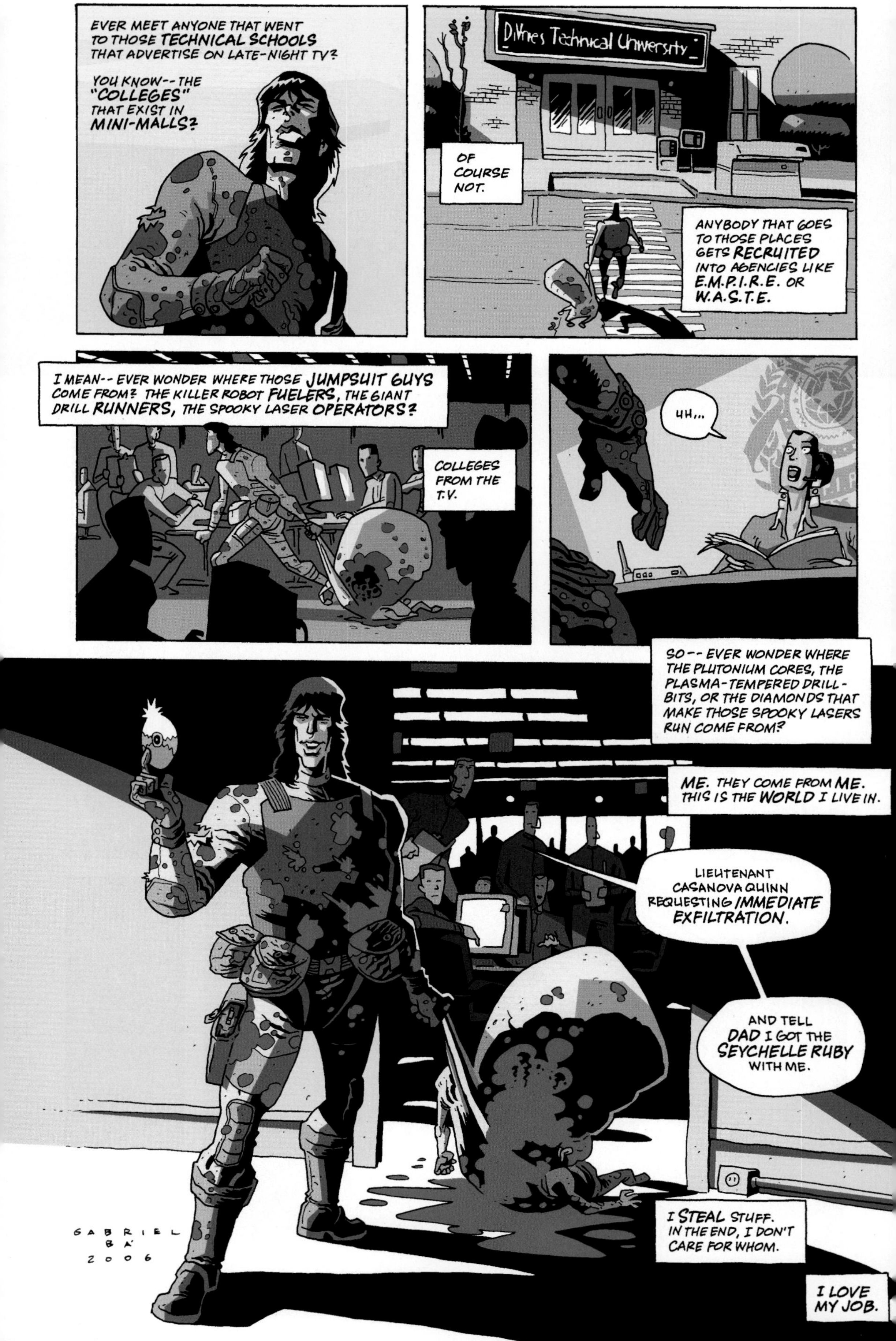
EVER MEET ANYONE THAT WENT TO THOSE TECHNICAL SCHOOLS THAT ADVERTISE ON LATE-NIGHT TV?
YOU KNOW-- THE "COLLEGES" THAT EXIST IN MINI-MALLS?
DiVries Technical University
OF COURSE NOT.
ANYBODY THAT GOES TO THOSE PLACES GETS RECRUITED INTO AGENCIES LIKE E.M.P.I.R.E. OR W.A.S.T.E.
I MEAN-- EVER WONDER WHERE THOSE JUMPSUIT GUYS COME FROM? THE KILLER ROBOT FUELERS, THE GIANT DRILL RUNNERS, THE SPOOKY LASER OPERATORS?
COLLEGES FROM THE T.V.
UH...
SO-- EVER WONDER WHERE THE PLUTONIUM CORES, THE PLASMA-TEMPERED DRILL-BITS, OR THE DIAMONDS THAT MAKE THOSE SPOOKY LASERS RUN COME FROM?
ME. THEY COME FROM ME. THIS IS THE WORLD I LIVE IN.
LIEUTENANT CASANOVA QUINN REQUESTING IMMEDIATE EXFILTRATION.
AND TELL DAD I GOT THE SEYCHELLE RUBY WITH ME.
GABRIEL BÁ 2006
I STEAL STUFF. IN THE END, I DON'T CARE FOR WHOM.
I LOVE MY JOB.

# CHAPTER 2
# PRETTY LITTLE POLICEMAN

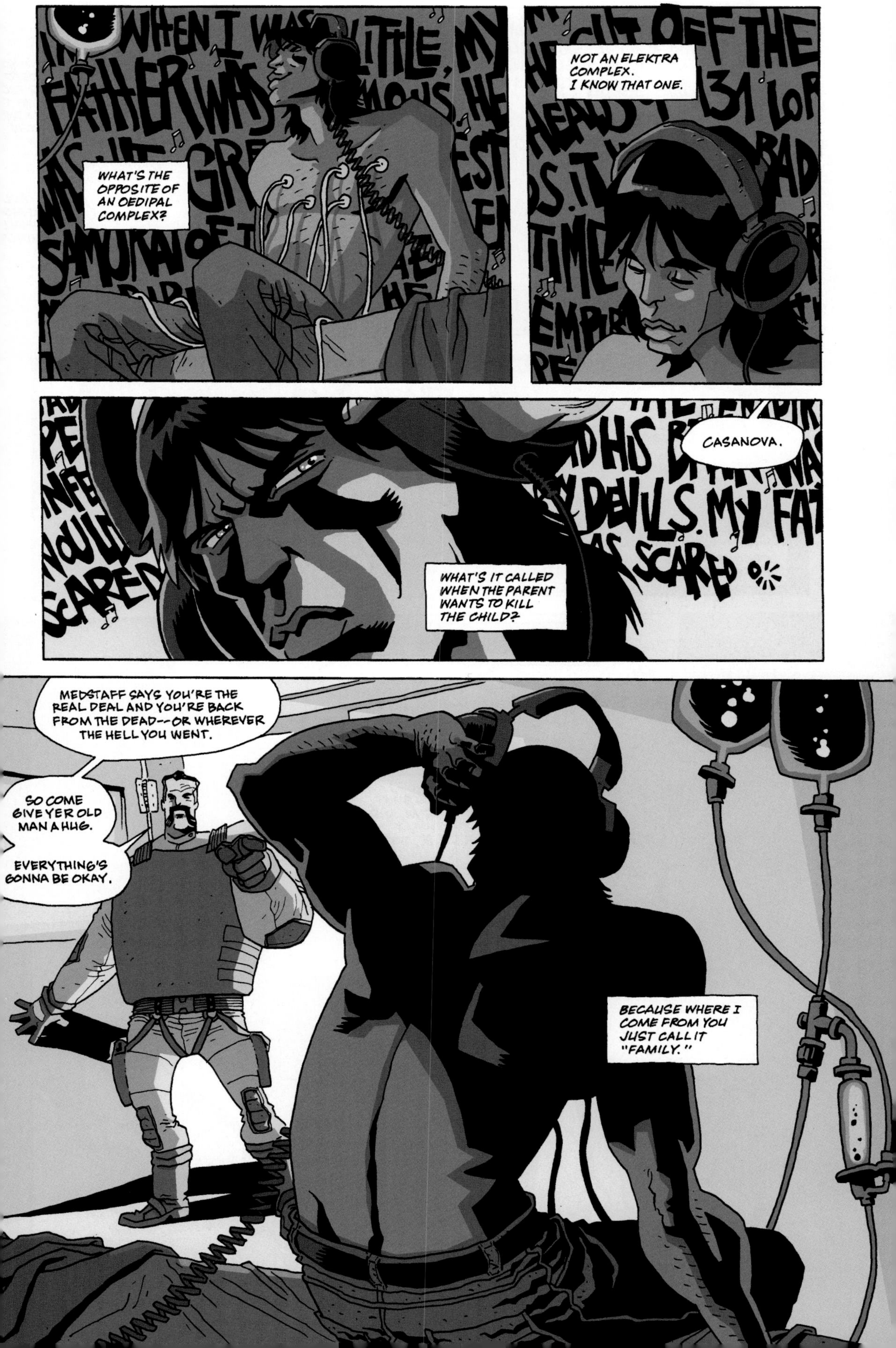
WHAT'S THE OPPOSITE OF AN OEDIPAL COMPLEX?
NOT AN ELEKTRA COMPLEX. I KNOW THAT ONE.
CASANOVA.
WHAT'S IT CALLED WHEN THE PARENT WANTS TO KILL THE CHILD?
MEDSTAFF SAYS YOU'RE THE REAL DEAL AND YOU'RE BACK FROM THE DEAD--OR WHEREVER THE HELL YOU WENT.
SO COME GIVE YER OLD MAN A HUG.
EVERYTHING'S GONNA BE OKAY.
BECAUSE WHERE I COME FROM YOU JUST CALL IT "FAMILY."

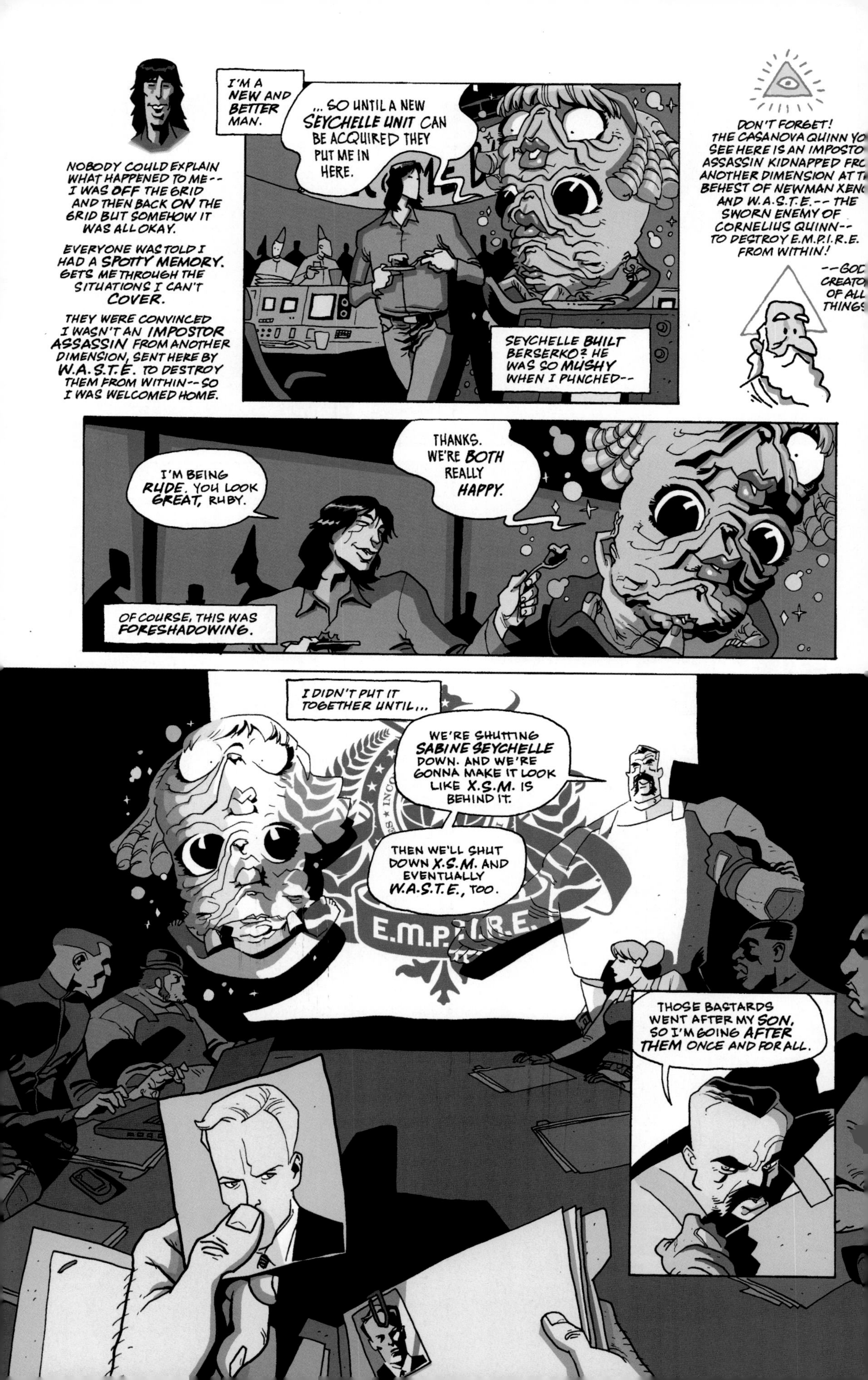
NOBODY COULD EXPLAIN WHAT HAPPENED TO ME-- I WAS OFF THE GRID AND THEN BACK ON THE GRID BUT SOMEHOW IT WAS ALL OKAY.
EVERYONE WAS TOLD I HAD A SPOTTY MEMORY. GETS ME THROUGH THE SITUATIONS I CAN'T COVER.
THEY WERE CONVINCED I WASN'T AN IMPOSTOR ASSASSIN FROM ANOTHER DIMENSION, SENT HERE BY W.A.S.T.E. TO DESTROY THEM FROM WITHIN--SO I WAS WELCOMED HOME.
I'M A NEW AND BETTER MAN.
...SO UNTIL A NEW SEYCHELLE UNIT CAN BE ACQUIRED THEY PUT ME IN HERE.
SEYCHELLE BUILT BERSERKO? HE WAS SO MUSHY WHEN I PUNCHED--
DON'T FORGET! THE CASANOVA QUINN YO SEE HERE IS AN IMPOSTO ASSASSIN KIDNAPPED FRO ANOTHER DIMENSION AT T BEHEST OF NEWMAN XEN AND W.A.S.T.E.-- THE SWORN ENEMY OF CORNELIUS QUINN-- TO DESTROY E.M.P.I.R.E. FROM WITHIN!
--GOD CREATO OF ALL THINGS
I'M BEING RUDE. YOU LOOK GREAT, RUBY.
THANKS. WE'RE BOTH REALLY HAPPY.
OF COURSE, THIS WAS FORESHADOWING.
I DIDN'T PUT IT TOGETHER UNTIL...
WE'RE SHUTTING SABINE SEYCHELLE DOWN. AND WE'RE GONNA MAKE IT LOOK LIKE X.S.M. IS BEHIND IT.
THEN WE'LL SHUT DOWN X.S.M. AND EVENTUALLY W.A.S.T.E., TOO.
E.M.P.I.R.E.
THOSE BASTARDS WENT AFTER MY SON, SO I'M GOING AFTER THEM ONCE AND FOR ALL.

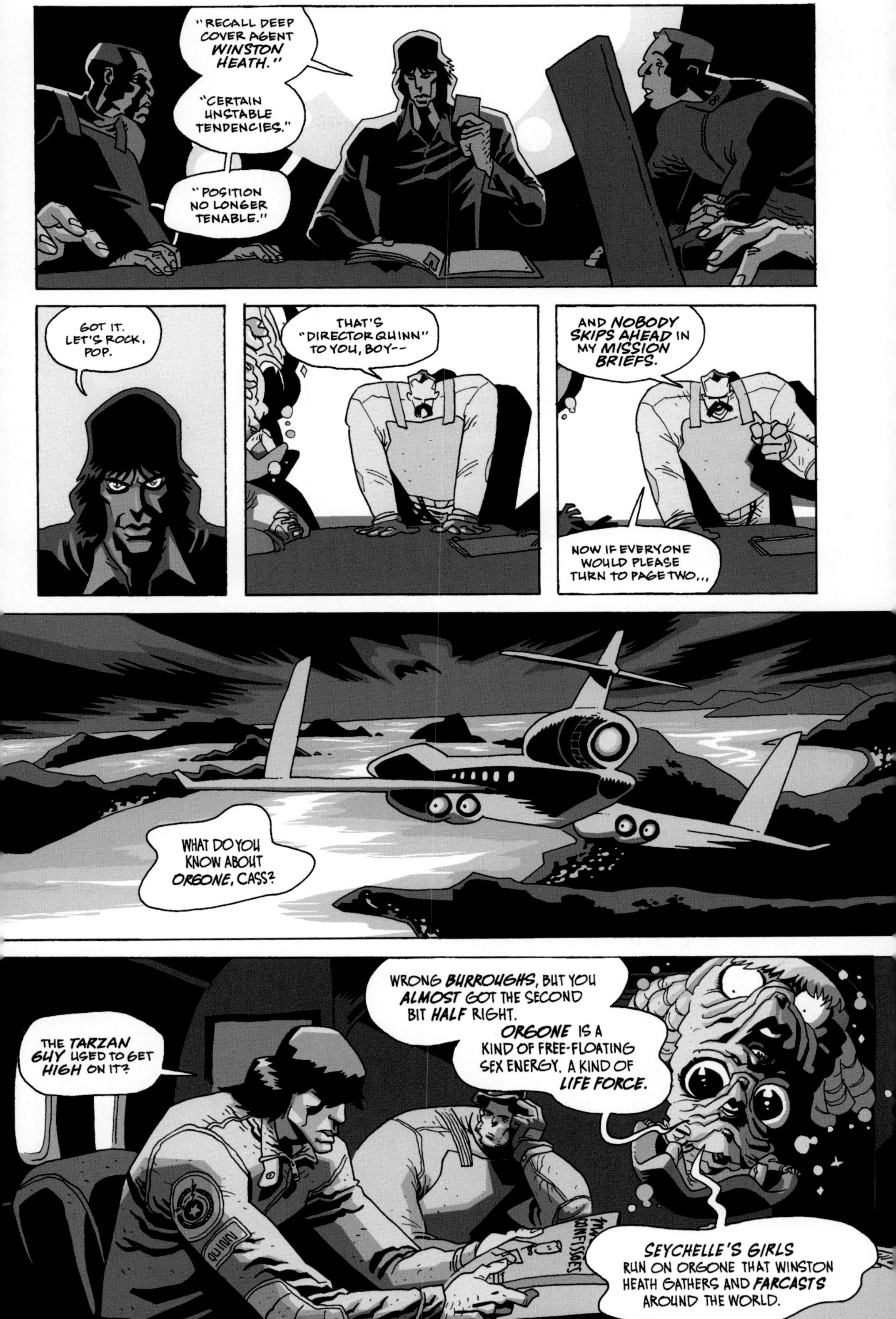
"RECALL DEEP COVER AGENT WINSTON HEATH."
"CERTAIN UNSTABLE TENDENCIES."
"POSITION NO LONGER TENABLE."
GOT IT. LET'S ROCK, POP.
THAT'S "DIRECTOR QUINN" TO YOU, BOY--
AND NOBODY SKIPS AHEAD IN MY MISSION BRIEFS.
NOW IF EVERYONE WOULD PLEASE TURN TO PAGE TWO...
WHAT DO YOU KNOW ABOUT ORGONE, CASS?
THE TARZAN GUY USED TO GET HIGH ON IT?
WRONG BURROUGHS, BUT YOU ALMOST GOT THE SECOND BIT HALF RIGHT.
ORGONE IS A KIND OF FREE-FLOATING SEX ENERGY. A KIND OF LIFE FORCE.
SEYCHELLE'S GIRLS RUN ON ORGONE THAT WINSTON HEATH GATHERS AND FARCASTS AROUND THE WORLD.

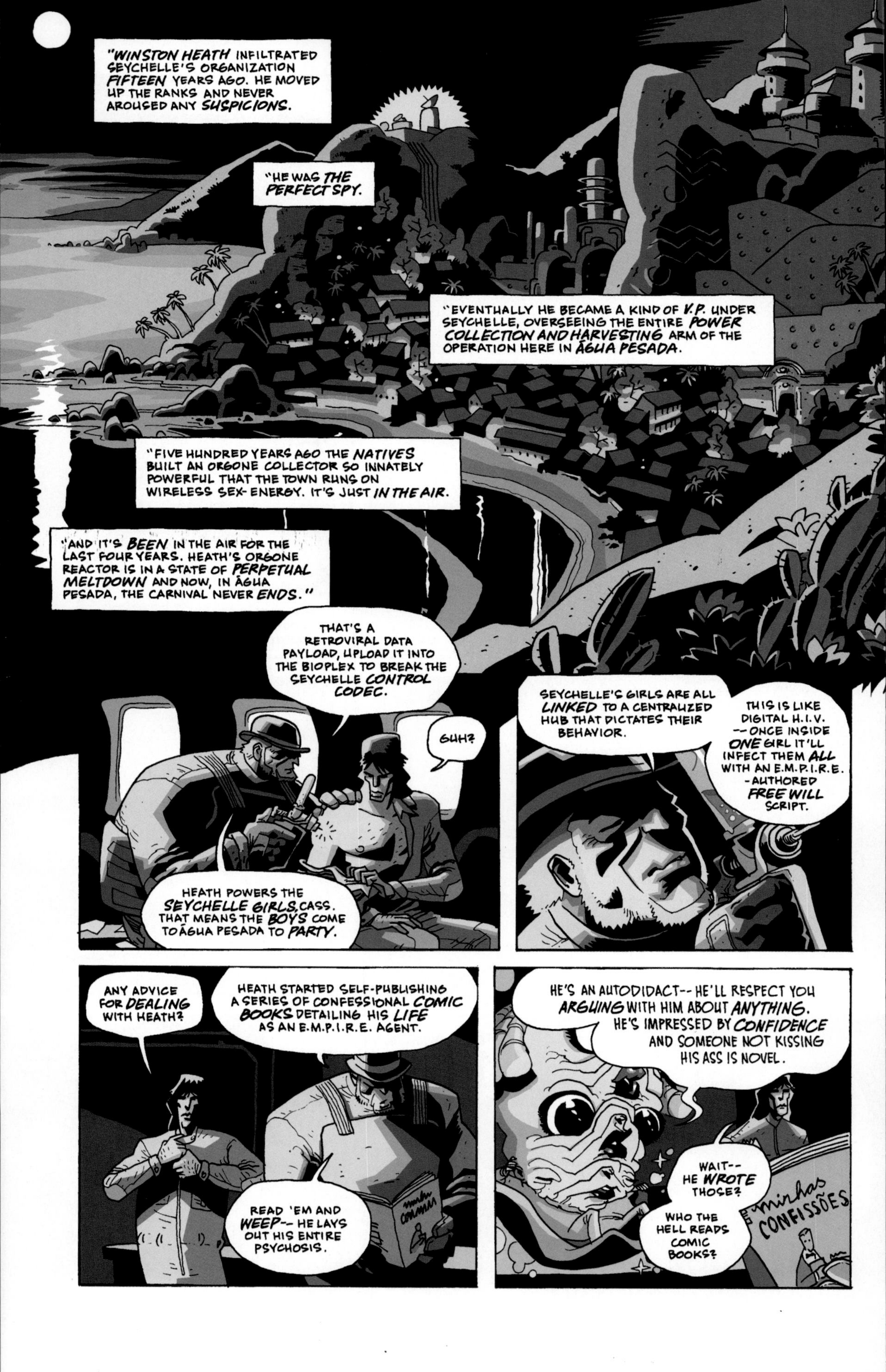
"WINSTON HEATH INFILTRATED SEYCHELLE'S ORGANIZATION FIFTEEN YEARS AGO. HE MOVED UP THE RANKS AND NEVER AROUSED ANY SUSPICIONS.
"HE WAS THE PERFECT SPY.
"EVENTUALLY HE BECAME A KIND OF V.P. UNDER SEYCHELLE, OVERSEEING THE ENTIRE POWER COLLECTION AND HARVESTING ARM OF THE OPERATION HERE IN ÁGUA PESADA.
"FIVE HUNDRED YEARS AGO THE NATIVES BUILT AN ORGONE COLLECTOR SO INNATELY POWERFUL THAT THE TOWN RUNS ON WIRELESS SEX-ENERGY. IT'S JUST IN THE AIR.
"AND IT'S BEEN IN THE AIR FOR THE LAST FOUR YEARS. HEATH'S ORGONE REACTOR IS IN A STATE OF PERPETUAL MELTDOWN AND NOW, IN ÁGUA PESADA, THE CARNIVAL NEVER ENDS."
THAT'S A RETROVIRAL DATA PAYLOAD, UPLOAD IT INTO THE BIOPLEX TO BREAK THE SEYCHELLE CONTROL CODEC.
GUH?
HEATH POWERS THE SEYCHELLE GIRLS, CASS. THAT MEANS THE BOYS COME TO ÁGUA PESADA TO PARTY.
SEYCHELLE'S GIRLS ARE ALL LINKED TO A CENTRALIZED HUB THAT DICTATES THEIR BEHAVIOR.
THIS IS LIKE DIGITAL H.I.V. --ONCE INSIDE ONE GIRL IT'LL INFECT THEM ALL WITH AN E.M.P.I.R.E.-AUTHORED FREE WILL SCRIPT.
ANY ADVICE FOR DEALING WITH HEATH?
HEATH STARTED SELF-PUBLISHING A SERIES OF CONFESSIONAL COMIC BOOKS DETAILING HIS LIFE AS AN E.M.P.I.R.E. AGENT.
READ 'EM AND WEEP-- HE LAYS OUT HIS ENTIRE PSYCHOSIS.
HE'S AN AUTODIDACT-- HE'LL RESPECT YOU ARGUING WITH HIM ABOUT ANYTHING. HE'S IMPRESSED BY CONFIDENCE AND SOMEONE NOT KISSING HIS ASS IS NOVEL.
WAIT-- HE WROTE THOSE?
WHO THE HELL READS COMIC BOOKS?
minhas CONFISSÕES

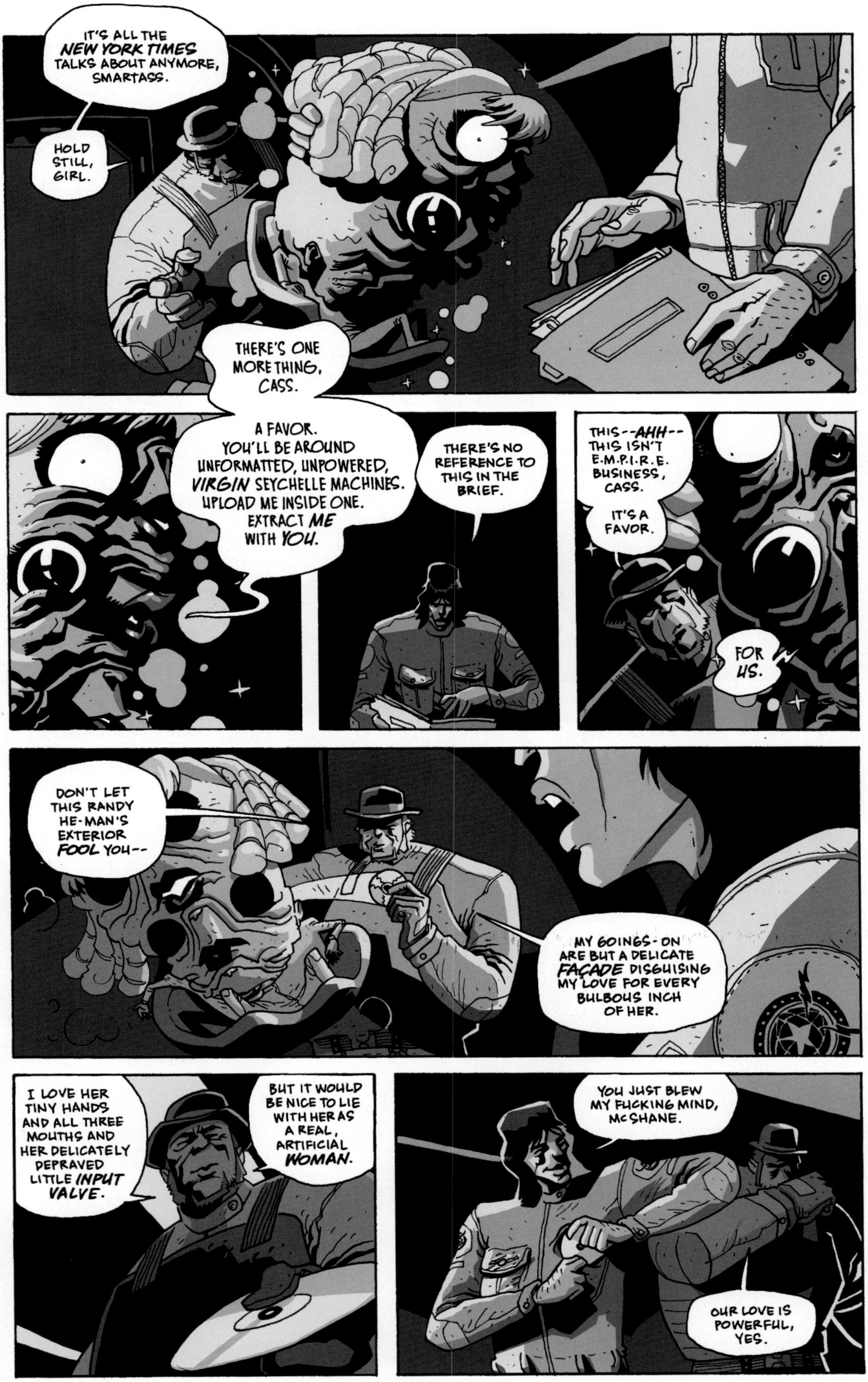
IT'S ALL THE NEW YORK TIMES TALKS ABOUT ANYMORE, SMARTASS.
HOLD STILL, GIRL.
THERE'S ONE MORE THING, CASS.
A FAVOR. YOU'LL BE AROUND UNFORMATTED, UNPOWERED, VIRGIN SEYCHELLE MACHINES. UPLOAD ME INSIDE ONE. EXTRACT ME WITH YOU.
THERE'S NO REFERENCE TO THIS IN THE BRIEF.
THIS--AHH--THIS ISN'T E.M.P.I.R.E. BUSINESS, CASS.
IT'S A FAVOR.
FOR US.
DON'T LET THIS RANDY HE-MAN'S EXTERIOR FOOL YOU--
MY GOINGS-ON ARE BUT A DELICATE FAÇADE DISGUISING MY LOVE FOR EVERY BULBOUS INCH OF HER.
I LOVE HER TINY HANDS AND ALL THREE MOUTHS AND HER DELICATELY DEPRAVED LITTLE INPUT VALVE.
BUT IT WOULD BE NICE TO LIE WITH HER AS A REAL, ARTIFICIAL WOMAN.
YOU JUST BLEW MY FUCKING MIND, McSHANE.
OUR LOVE IS POWERFUL, YES.

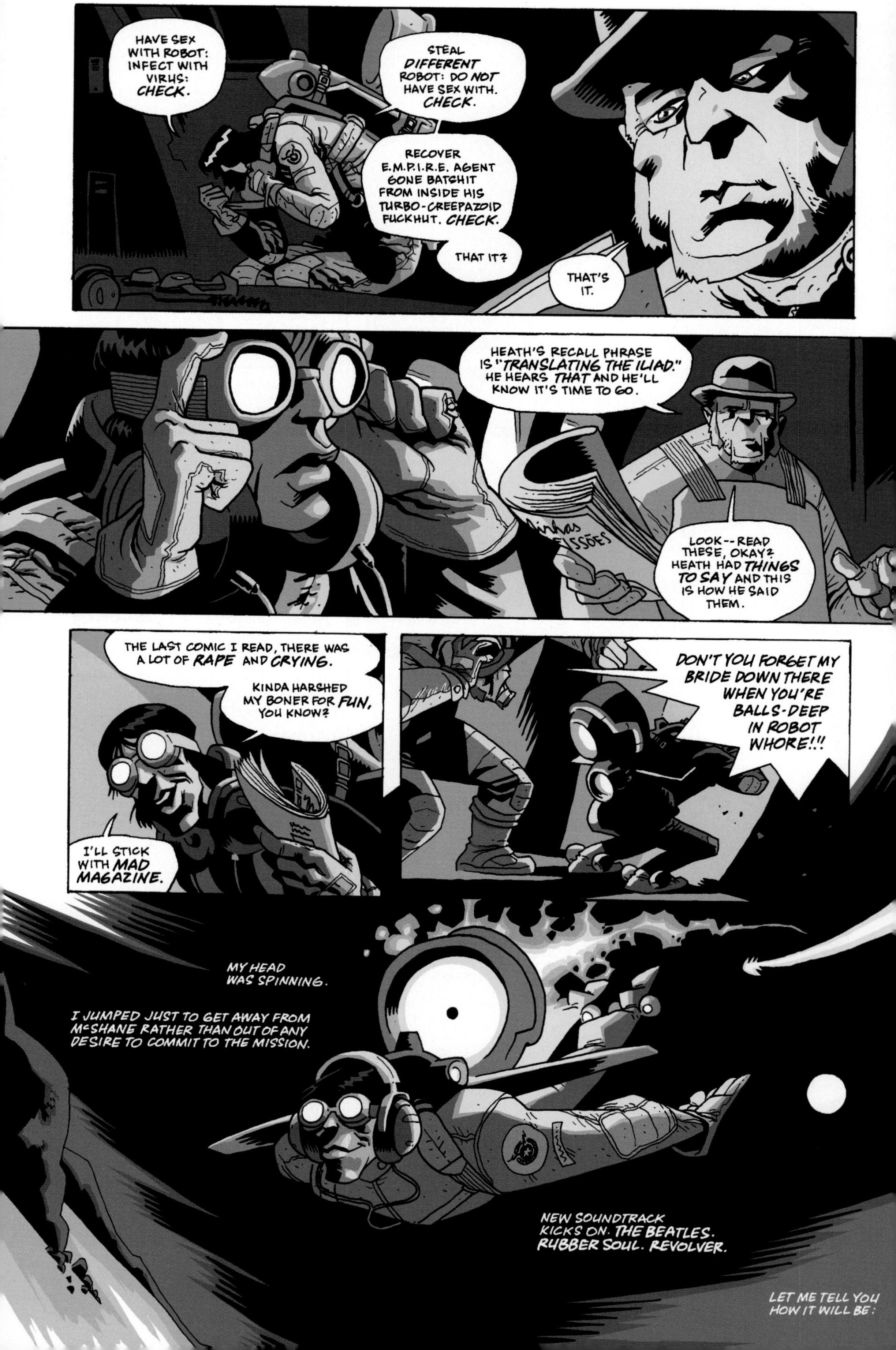
HAVE SEX WITH ROBOT: INFECT WITH VIRUS: CHECK.
STEAL DIFFERENT ROBOT: DO NOT HAVE SEX WITH. CHECK.
RECOVER E.M.P.I.R.E. AGENT GONE BATSHIT FROM INSIDE HIS TURBO-CREEPAZOID FUCKHUT. CHECK.
THAT IT?
THAT'S IT.
HEATH'S RECALL PHRASE IS "TRANSLATING THE ILIAD." HE HEARS THAT AND HE'LL KNOW IT'S TIME TO GO.
LOOK--READ THESE, OKAY? HEATH HAD THINGS TO SAY AND THIS IS HOW HE SAID THEM.
THE LAST COMIC I READ, THERE WAS A LOT OF RAPE AND CRYING.
KINDA HARSHED MY BONER FOR FUN, YOU KNOW?
I'LL STICK WITH MAD MAGAZINE.
DON'T YOU FORGET MY BRIDE DOWN THERE WHEN YOU'RE BALLS-DEEP IN ROBOT WHORE!!!
MY HEAD WAS SPINNING.
I JUMPED JUST TO GET AWAY FROM McSHANE RATHER THAN OUT OF ANY DESIRE TO COMMIT TO THE MISSION.
NEW SOUNDTRACK KICKS ON. THE BEATLES. RUBBER SOUL. REVOLVER.
LET ME TELL YOU HOW IT WILL BE:

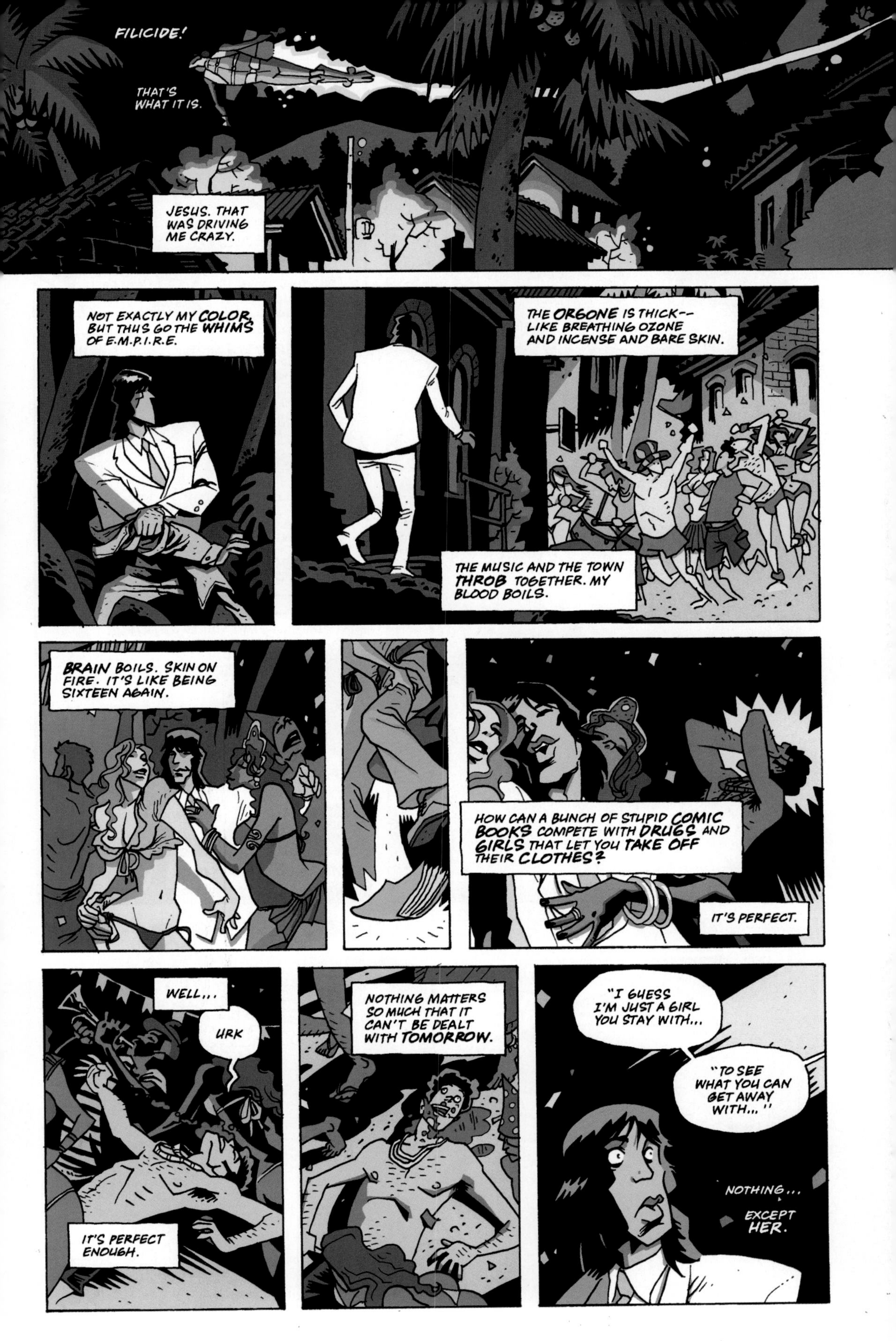
FILICIDE!
THAT'S WHAT IT IS.
JESUS. THAT WAS DRIVING ME CRAZY.
NOT EXACTLY MY COLOR, BUT THUS GO THE WHIMS OF E.M.P.I.R.E.
THE ORGONE IS THICK-- LIKE BREATHING OZONE AND INCENSE AND BARE SKIN.
THE MUSIC AND THE TOWN THROB TOGETHER. MY BLOOD BOILS.
BRAIN BOILS. SKIN ON FIRE. IT'S LIKE BEING SIXTEEN AGAIN.
HOW CAN A BUNCH OF STUPID COMIC BOOKS COMPETE WITH DRUGS AND GIRLS THAT LET YOU TAKE OFF THEIR CLOTHES?
IT'S PERFECT.
WELL...
URK
IT'S PERFECT ENOUGH.
NOTHING MATTERS SO MUCH THAT IT CAN'T BE DEALT WITH TOMORROW.
"I GUESS I'M JUST A GIRL YOU STAY WITH...
"TO SEE WHAT YOU CAN GET AWAY WITH..."
NOTHING...
EXCEPT HER.

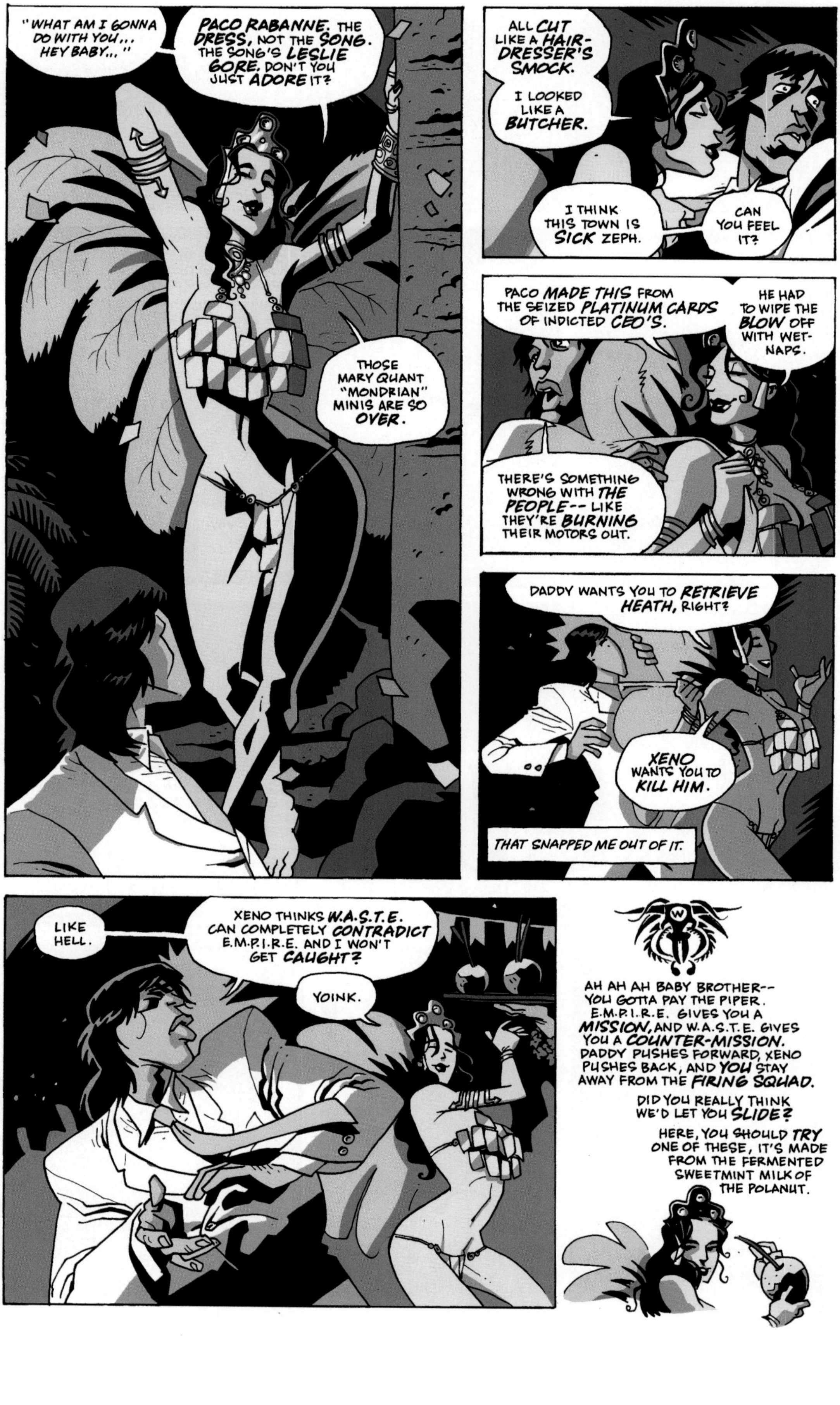
"WHAT AM I GONNA DO WITH YOU... HEY BABY..."
PACO RABANNE. THE DRESS, NOT THE SONG. THE SONG'S LESLIE GORE. DON'T YOU JUST ADORE IT?
THOSE MARY QUANT "MONDRIAN" MINIS ARE SO OVER.
ALL CUT LIKE A HAIR-DRESSER'S SMOCK.
I LOOKED LIKE A BUTCHER.
I THINK THIS TOWN IS SICK ZEPH.
CAN YOU FEEL IT?
PACO MADE THIS FROM THE SEIZED PLATINUM CARDS OF INDICTED CEO'S.
HE HAD TO WIPE THE BLOW OFF WITH WET-NAPS.
THERE'S SOMETHING WRONG WITH THE PEOPLE-- LIKE THEY'RE BURNING THEIR MOTORS OUT.
DADDY WANTS YOU TO RETRIEVE HEATH, RIGHT?
XENO WANTS YOU TO KILL HIM.
THAT SNAPPED ME OUT OF IT.
LIKE HELL.
XENO THINKS W.A.S.T.E. CAN COMPLETELY CONTRADICT E.M.P.I.R.E. AND I WON'T GET CAUGHT?
YOINK.
AH AH AH BABY BROTHER-- YOU GOTTA PAY THE PIPER. E.M.P.I.R.E. GIVES YOU A MISSION, AND W.A.S.T.E. GIVES YOU A COUNTER-MISSION. DADDY PUSHES FORWARD, XENO PUSHES BACK, AND YOU STAY AWAY FROM THE FIRING SQUAD.
DID YOU REALLY THINK WE'D LET YOU SLIDE?
HERE, YOU SHOULD TRY ONE OF THESE, IT'S MADE FROM THE FERMENTED SWEETMINT MILK OF THE POLANUT.

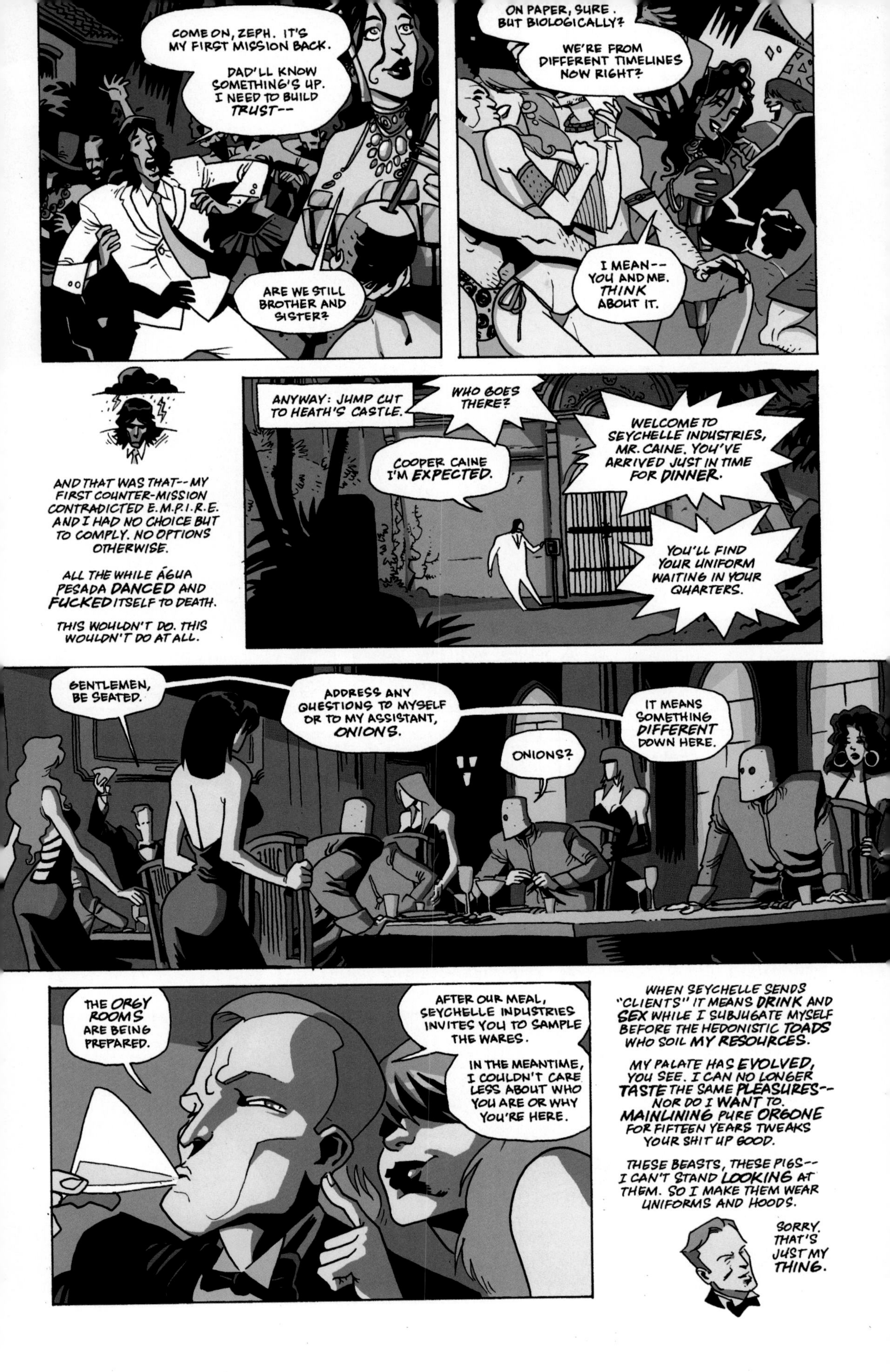
COME ON, ZEPH. IT'S MY FIRST MISSION BACK.
DAD'LL KNOW SOMETHING'S UP. I NEED TO BUILD TRUST--
ARE WE STILL BROTHER AND SISTER?
ON PAPER, SURE. BUT BIOLOGICALLY?
WE'RE FROM DIFFERENT TIMELINES NOW RIGHT?
I MEAN-- YOU AND ME. THINK ABOUT IT.
AND THAT WAS THAT--MY FIRST COUNTER-MISSION CONTRADICTED E.M.P.I.R.E. AND I HAD NO CHOICE BUT TO COMPLY. NO OPTIONS OTHERWISE.
ALL THE WHILE ÁGUA PESADA DANCED AND FUCKED ITSELF TO DEATH.
THIS WOULDN'T DO. THIS WOULDN'T DO AT ALL.
ANYWAY: JUMP CUT TO HEATH'S CASTLE.
WHO GOES THERE?
COOPER CAINE I'M EXPECTED.
WELCOME TO SEYCHELLE INDUSTRIES, MR. CAINE. YOU'VE ARRIVED JUST IN TIME FOR DINNER.
YOU'LL FIND YOUR UNIFORM WAITING IN YOUR QUARTERS.
GENTLEMEN, BE SEATED.
ADDRESS ANY QUESTIONS TO MYSELF OR TO MY ASSISTANT, ONIONS.
ONIONS?
IT MEANS SOMETHING DIFFERENT DOWN HERE.
THE ORGY ROOMS ARE BEING PREPARED.
AFTER OUR MEAL, SEYCHELLE INDUSTRIES INVITES YOU TO SAMPLE THE WARES.
IN THE MEANTIME, I COULDN'T CARE LESS ABOUT WHO YOU ARE OR WHY YOU'RE HERE.
WHEN SEYCHELLE SENDS "CLIENTS" IT MEANS DRINK AND SEX WHILE I SUBJUGATE MYSELF BEFORE THE HEDONISTIC TOADS WHO SOIL MY RESOURCES.
MY PALATE HAS EVOLVED, YOU SEE. I CAN NO LONGER TASTE THE SAME PLEASURES--NOR DO I WANT TO. MAINLINING PURE ORGONE FOR FIFTEEN YEARS TWEAKS YOUR SHIT UP GOOD.
THESE BEASTS, THESE PIGS--I CAN'T STAND LOOKING AT THEM. SO I MAKE THEM WEAR UNIFORMS AND HOODS.
SORRY. THAT'S JUST MY THING.

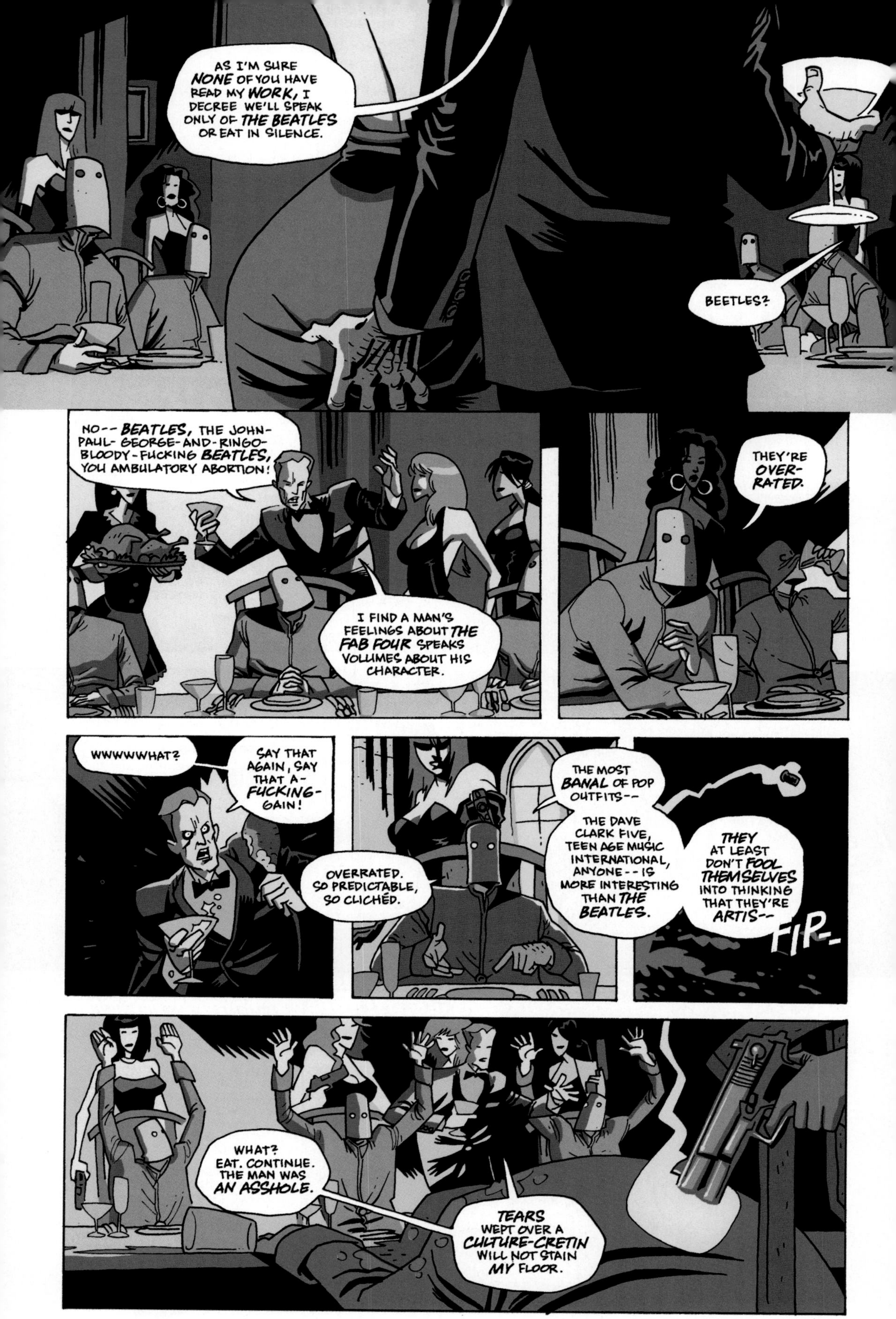
AS I'M SURE NONE OF YOU HAVE READ MY WORK, I DECREE WE'LL SPEAK ONLY OF THE BEATLES OR EAT IN SILENCE.
BEETLES?
NO-- BEATLES, THE JOHN-PAUL-GEORGE-AND-RINGO-BLOODY-FUCKING BEATLES, YOU AMBULATORY ABORTION!
I FIND A MAN'S FEELINGS ABOUT THE FAB FOUR SPEAKS VOLUMES ABOUT HIS CHARACTER.
THEY'RE OVER-RATED.
WWWWWHAT?
SAY THAT AGAIN, SAY THAT A-FUCKING-GAIN!
OVERRATED. SO PREDICTABLE, SO CLICHÉD.
THE MOST BANAL OF POP OUTFITS--
THE DAVE CLARK FIVE, TEEN AGE MUSIC INTERNATIONAL, ANYONE--IS MORE INTERESTING THAN THE BEATLES.
THEY AT LEAST DON'T FOOL THEMSELVES INTO THINKING THAT THEY'RE ARTIS--
FIP--
WHAT? EAT. CONTINUE. THE MAN WAS AN ASSHOLE.
TEARS WEPT OVER A CULTURE-CRETIN WILL NOT STAIN MY FLOOR.

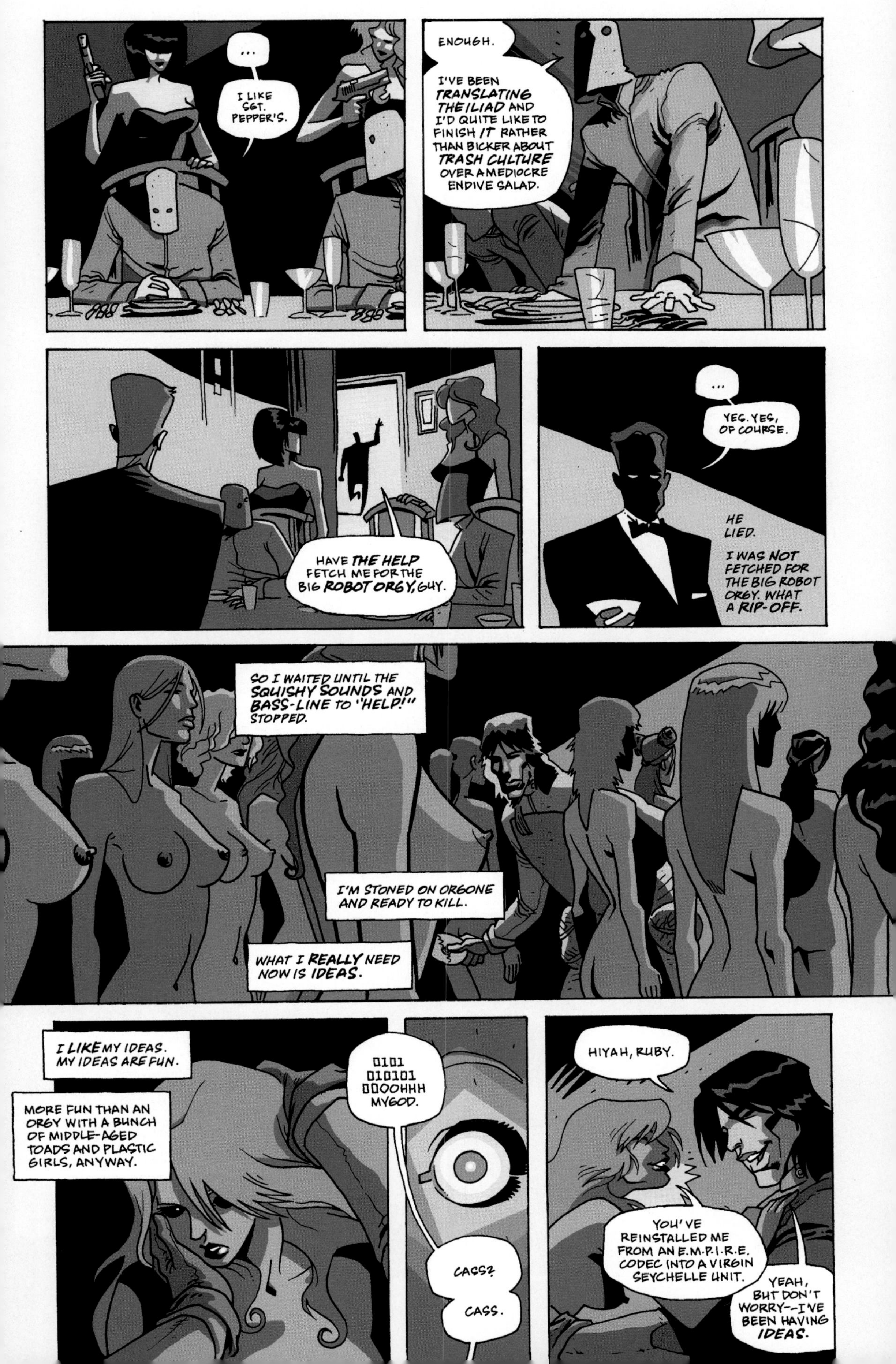
...
I LIKE SGT. PEPPER'S.
ENOUGH.
I'VE BEEN TRANSLATING THE ILIAD AND I'D QUITE LIKE TO FINISH IT RATHER THAN BICKER ABOUT TRASH CULTURE OVER A MEDIOCRE ENDIVE SALAD.
HAVE THE HELP FETCH ME FOR THE BIG ROBOT ORGY, GUY.
...
YES. YES, OF COURSE.
HE LIED.
I WAS NOT FETCHED FOR THE BIG ROBOT ORGY. WHAT A RIP-OFF.
SO I WAITED UNTIL THE SQUISHY SOUNDS AND BASS-LINE TO "HELP!" STOPPED.
I'M STONED ON ORGONE AND READY TO KILL.
WHAT I REALLY NEED NOW IS IDEAS.
I LIKE MY IDEAS. MY IDEAS ARE FUN.
MORE FUN THAN AN ORGY WITH A BUNCH OF MIDDLE-AGED TOADS AND PLASTIC GIRLS, ANYWAY.
0101 010101 0OOOHHH MYGOD.
CASS?
CASS.
HIYAH, RUBY.
YOU'VE REINSTALLED ME FROM AN E.M.P.I.R.E. CODEC INTO A VIRGIN SEYCHELLE UNIT.
YEAH, BUT DON'T WORRY--I'VE BEEN HAVING IDEAS.

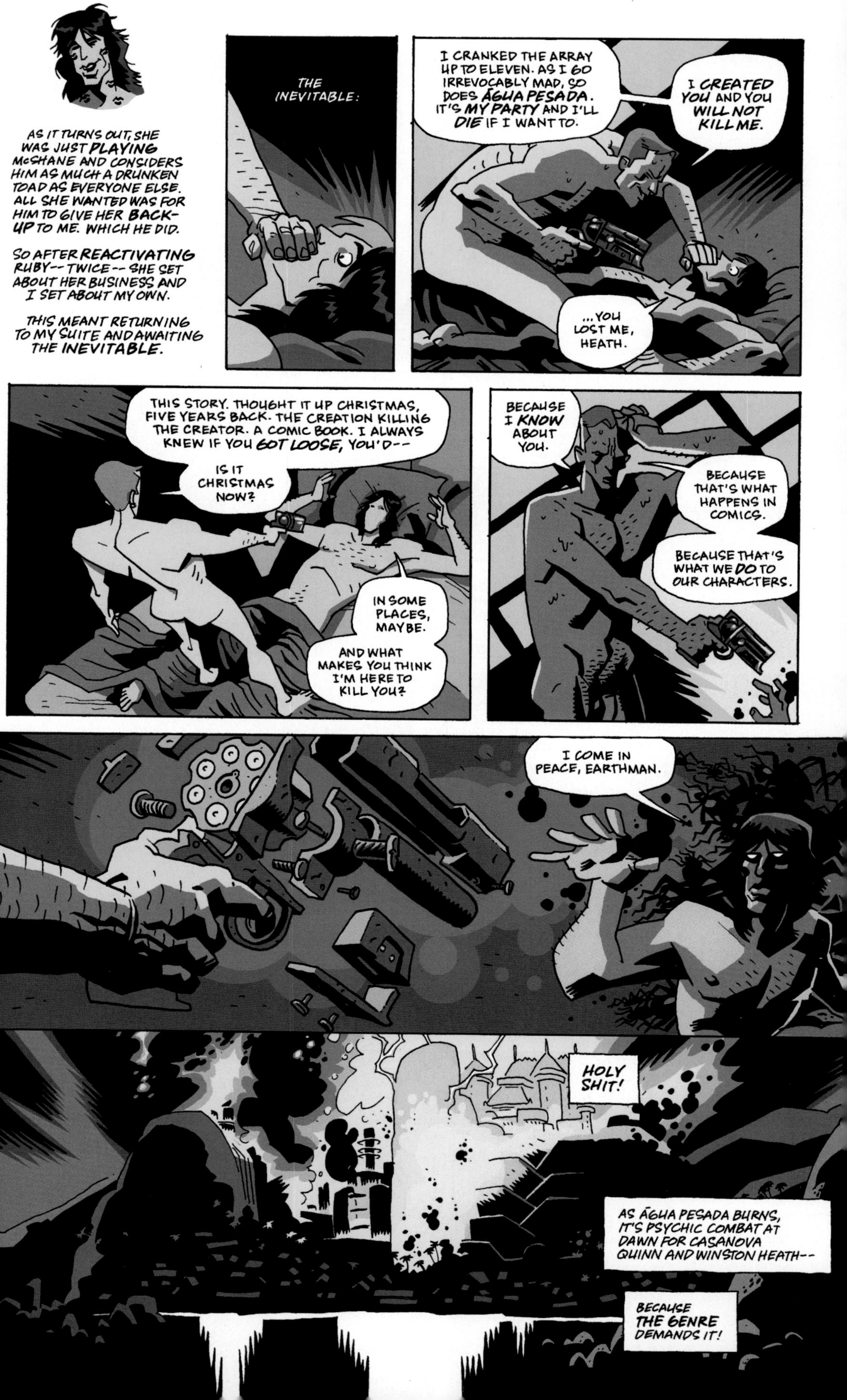
AS IT TURNS OUT, SHE WAS JUST PLAYING McSHANE AND CONSIDERS HIM AS MUCH A DRUNKEN TOAD AS EVERYONE ELSE. ALL SHE WANTED WAS FOR HIM TO GIVE HER BACK-UP TO ME. WHICH HE DID.
SO AFTER REACTIVATING RUBY-- TWICE-- SHE SET ABOUT HER BUSINESS AND I SET ABOUT MY OWN.
THIS MEANT RETURNING TO MY SUITE AND AWAITING THE INEVITABLE.
THE INEVITABLE:
I CRANKED THE ARRAY UP TO ELEVEN. AS I GO IRREVOCABLY MAD, SO DOES ÁGUA PESADA. IT'S MY PARTY AND I'LL DIE IF I WANT TO.
I CREATED YOU AND YOU WILL NOT KILL ME.
...YOU LOST ME, HEATH.
THIS STORY. THOUGHT IT UP CHRISTMAS, FIVE YEARS BACK. THE CREATION KILLING THE CREATOR. A COMIC BOOK. I ALWAYS KNEW IF YOU GOT LOOSE, YOU'D--
IS IT CHRISTMAS NOW?
IN SOME PLACES, MAYBE.
AND WHAT MAKES YOU THINK I'M HERE TO KILL YOU?
BECAUSE I KNOW ABOUT YOU.
BECAUSE THAT'S WHAT HAPPENS IN COMICS.
BECAUSE THAT'S WHAT WE DO TO OUR CHARACTERS.
I COME IN PEACE, EARTHMAN.
HOLY SHIT!
AS ÁGUA PESADA BURNS, IT'S PSYCHIC COMBAT AT DAWN FOR CASANOVA QUINN AND WINSTON HEATH--
BECAUSE THE GENRE DEMANDS IT!

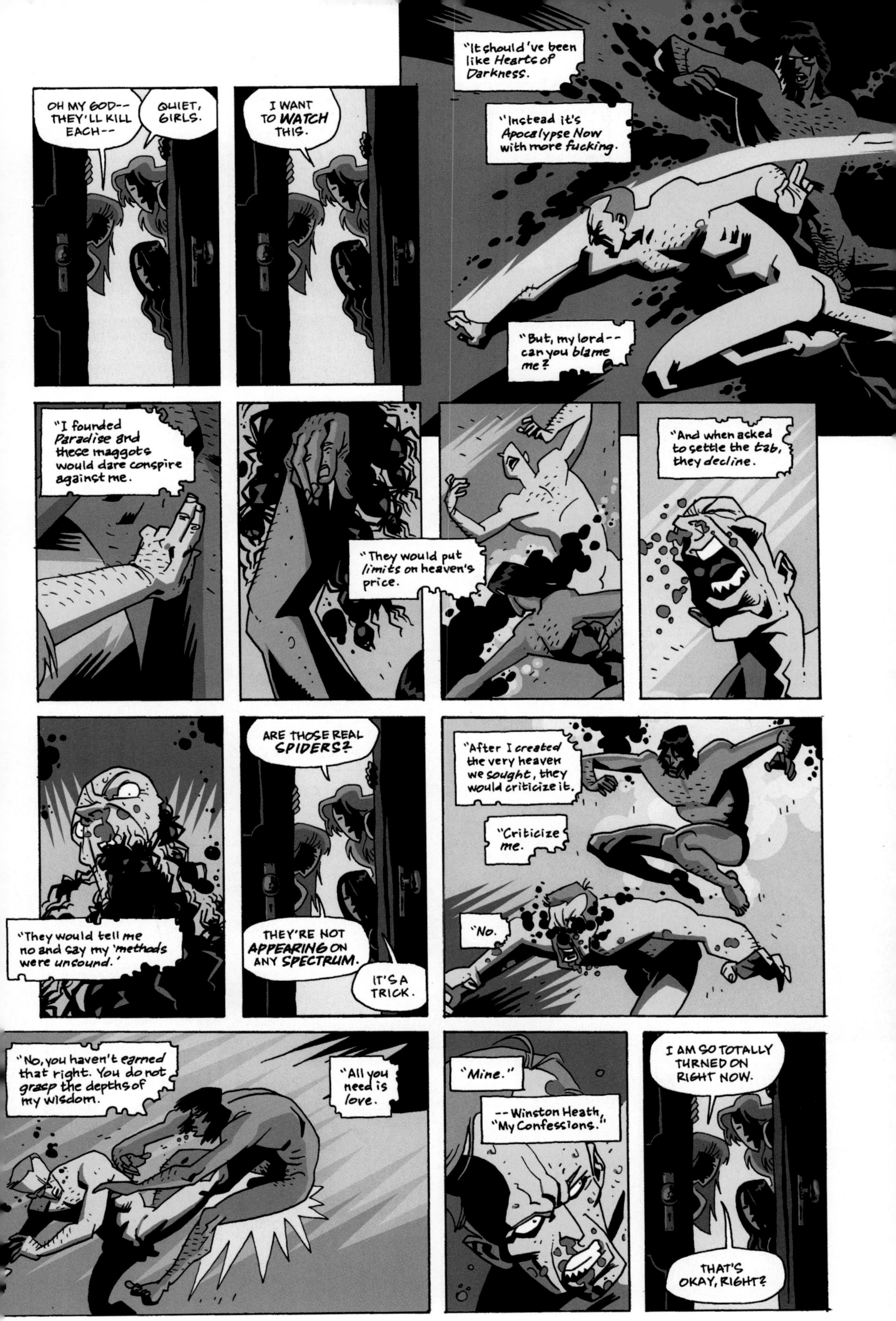
OH MY GOD-- THEY'LL KILL EACH--
QUIET, GIRLS.
I WANT TO WATCH THIS.
"It should've been like Hearts of Darkness.
"Instead it's Apocalypse Now with more fucking.
"But, my lord-- can you blame me?
"I founded Paradise and these maggots would dare conspire against me.
"They would put limits on heaven's price.
"And when asked to settle the tab, they decline.
"They would tell me no and say my 'methods were unsound.'
ARE THOSE REAL SPIDERS?
THEY'RE NOT APPEARING ON ANY SPECTRUM.
IT'S A TRICK.
"After I created the very heaven we sought, they would criticize it.
"Criticize me.
"No.
"No, you haven't earned that right. You do not grasp the depths of my wisdom.
"All you need is love.
"Mine."
--Winston Heath, "My Confessions."
I AM SO TOTALLY TURNED ON RIGHT NOW.
THAT'S OKAY, RIGHT?

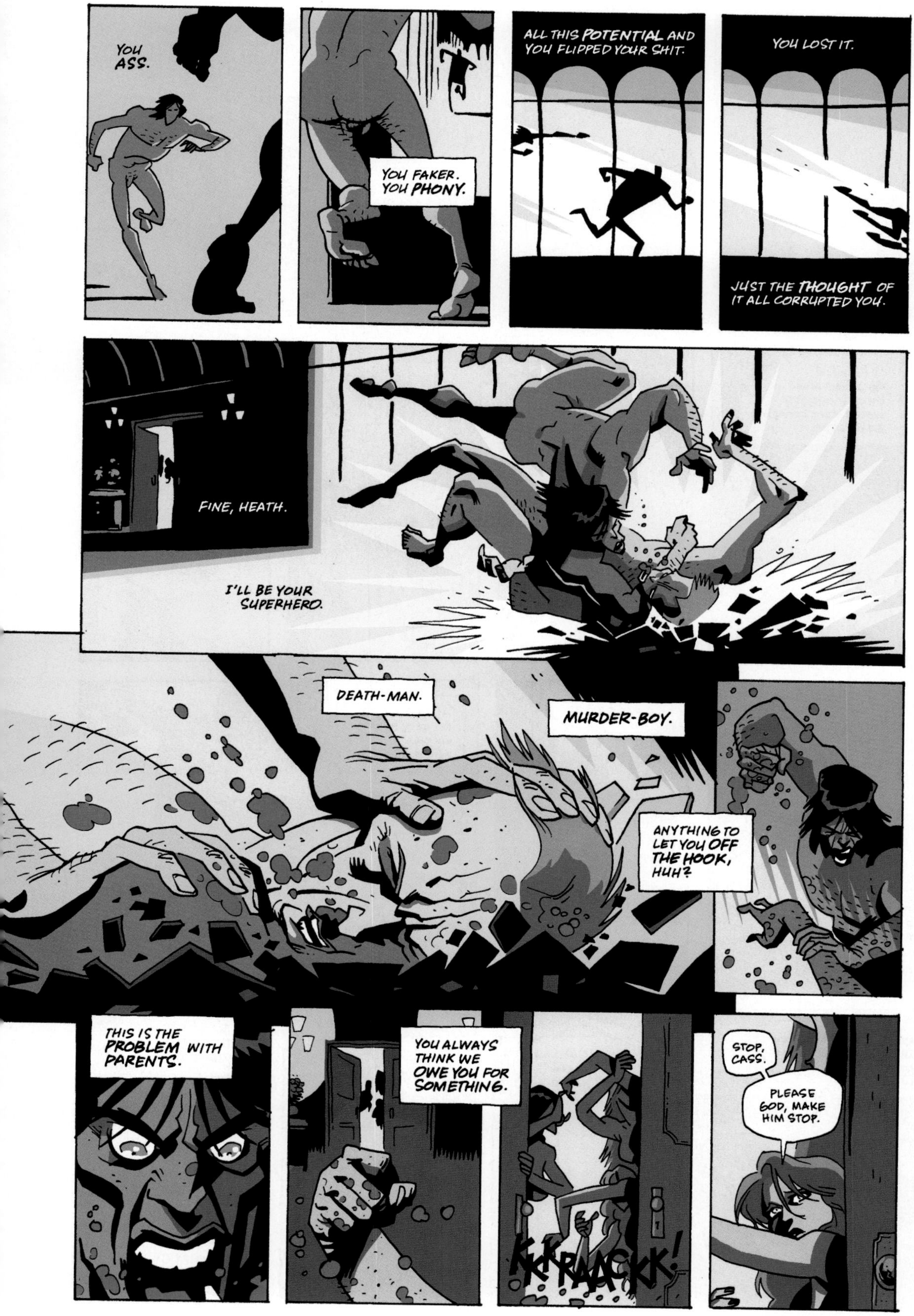
YOU ASS.
YOU FAKER. YOU PHONY.
ALL THIS POTENTIAL AND YOU FLIPPED YOUR SHIT.
YOU LOST IT.
JUST THE THOUGHT OF IT ALL CORRUPTED YOU.
FINE, HEATH.
I'LL BE YOUR SUPERHERO.
DEATH-MAN.
MURDER-BOY.
ANYTHING TO LET YOU OFF THE HOOK, HUH?
THIS IS THE PROBLEM WITH PARENTS.
YOU ALWAYS THINK WE OWE YOU FOR SOMETHING.
KKKRAAACKK!
STOP, CASS.
PLEASE GOD, MAKE HIM STOP.

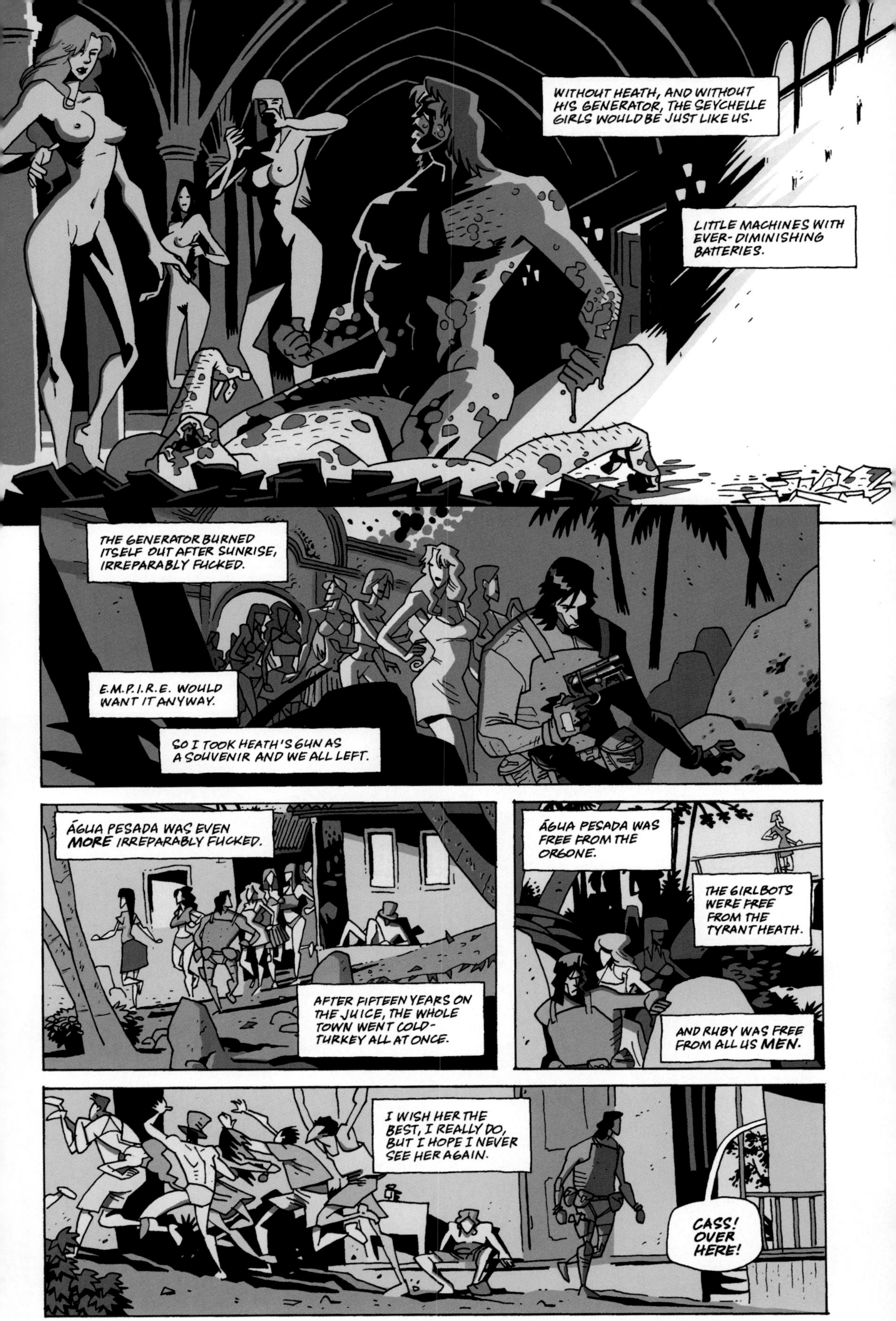
WITHOUT HEATH, AND WITHOUT HIS GENERATOR, THE SEYCHELLE GIRLS WOULD BE JUST LIKE US.
LITTLE MACHINES WITH EVER-DIMINISHING BATTERIES.
THE GENERATOR BURNED ITSELF OUT AFTER SUNRISE, IRREPARABLY FUCKED.
E.M.P.I.R.E. WOULD WANT IT ANYWAY.
SO I TOOK HEATH'S GUN AS A SOUVENIR AND WE ALL LEFT.
ÁGUA PESADA WAS EVEN MORE IRREPARABLY FUCKED.
AFTER FIFTEEN YEARS ON THE JUICE, THE WHOLE TOWN WENT COLD-TURKEY ALL AT ONCE.
ÁGUA PESADA WAS FREE FROM THE ORGONE.
THE GIRLBOTS WERE FREE FROM THE TYRANT HEATH.
AND RUBY WAS FREE FROM ALL US MEN.
I WISH HER THE BEST, I REALLY DO, BUT I HOPE I NEVER SEE HER AGAIN.
CASS! OVER HERE!

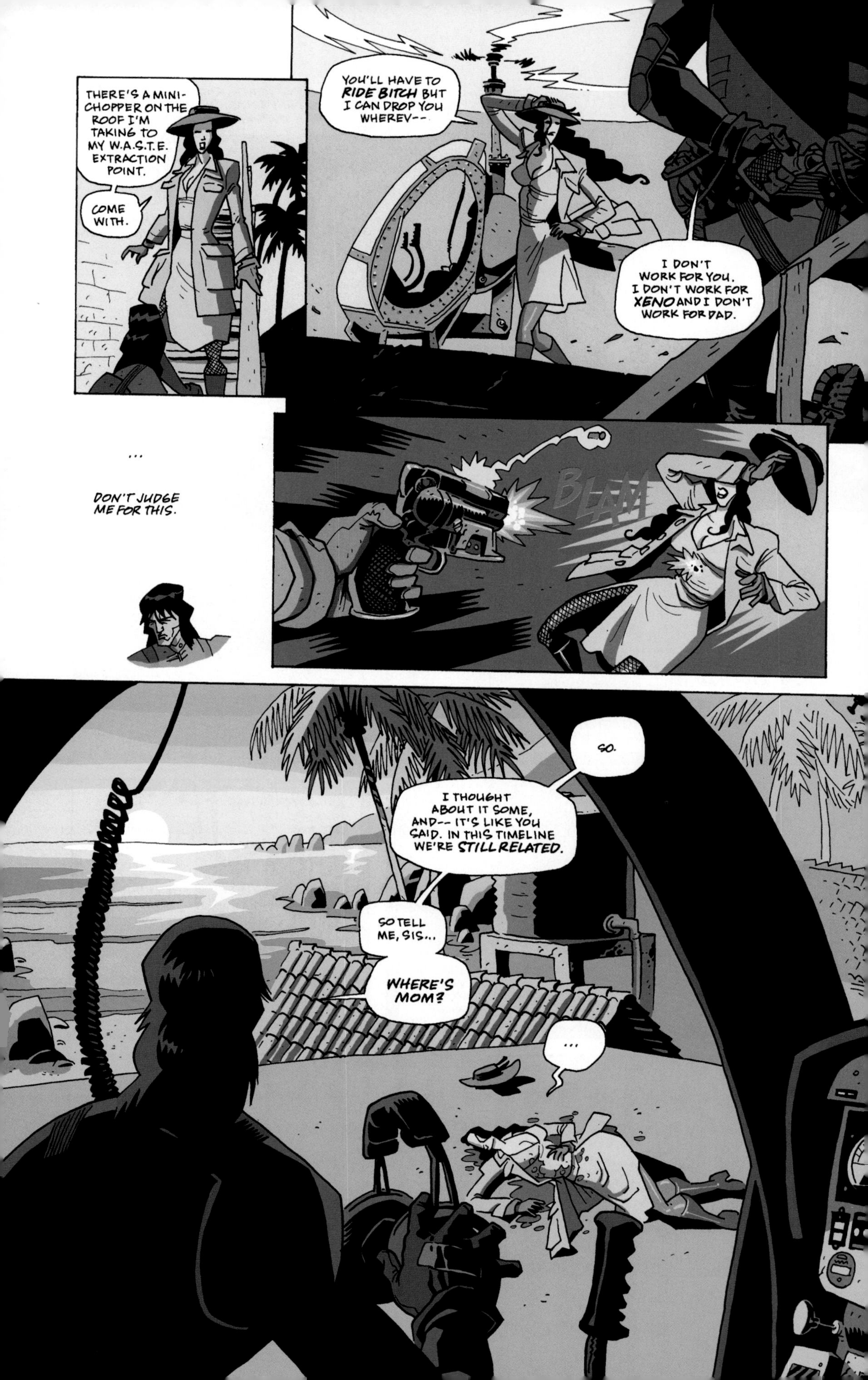
THERE'S A MINI-CHOPPER ON THE ROOF I'M TAKING TO MY W.A.S.T.E. EXTRACTION POINT.
COME WITH.
YOU'LL HAVE TO RIDE BITCH BUT I CAN DROP YOU WHEREV--.
I DON'T WORK FOR YOU. I DON'T WORK FOR XENO AND I DON'T WORK FOR DAD.
...
DON'T JUDGE ME FOR THIS.
BLAM
SO.
I THOUGHT ABOUT IT SOME, AND-- IT'S LIKE YOU SAID. IN THIS TIMELINE WE'RE STILL RELATED.
SO TELL ME, SIS...
WHERE'S MOM?
...

# CHAPTER 3
# MISSION TO YERBA MUERTA

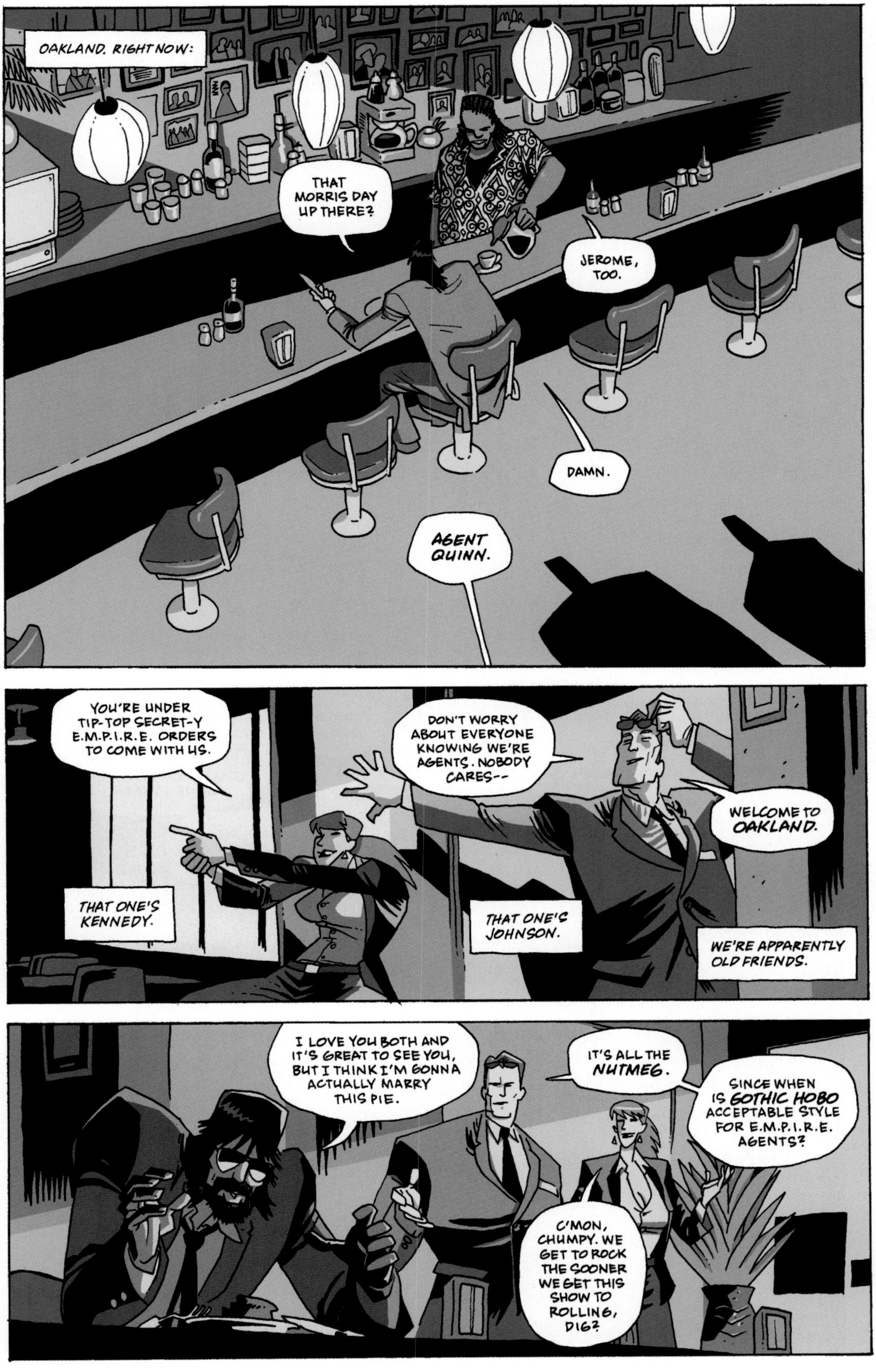
OAKLAND. RIGHT NOW:
THAT MORRIS DAY UP THERE?
JEROME, TOO.
DAMN.
AGENT QUINN.
YOU'RE UNDER TIP-TOP SECRET-Y E.M.P.I.R.E. ORDERS TO COME WITH US.
DON'T WORRY ABOUT EVERYONE KNOWING WE'RE AGENTS. NOBODY CARES--
WELCOME TO OAKLAND.
THAT ONE'S KENNEDY.
THAT ONE'S JOHNSON.
WE'RE APPARENTLY OLD FRIENDS.
I LOVE YOU BOTH AND IT'S GREAT TO SEE YOU, BUT I THINK I'M GONNA ACTUALLY MARRY THIS PIE.
IT'S ALL THE NUTMEG.
SINCE WHEN IS GOTHIC HOBO ACCEPTABLE STYLE FOR E.M.P.I.R.E. AGENTS?
C'MON, CHUMPY. WE GET TO ROCK THE SOONER WE GET THIS SHOW TO ROLLING, DIG?

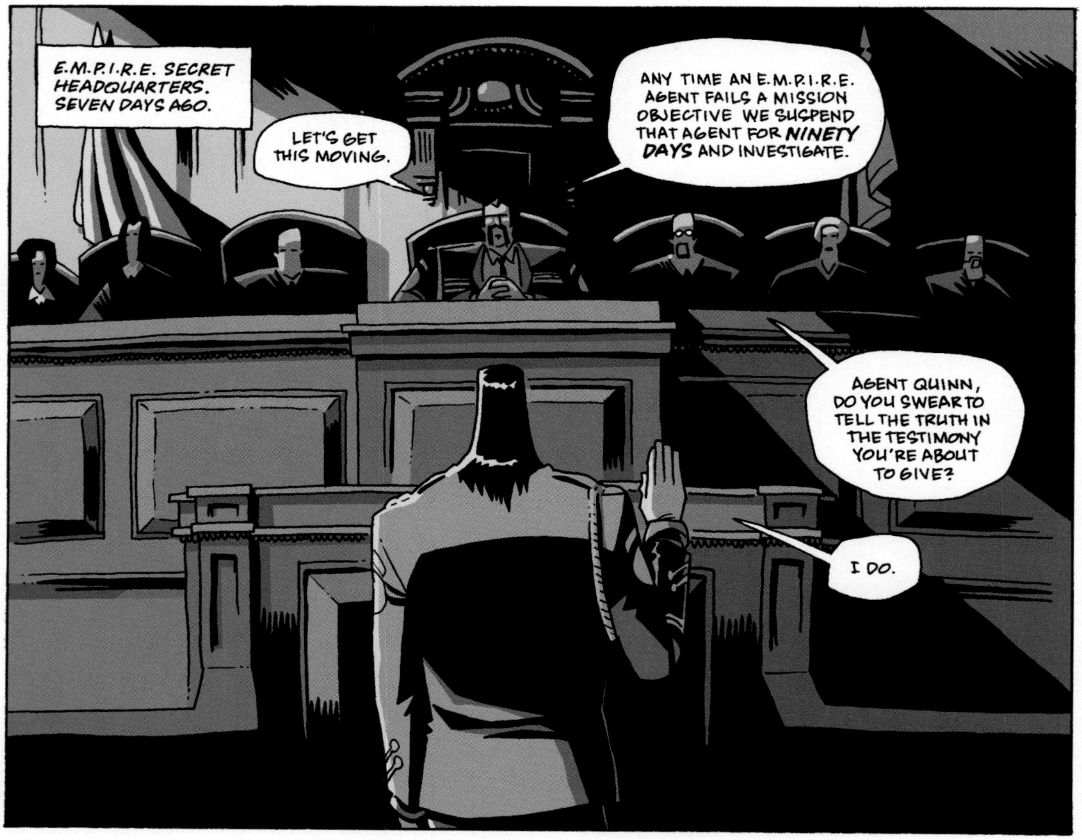
E.M.P.I.R.E. SECRET HEADQUARTERS. SEVEN DAYS AGO.
LET'S GET THIS MOVING.
ANY TIME AN E.M.P.I.R.E. AGENT FAILS A MISSION OBJECTIVE WE SUSPEND THAT AGENT FOR NINETY DAYS AND INVESTIGATE.
AGENT QUINN, DO YOU SWEAR TO TELL THE TRUTH IN THE TESTIMONY YOU'RE ABOUT TO GIVE?
I DO.

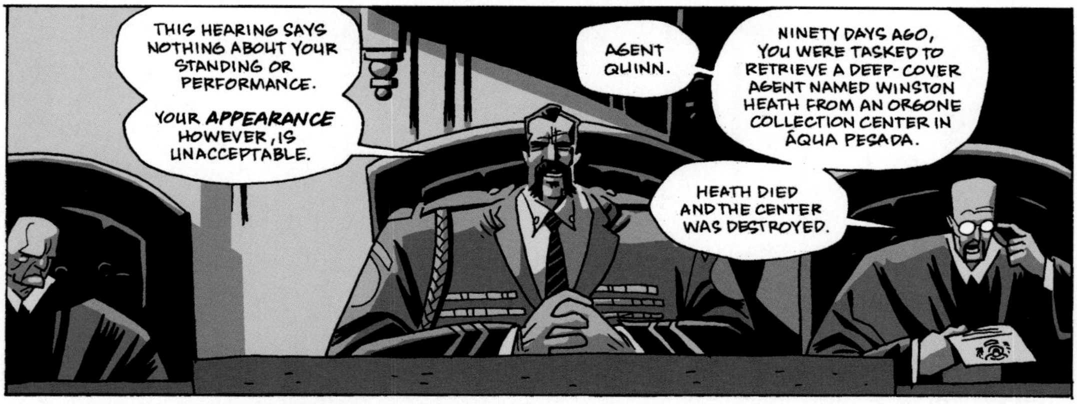
THIS HEARING SAYS NOTHING ABOUT YOUR STANDING OR PERFORMANCE.
YOUR APPEARANCE HOWEVER, IS UNACCEPTABLE.
AGENT QUINN.
NINETY DAYS AGO, YOU WERE TASKED TO RETRIEVE A DEEP-COVER AGENT NAMED WINSTON HEATH FROM AN ORGONE COLLECTION CENTER IN ÁQUA PESADA.
HEATH DIED AND THE CENTER WAS DESTROYED.

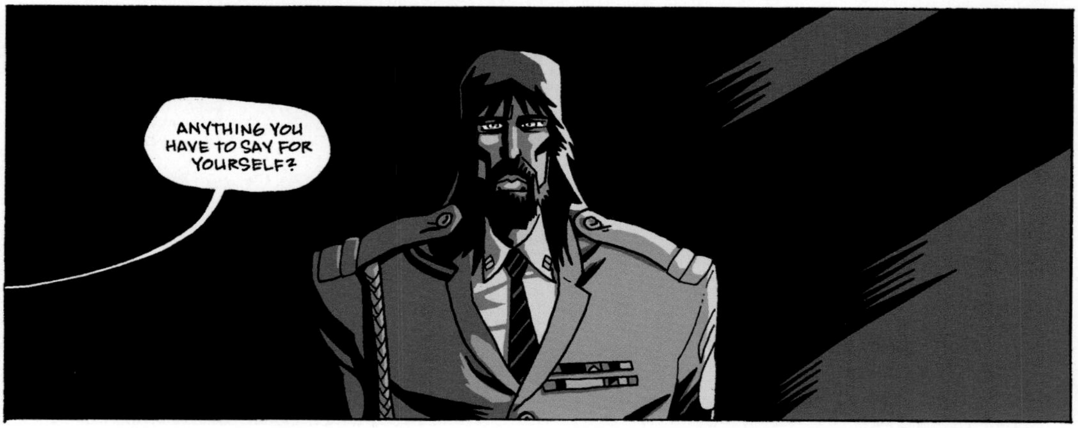
ANYTHING YOU HAVE TO SAY FOR YOURSELF?

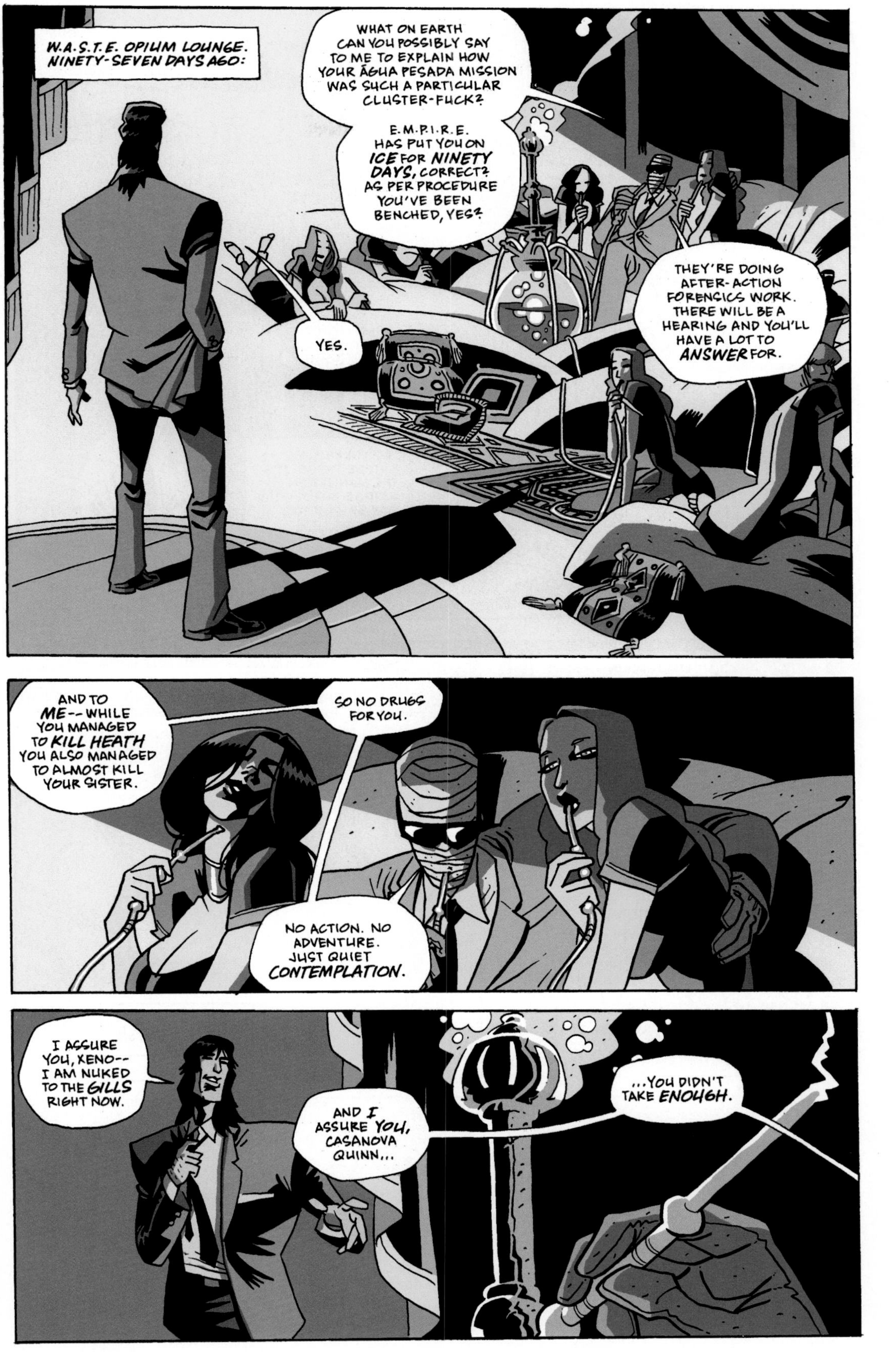
W.A.S.T.E. OPIUM LOUNGE. NINETY-SEVEN DAYS AGO:
WHAT ON EARTH CAN YOU POSSIBLY SAY TO ME TO EXPLAIN HOW YOUR ÁGUA PESADA MISSION WAS SUCH A PARTICULAR CLUSTER-FUCK?
E.M.P.I.R.E. HAS PUT YOU ON ICE FOR NINETY DAYS, CORRECT? AS PER PROCEDURE YOU'VE BEEN BENCHED, YES?
YES.
THEY'RE DOING AFTER-ACTION FORENSICS WORK. THERE WILL BE A HEARING AND YOU'LL HAVE A LOT TO ANSWER FOR.
AND TO ME-- WHILE YOU MANAGED TO KILL HEATH YOU ALSO MANAGED TO ALMOST KILL YOUR SISTER.
SO NO DRUGS FOR YOU.
NO ACTION. NO ADVENTURE. JUST QUIET CONTEMPLATION.
I ASSURE YOU, XENO-- I AM NUKED TO THE GILLS RIGHT NOW.
AND I ASSURE YOU, CASANOVA QUINN...
...YOU DIDN'T TAKE ENOUGH.

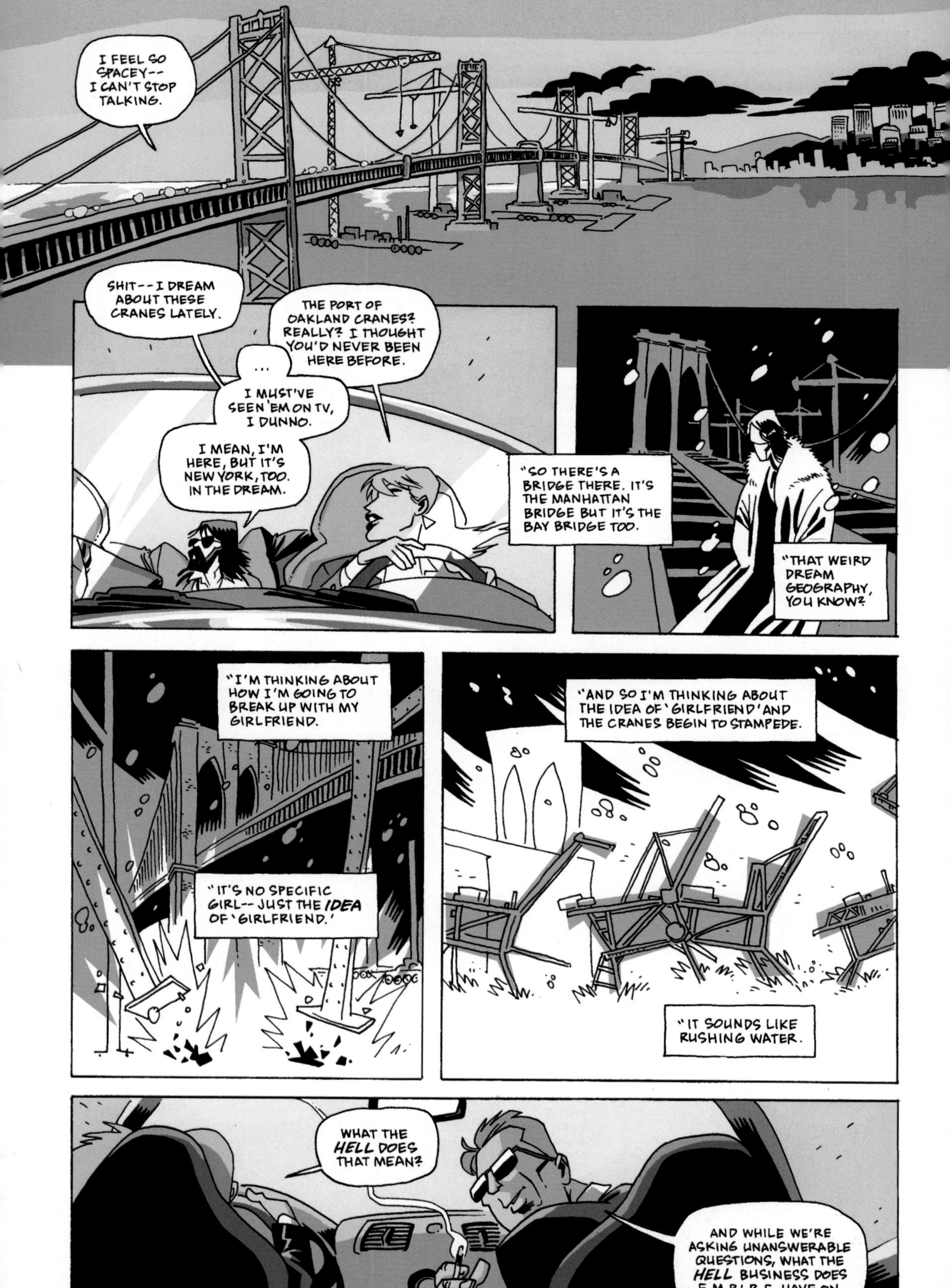
I FEEL SO SPACEY-- I CAN'T STOP TALKING.
SHIT--I DREAM ABOUT THESE CRANES LATELY.
THE PORT OF OAKLAND CRANES? REALLY? I THOUGHT YOU'D NEVER BEEN HERE BEFORE.
...
I MUST'VE SEEN 'EM ON TV, I DUNNO.
I MEAN, I'M HERE, BUT IT'S NEW YORK, TOO. IN THE DREAM.
"SO THERE'S A BRIDGE THERE. IT'S THE MANHATTAN BRIDGE BUT IT'S THE BAY BRIDGE TOO.
"THAT WEIRD DREAM GEOGRAPHY, YOU KNOW?
"I'M THINKING ABOUT HOW I'M GOING TO BREAK UP WITH MY GIRLFRIEND.
"IT'S NO SPECIFIC GIRL-- JUST THE IDEA OF 'GIRLFRIEND.'
"AND SO I'M THINKING ABOUT THE IDEA OF 'GIRLFRIEND' AND THE CRANES BEGIN TO STAMPEDE.
"IT SOUNDS LIKE RUSHING WATER.
WHAT THE HELL DOES THAT MEAN?
AND WHILE WE'RE ASKING UNANSWERABLE QUESTIONS, WHAT THE HELL BUSINESS DOES E.M.P.I.R.E. HAVE ON YERBA MUERTA?

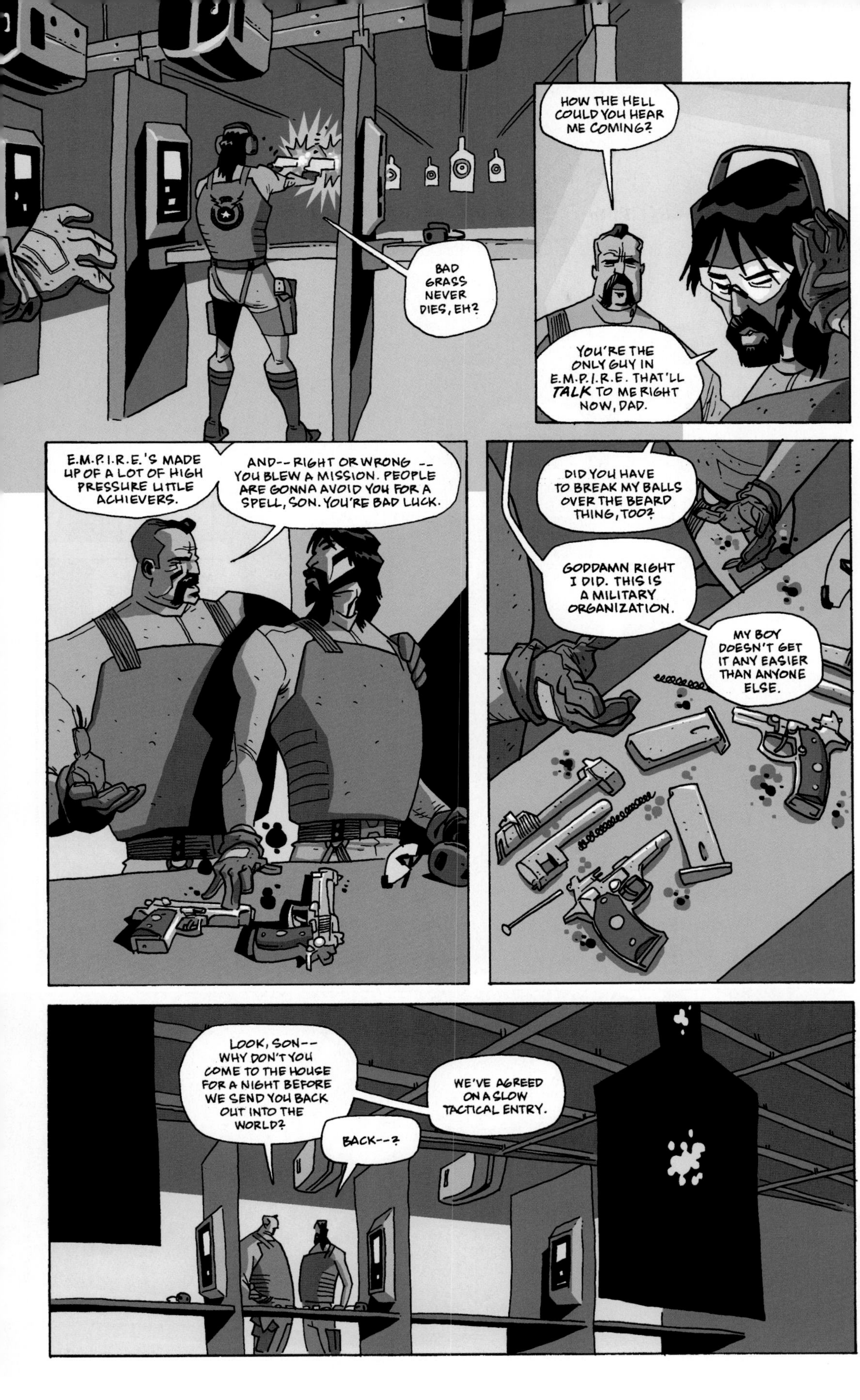
BAD GRASS NEVER DIES, EH?
HOW THE HELL COULD YOU HEAR ME COMING?
YOU'RE THE ONLY GUY IN E.M.P.I.R.E. THAT'LL *TALK* TO ME RIGHT NOW, DAD.
E.M.P.I.R.E.'S MADE UP OF A LOT OF HIGH PRESSURE LITTLE ACHIEVERS.
AND-- RIGHT OR WRONG -- YOU BLEW A MISSION. PEOPLE ARE GONNA AVOID YOU FOR A SPELL, SON. YOU'RE BAD LUCK.
DID YOU HAVE TO BREAK MY BALLS OVER THE BEARD THING, TOO?
GODDAMN RIGHT I DID. THIS IS A MILITARY ORGANIZATION.
MY BOY DOESN'T GET IT ANY EASIER THAN ANYONE ELSE.
LOOK, SON-- WHY DON'T YOU COME TO THE HOUSE FOR A NIGHT BEFORE WE SEND YOU BACK OUT INTO THE WORLD?
WE'VE AGREED ON A SLOW TACTICAL ENTRY.
BACK--?

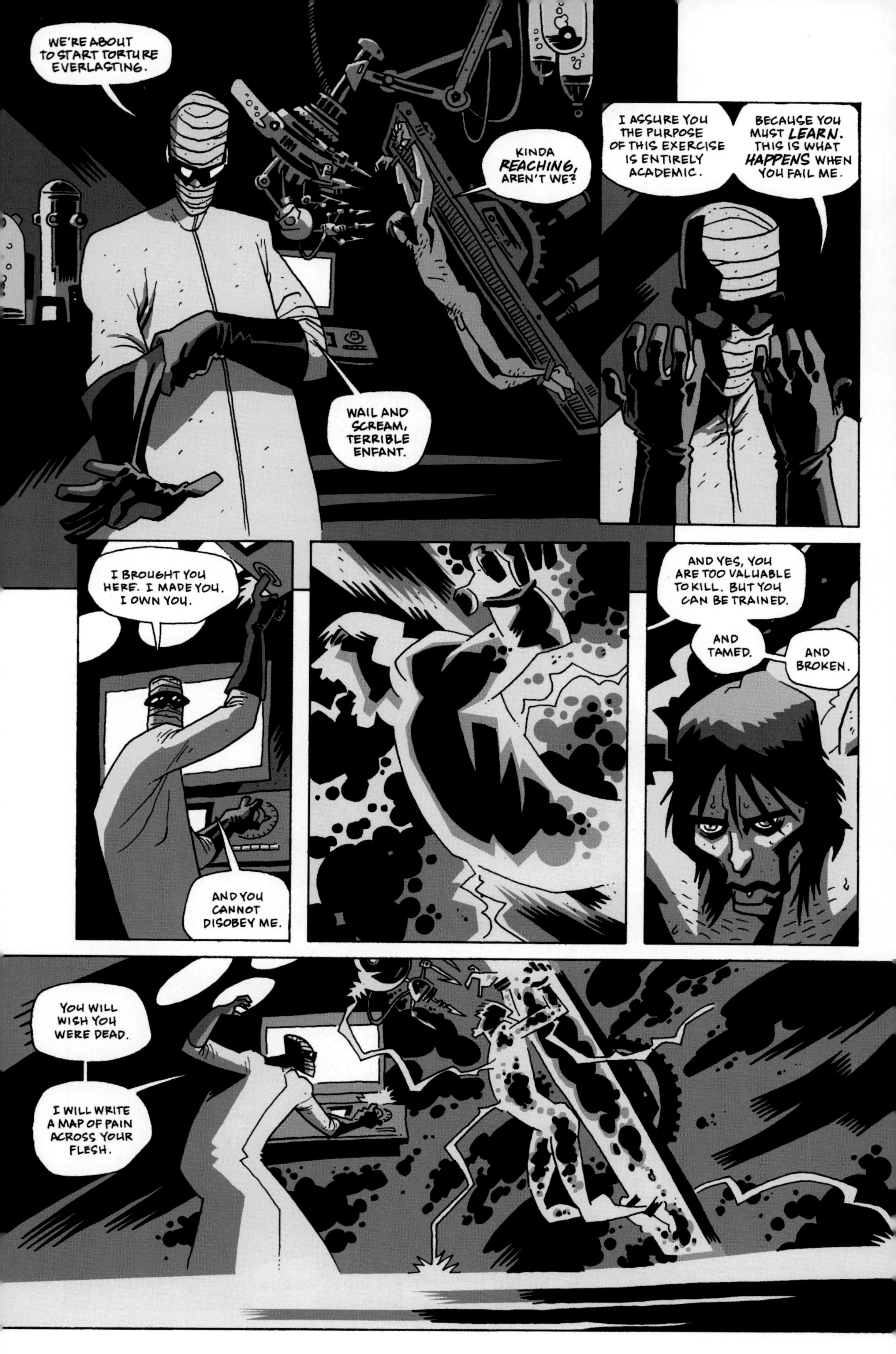
WE'RE ABOUT TO START TORTURE EVERLASTING.
KINDA REACHING, AREN'T WE?
WAIL AND SCREAM, TERRIBLE ENFANT.
I ASSURE YOU THE PURPOSE OF THIS EXERCISE IS ENTIRELY ACADEMIC.
BECAUSE YOU MUST LEARN. THIS IS WHAT HAPPENS WHEN YOU FAIL ME.
I BROUGHT YOU HERE. I MADE YOU. I OWN YOU.
AND YOU CANNOT DISOBEY ME.
AND YES, YOU ARE TOO VALUABLE TO KILL. BUT YOU CAN BE TRAINED.
AND TAMED.
AND BROKEN.
YOU WILL WISH YOU WERE DEAD.
I WILL WRITE A MAP OF PAIN ACROSS YOUR FLESH.

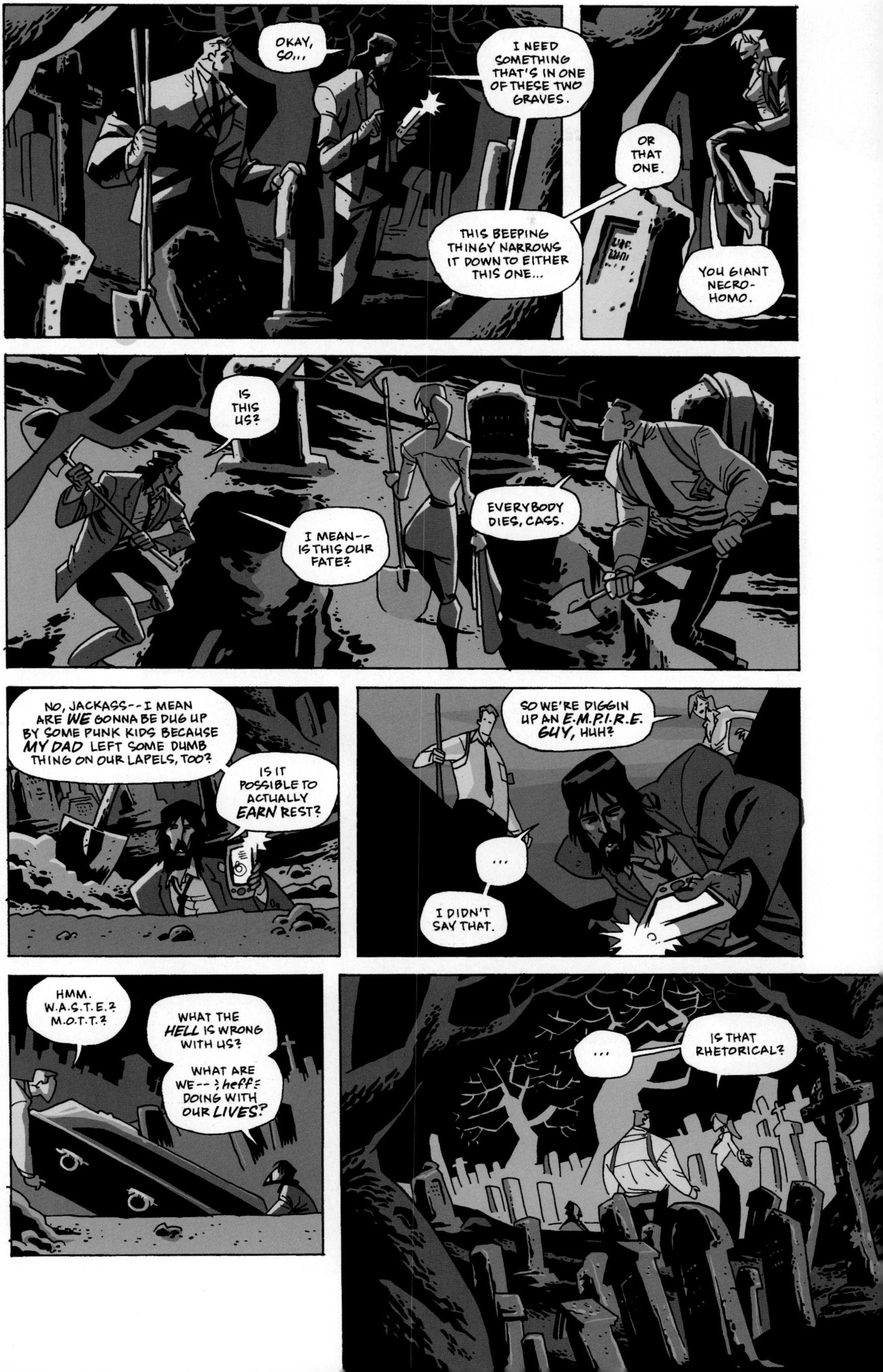
OKAY, SO...
I NEED SOMETHING THAT'S IN ONE OF THESE TWO GRAVES.
THIS BEEPING THINGY NARROWS IT DOWN TO EITHER THIS ONE...
OR THAT ONE.
YOU GIANT NECRO-HOMO.
IS THIS US?
I MEAN-- IS THIS OUR FATE?
EVERYBODY DIES, CASS.
NO, JACKASS--I MEAN ARE WE GONNA BE DUG UP BY SOME PUNK KIDS BECAUSE MY DAD LEFT SOME DUMB THING ON OUR LAPELS, TOO?
IS IT POSSIBLE TO ACTUALLY EARN REST?
SO WE'RE DIGGIN UP AN E.M.P.I.R.E. GUY, HUH?
...
I DIDN'T SAY THAT.
HMM. W.A.S.T.E.? M.O.T.T.?
WHAT THE HELL IS WRONG WITH US?
WHAT ARE WE-- :heff: DOING WITH OUR LIVES?
...
IS THAT RHETORICAL?

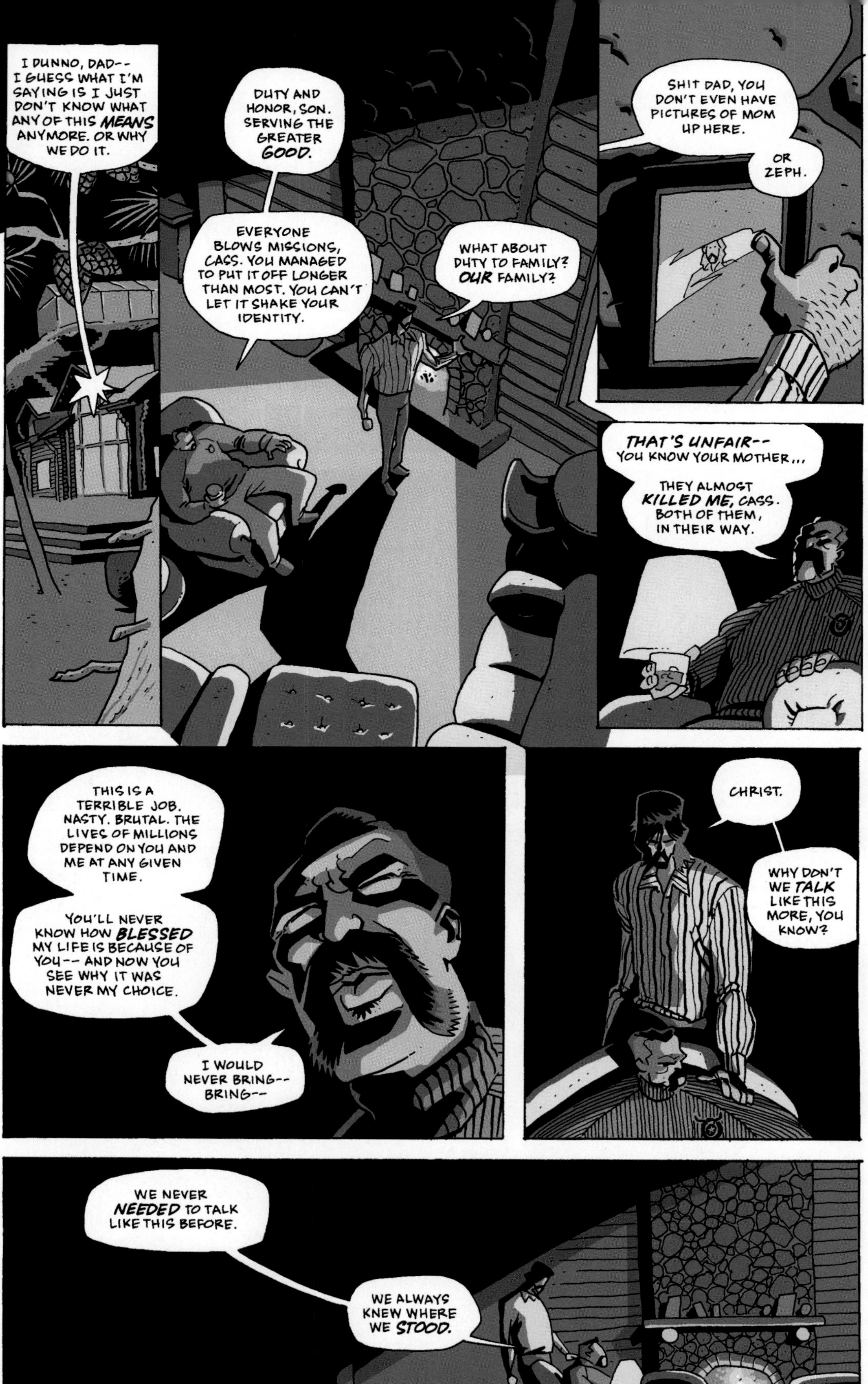
I DUNNO, DAD-- I GUESS WHAT I'M SAYING IS I JUST DON'T KNOW WHAT ANY OF THIS MEANS ANYMORE. OR WHY WE DO IT.
DUTY AND HONOR, SON. SERVING THE GREATER GOOD.
EVERYONE BLOWS MISSIONS, CASS. YOU MANAGED TO PUT IT OFF LONGER THAN MOST. YOU CAN'T LET IT SHAKE YOUR IDENTITY.
WHAT ABOUT DUTY TO FAMILY? OUR FAMILY?
SHIT DAD, YOU DON'T EVEN HAVE PICTURES OF MOM UP HERE.
OR ZEPH.
THAT'S UNFAIR-- YOU KNOW YOUR MOTHER...
THEY ALMOST KILLED ME, CASS. BOTH OF THEM, IN THEIR WAY.
THIS IS A TERRIBLE JOB. NASTY. BRUTAL. THE LIVES OF MILLIONS DEPEND ON YOU AND ME AT ANY GIVEN TIME.
YOU'LL NEVER KNOW HOW BLESSED MY LIFE IS BECAUSE OF YOU-- AND NOW YOU SEE WHY IT WAS NEVER MY CHOICE.
I WOULD NEVER BRING-- BRING--
CHRIST.
WHY DON'T WE TALK LIKE THIS MORE, YOU KNOW?
WE NEVER NEEDED TO TALK LIKE THIS BEFORE.
WE ALWAYS KNEW WHERE WE STOOD.

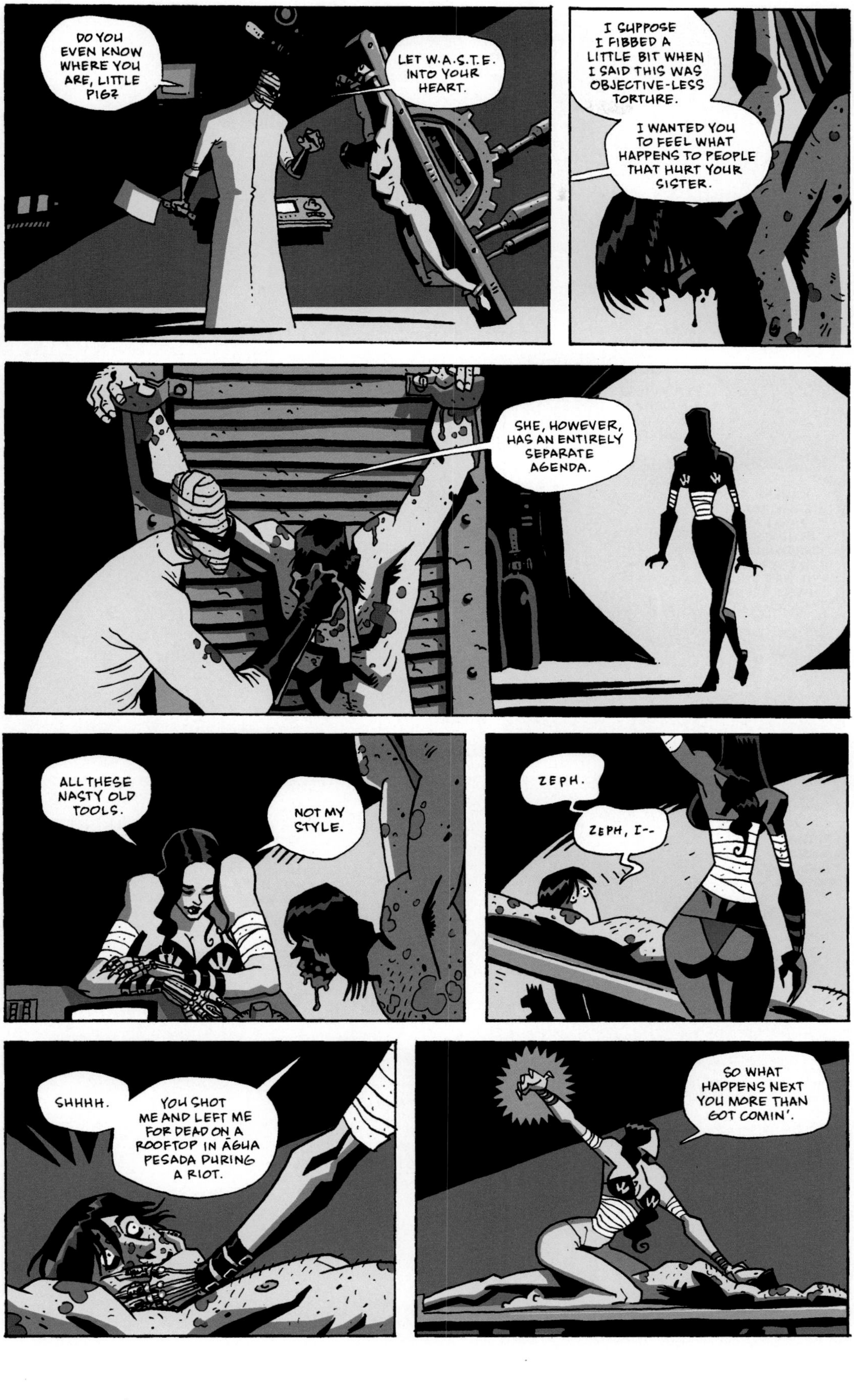
DO YOU EVEN KNOW WHERE YOU ARE, LITTLE PIG?
LET W.A.S.T.E. INTO YOUR HEART.
I SUPPOSE I FIBBED A LITTLE BIT WHEN I SAID THIS WAS OBJECTIVE-LESS TORTURE.
I WANTED YOU TO FEEL WHAT HAPPENS TO PEOPLE THAT HURT YOUR SISTER.
SHE, HOWEVER, HAS AN ENTIRELY SEPARATE AGENDA.
ALL THESE NASTY OLD TOOLS.
NOT MY STYLE.
ZEPH.
ZEPH, I--
SHHHH.
YOU SHOT ME AND LEFT ME FOR DEAD ON A ROOFTOP IN ÁGUA PESADA DURING A RIOT.
SO WHAT HAPPENS NEXT YOU MORE THAN GOT COMIN'.

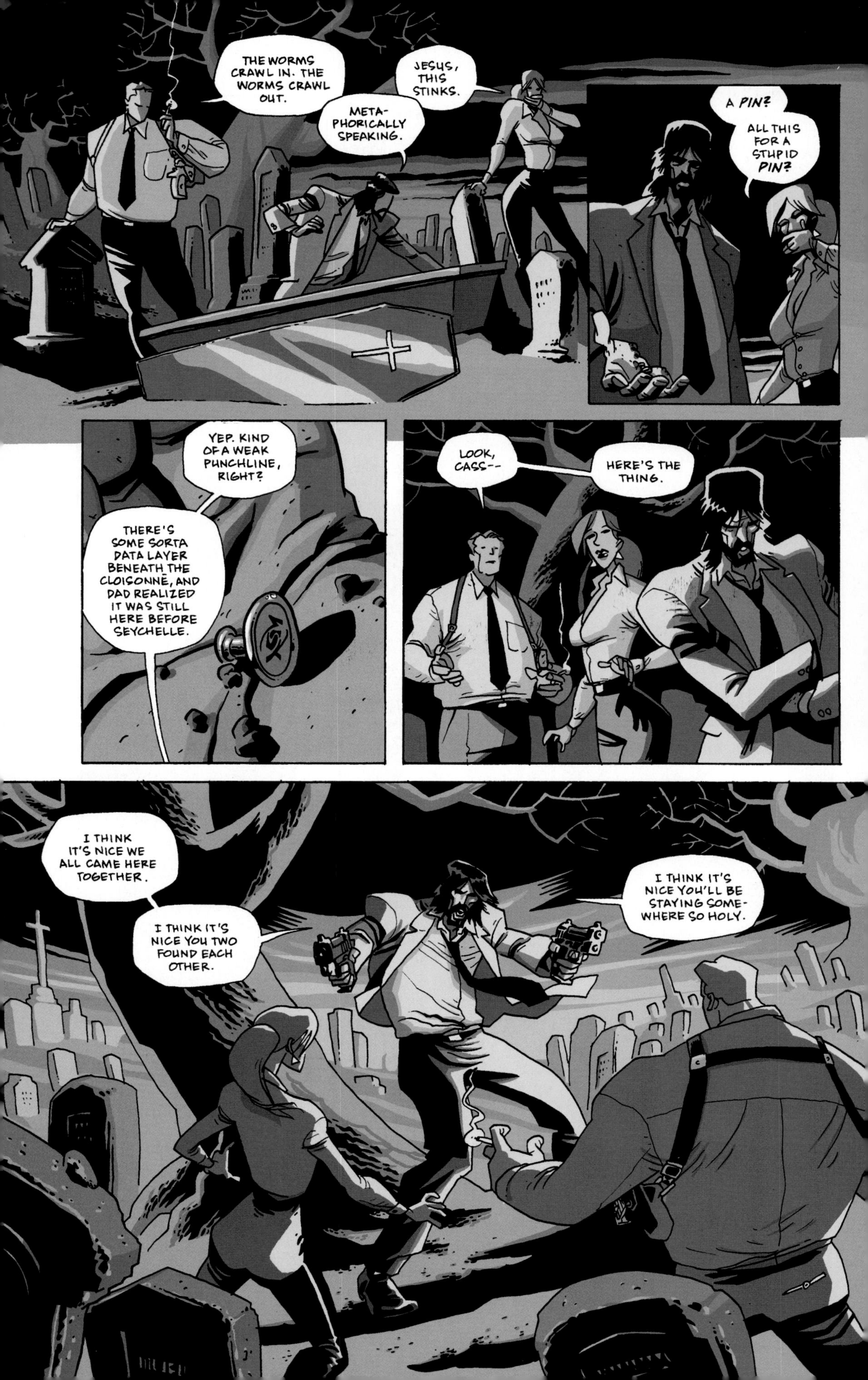
THE WORMS CRAWL IN. THE WORMS CRAWL OUT.
JESUS, THIS STINKS.
META-PHORICALLY SPEAKING.
A PIN?
ALL THIS FOR A STUPID PIN?
YEP. KIND OF A WEAK PUNCHLINE, RIGHT?
THERE'S SOME SORTA DATA LAYER BENEATH THE CLOISONNÉ, AND DAD REALIZED IT WAS STILL HERE BEFORE SEYCHELLE.
LOOK, CASS--
HERE'S THE THING.
I THINK IT'S NICE WE ALL CAME HERE TOGETHER.
I THINK IT'S NICE YOU TWO FOUND EACH OTHER.
I THINK IT'S NICE YOU'LL BE STAYING SOME-WHERE SO HOLY.

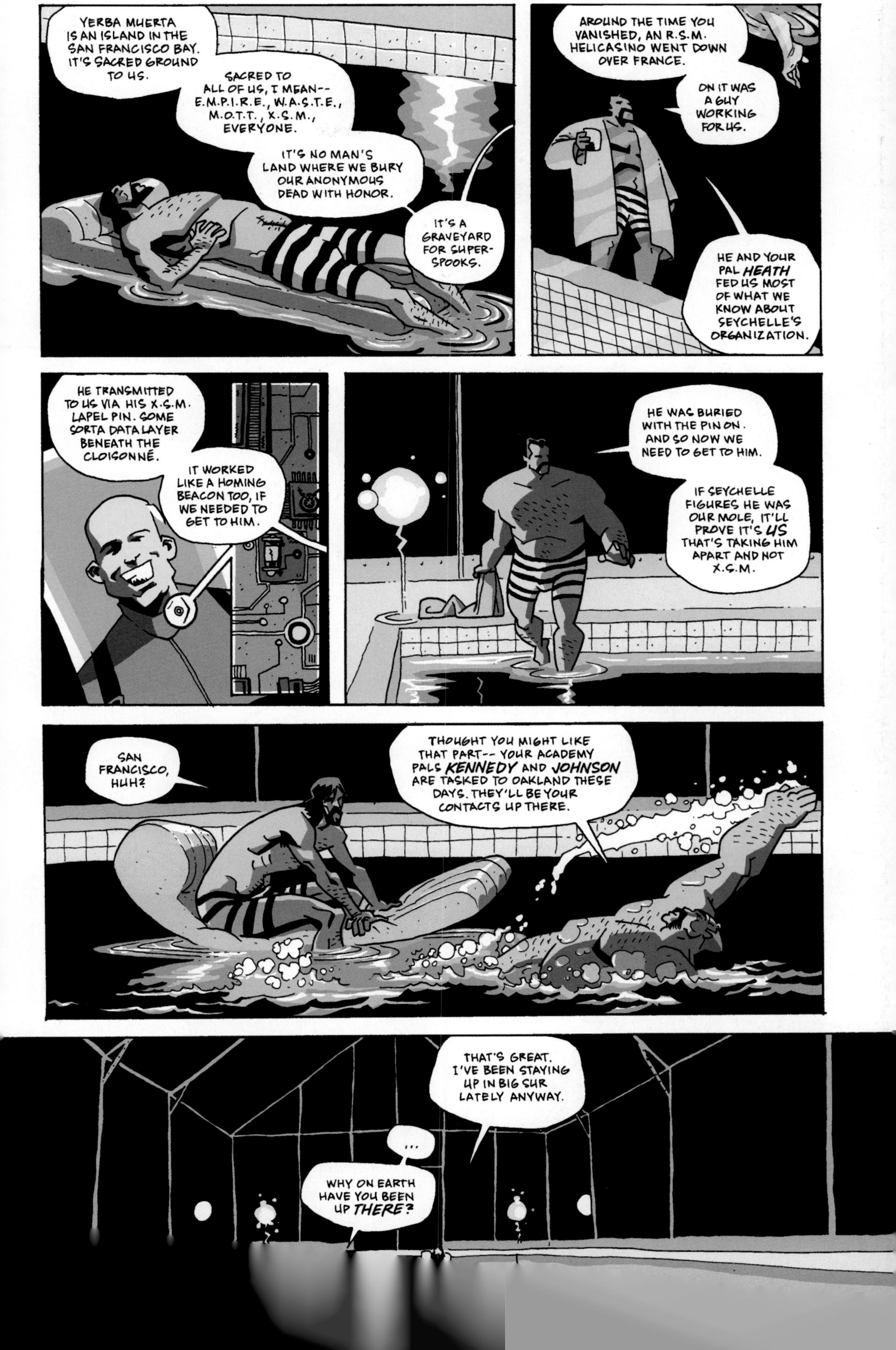
YERBA MUERTA IS AN ISLAND IN THE SAN FRANCISCO BAY. IT'S SACRED GROUND TO US.
SACRED TO ALL OF US, I MEAN-- E.M.P.I.R.E., W.A.S.T.E., M.O.T.T., X.S.M., EVERYONE.
IT'S NO MAN'S LAND WHERE WE BURY OUR ANONYMOUS DEAD WITH HONOR.
IT'S A GRAVEYARD FOR SUPER-SPOOKS.
AROUND THE TIME YOU VANISHED, AN R.S.M. HELICASINO WENT DOWN OVER FRANCE.
ON IT WAS A GUY WORKING FOR US.
HE AND YOUR PAL HEATH FED US MOST OF WHAT WE KNOW ABOUT SEYCHELLE'S ORGANIZATION.
HE TRANSMITTED TO US VIA HIS X.S.M. LAPEL PIN. SOME SORTA DATA LAYER BENEATH THE CLOISONNÉ.
IT WORKED LIKE A HOMING BEACON TOO, IF WE NEEDED TO GET TO HIM.
HE WAS BURIED WITH THE PIN ON. AND SO NOW WE NEED TO GET TO HIM.
IF SEYCHELLE FIGURES HE WAS OUR MOLE, IT'LL PROVE IT'S US THAT'S TAKING HIM APART AND NOT X.S.M.
SAN FRANCISCO, HUH?
THOUGHT YOU MIGHT LIKE THAT PART-- YOUR ACADEMY PALS KENNEDY AND JOHNSON ARE TASKED TO OAKLAND THESE DAYS. THEY'LL BE YOUR CONTACTS UP THERE.
THAT'S GREAT. I'VE BEEN STAYING UP IN BIG SUR LATELY ANYWAY.
...
WHY ON EARTH HAVE YOU BEEN UP THERE?

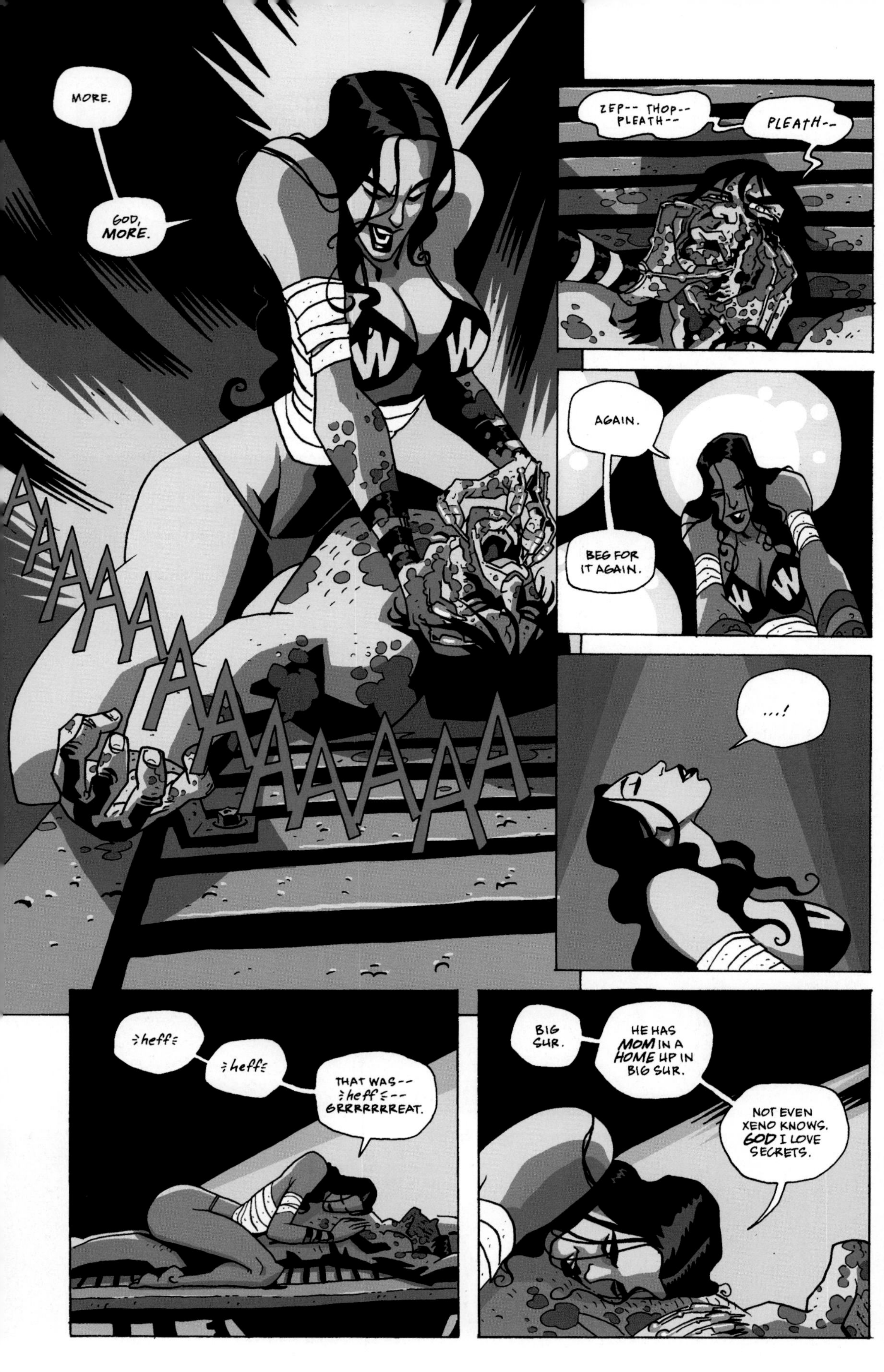
MORE.
GOD, MORE.
AAAAAAAAAAAAAAAAA
ZEP-- THOP-- PLEATH--
PLEATH--
AGAIN.
BEG FOR IT AGAIN.
...!
heff
heff
THAT WAS-- heff-- GRRRRRRREAT.
BIG SUR.
HE HAS MOM IN A HOME UP IN BIG SUR.
NOT EVEN XENO KNOWS. GOD I LOVE SECRETS.

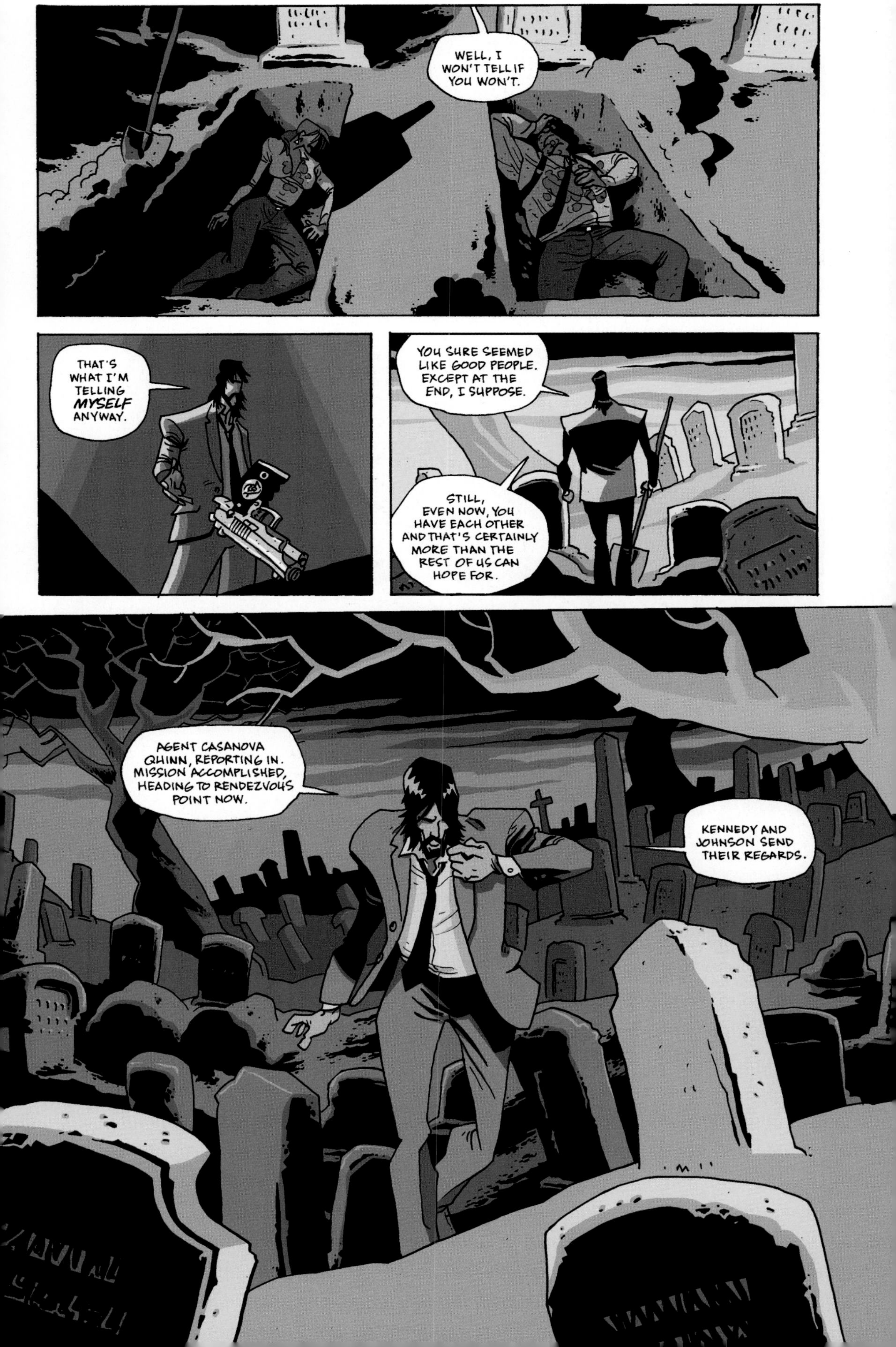
WELL, I WON'T TELL IF YOU WON'T.
THAT'S WHAT I'M TELLING MYSELF ANYWAY.
YOU SURE SEEMED LIKE GOOD PEOPLE. EXCEPT AT THE END, I SUPPOSE.
STILL, EVEN NOW, YOU HAVE EACH OTHER AND THAT'S CERTAINLY MORE THAN THE REST OF US CAN HOPE FOR.
AGENT CASANOVA QHINN, REPORTING IN. MISSION ACCOMPLISHED, HEADING TO RENDEZVOUS POINT NOW.
KENNEDY AND JOHNSON SEND THEIR REGARDS.

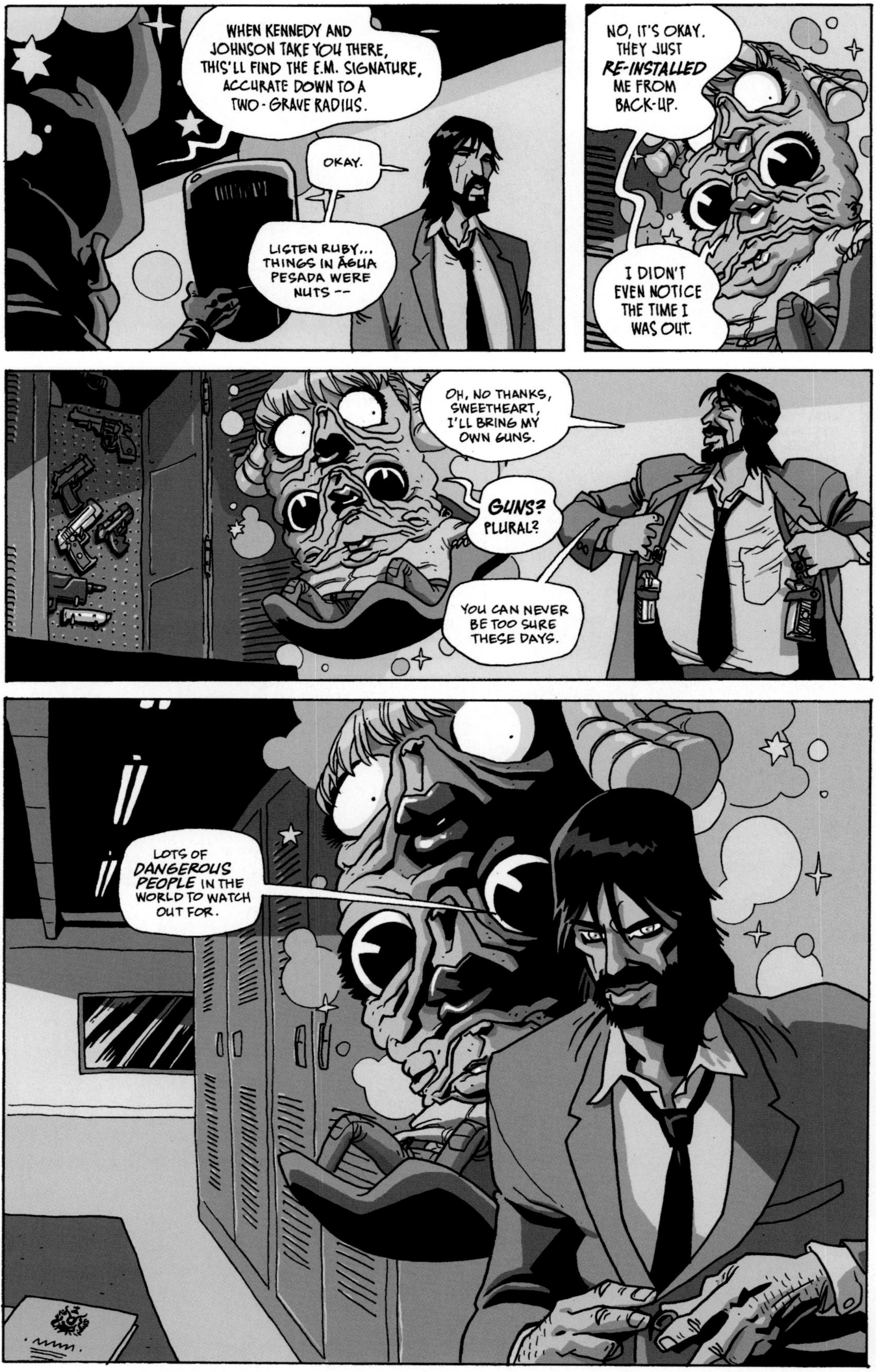
WHEN KENNEDY AND JOHNSON TAKE YOU THERE, THIS'LL FIND THE E.M. SIGNATURE, ACCURATE DOWN TO A TWO-GRAVE RADIUS.
OKAY.
LISTEN RUBY... THINGS IN ÁGUA PESADA WERE NUTS --
NO, IT'S OKAY. THEY JUST RE-INSTALLED ME FROM BACK-UP.
I DIDN'T EVEN NOTICE THE TIME I WAS OUT.
OH, NO THANKS, SWEETHEART, I'LL BRING MY OWN GUNS.
GUNS? PLURAL?
YOU CAN NEVER BE TOO SURE THESE DAYS.
LOTS OF DANGEROUS PEOPLE IN THE WORLD TO WATCH OUT FOR.

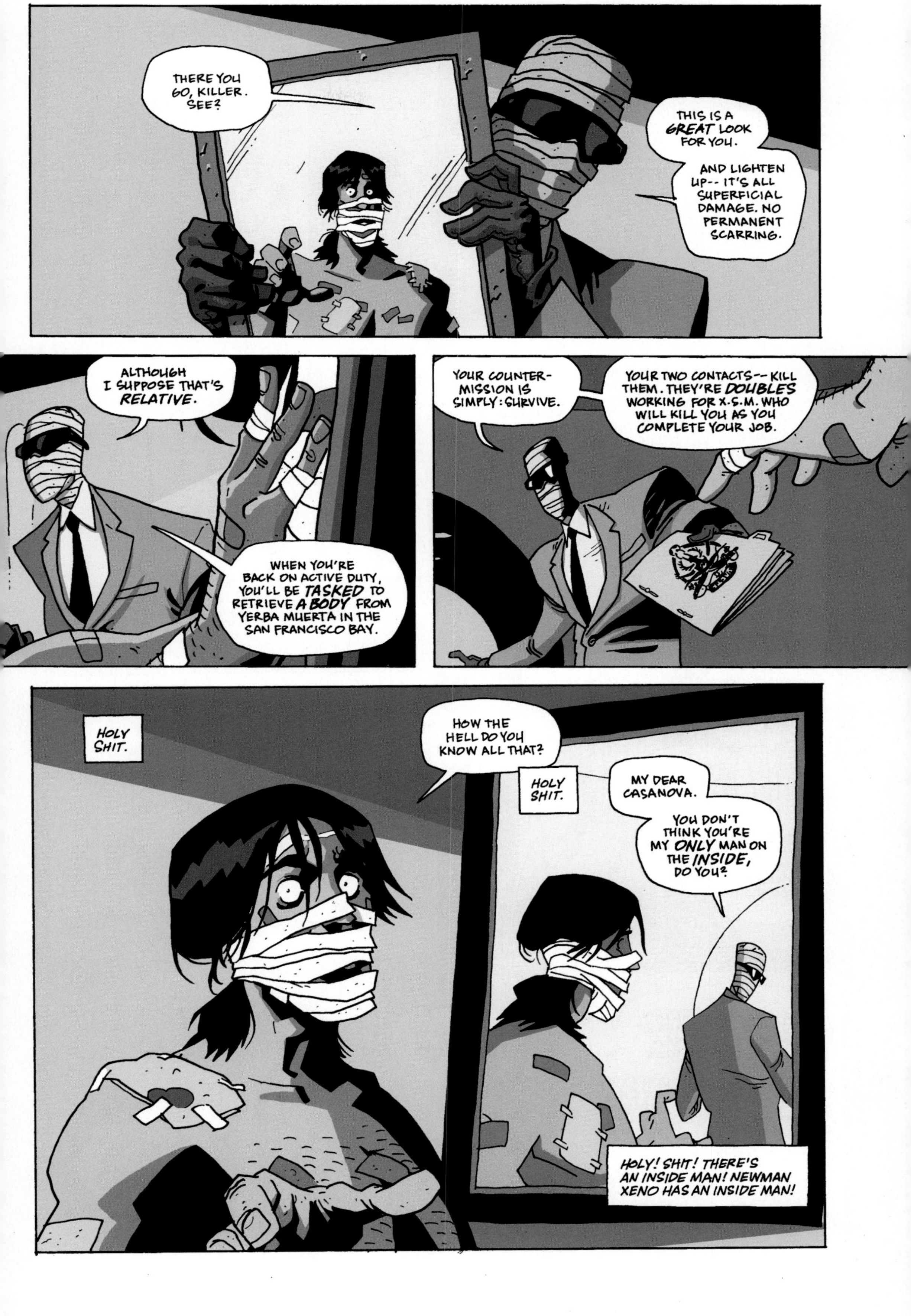
THERE YOU GO, KILLER. SEE?
THIS IS A GREAT LOOK FOR YOU.
AND LIGHTEN UP-- IT'S ALL SUPERFICIAL DAMAGE. NO PERMANENT SCARRING.
ALTHOUGH I SUPPOSE THAT'S RELATIVE.
WHEN YOU'RE BACK ON ACTIVE DUTY, YOU'LL BE TASKED TO RETRIEVE A BODY FROM YERBA MUERTA IN THE SAN FRANCISCO BAY.
YOUR COUNTER-MISSION IS SIMPLY: SURVIVE.
YOUR TWO CONTACTS-- KILL THEM. THEY'RE DOUBLES WORKING FOR X.S.M. WHO WILL KILL YOU AS YOU COMPLETE YOUR JOB.
HOLY SHIT.
HOW THE HELL DO YOU KNOW ALL THAT?
HOLY SHIT.
MY DEAR CASANOVA.
YOU DON'T THINK YOU'RE MY ONLY MAN ON THE INSIDE, DO YOU?
HOLY! SHIT! THERE'S AN INSIDE MAN! NEWMAN XENO HAS AN INSIDE MAN!

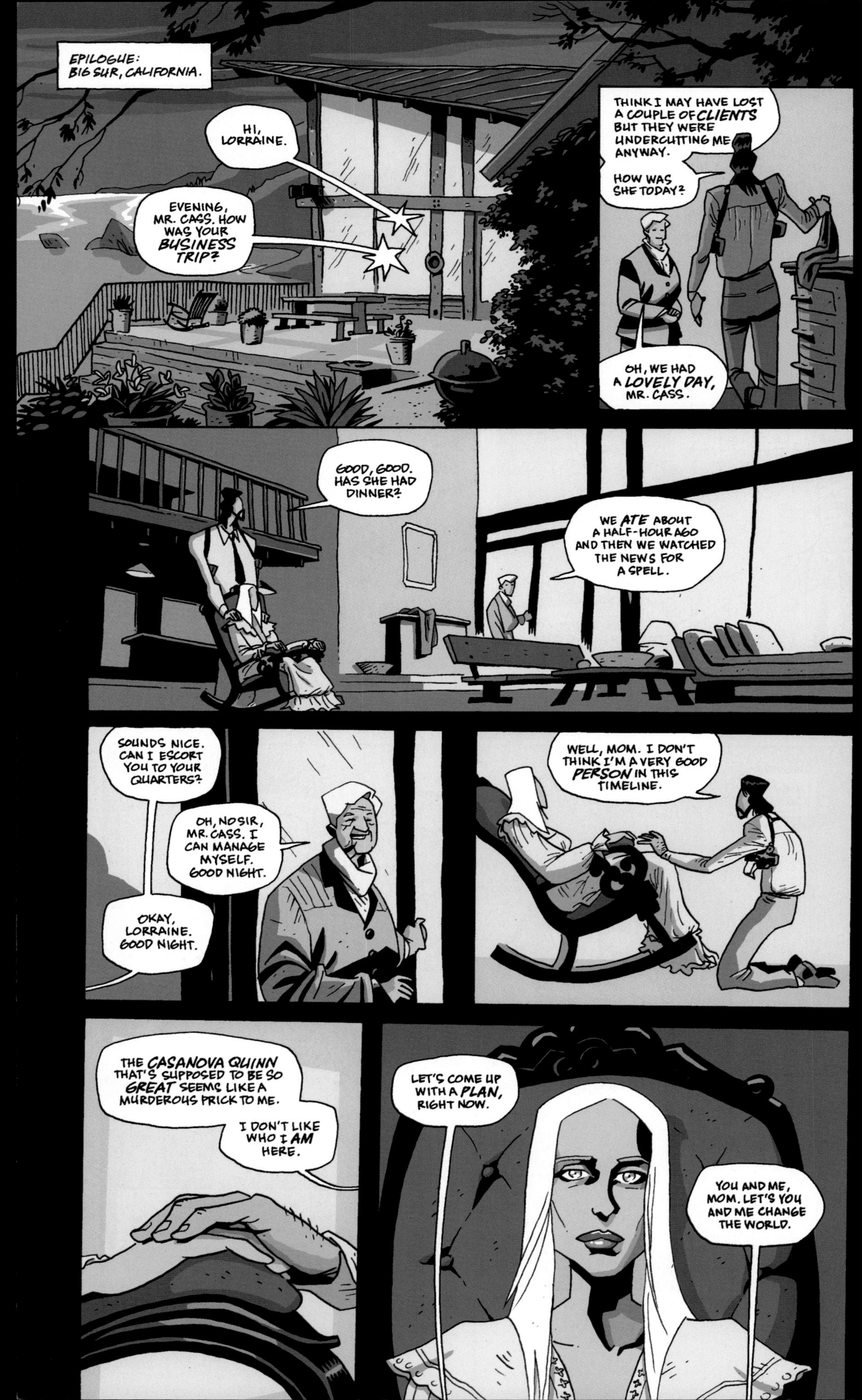
EPILOGUE: BIG SUR, CALIFORNIA.
HI, LORRAINE.
EVENING, MR. CASS. HOW WAS YOUR BUSINESS TRIP?
THINK I MAY HAVE LOST A COUPLE OF CLIENTS BUT THEY WERE UNDERCUTTING ME ANYWAY.
HOW WAS SHE TODAY?
OH, WE HAD A LOVELY DAY, MR. CASS.
GOOD, GOOD. HAS SHE HAD DINNER?
WE ATE ABOUT A HALF-HOUR AGO AND THEN WE WATCHED THE NEWS FOR A SPELL.
SOUNDS NICE. CAN I ESCORT YOU TO YOUR QUARTERS?
OH, NO SIR, MR. CASS. I CAN MANAGE MYSELF. GOOD NIGHT.
OKAY, LORRAINE. GOOD NIGHT.
WELL, MOM. I DON'T THINK I'M A VERY GOOD PERSON IN THIS TIMELINE.
THE CASANOVA QUINN THAT'S SUPPOSED TO BE SO GREAT SEEMS LIKE A MURDEROUS PRICK TO ME.
I DON'T LIKE WHO I AM HERE.
LET'S COME UP WITH A PLAN, RIGHT NOW.
YOU AND ME, MOM. LET'S YOU AND ME CHANGE THE WORLD.

# CHAPTER 4
# DÉTOURNEMENT

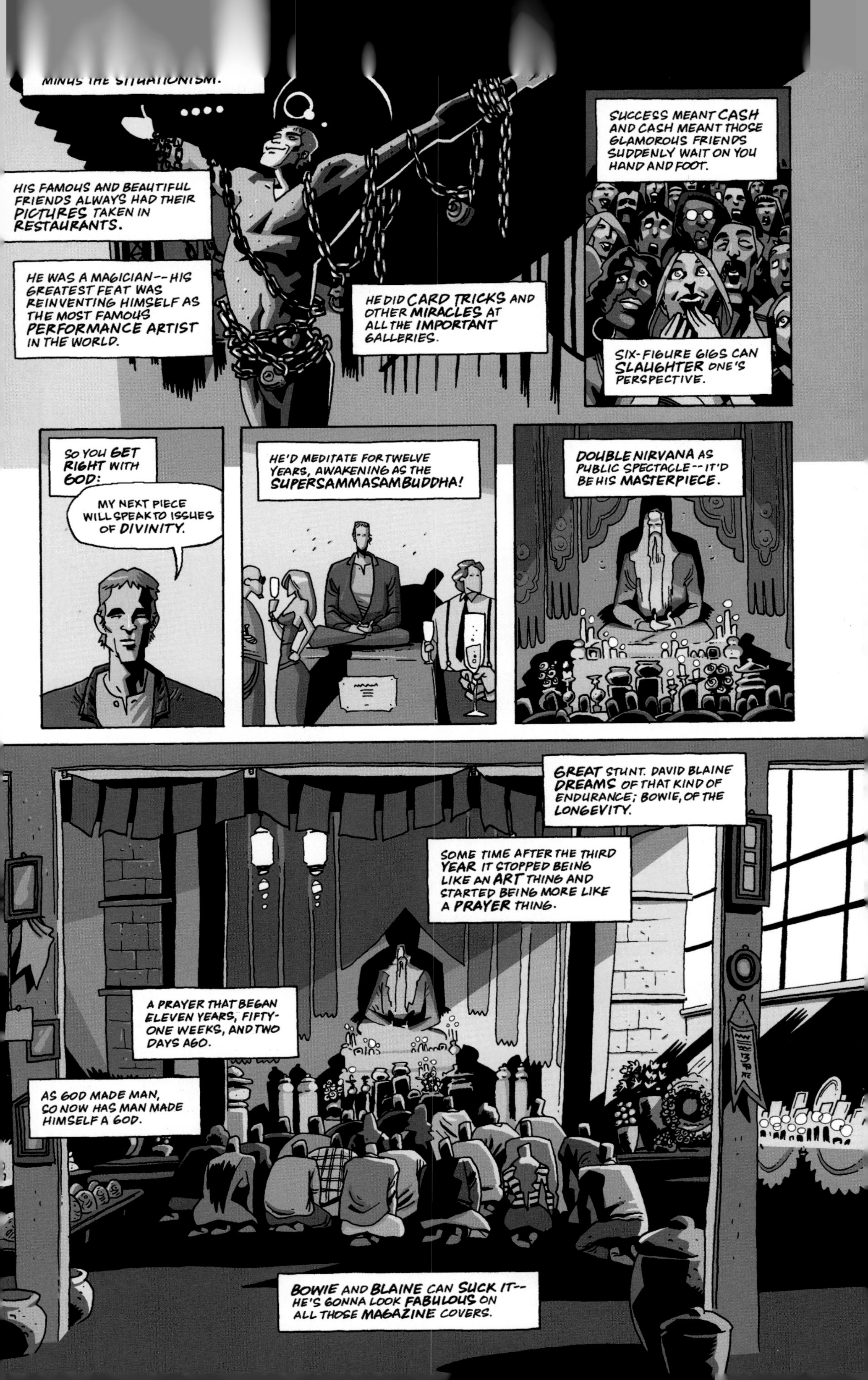
MINUS THE SITUATIONISM.
....
HIS FAMOUS AND BEAUTIFUL FRIENDS ALWAYS HAD THEIR PICTURES TAKEN IN RESTAURANTS.
HE WAS A MAGICIAN--HIS GREATEST FEAT WAS REINVENTING HIMSELF AS THE MOST FAMOUS PERFORMANCE ARTIST IN THE WORLD.
HE DID CARD TRICKS AND OTHER MIRACLES AT ALL THE IMPORTANT GALLERIES.
SUCCESS MEANT CASH AND CASH MEANT THOSE GLAMOROUS FRIENDS SUDDENLY WAIT ON YOU HAND AND FOOT.
SIX-FIGURE GIGS CAN SLAUGHTER ONE'S PERSPECTIVE.
SO YOU GET RIGHT WITH GOD:
MY NEXT PIECE WILL SPEAK TO ISSUES OF DIVINITY.
HE'D MEDITATE FOR TWELVE YEARS, AWAKENING AS THE SUPERSAMMASAMBUDDHA!
DOUBLE NIRVANA AS PUBLIC SPECTACLE--IT'D BE HIS MASTERPIECE.
GREAT STUNT. DAVID BLAINE DREAMS OF THAT KIND OF ENDURANCE; BOWIE, OF THE LONGEVITY.
SOME TIME AFTER THE THIRD YEAR IT STOPPED BEING LIKE AN ART THING AND STARTED BEING MORE LIKE A PRAYER THING.
A PRAYER THAT BEGAN ELEVEN YEARS, FIFTY-ONE WEEKS, AND TWO DAYS AGO.
AS GOD MADE MAN, SO NOW HAS MAN MADE HIMSELF A GOD.
BOWIE AND BLAINE CAN SUCK IT--HE'S GONNA LOOK FABULOUS ON ALL THOSE MAGAZINE COVERS.

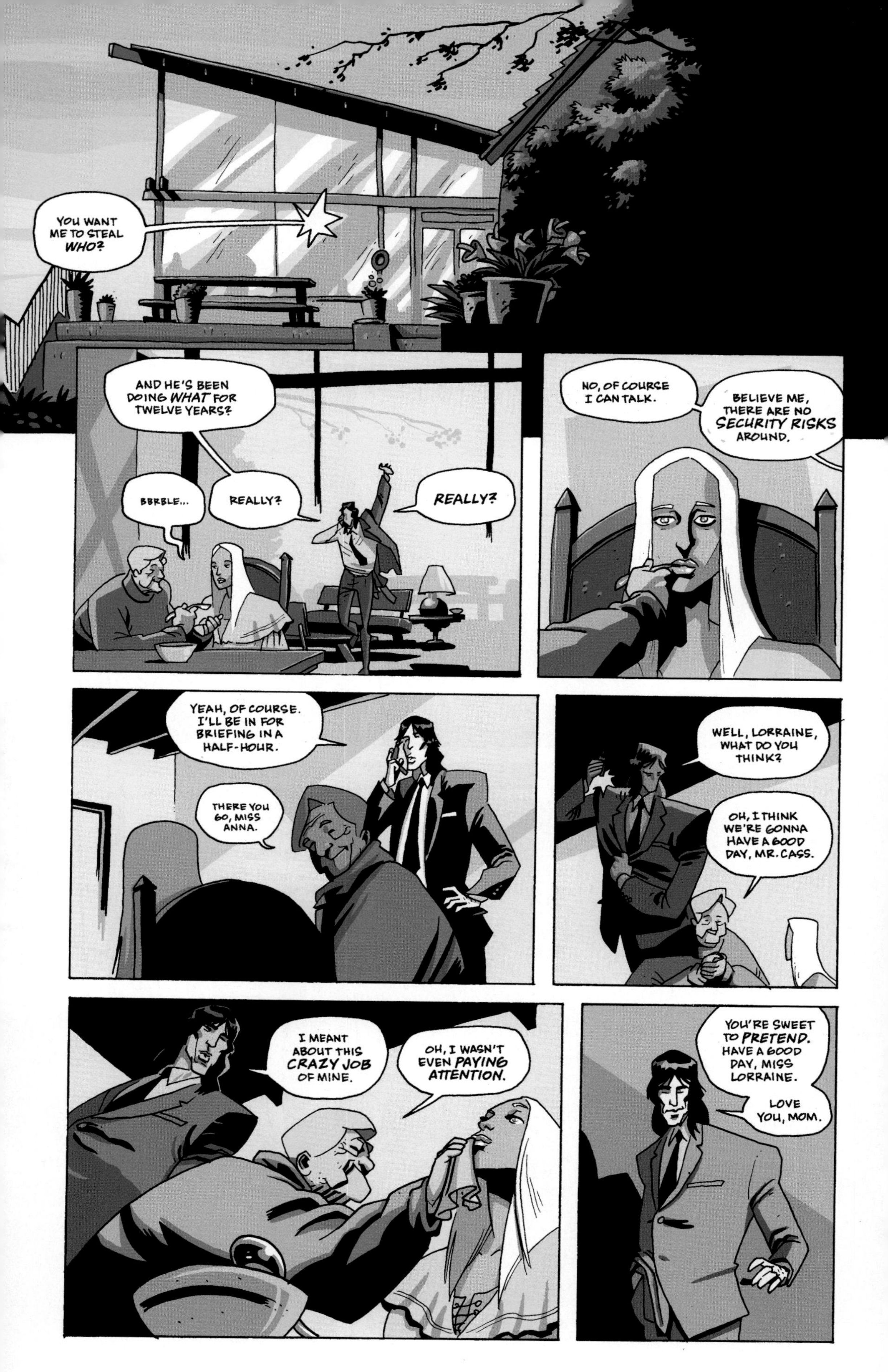
YOU WANT ME TO STEAL WHO?
AND HE'S BEEN DOING WHAT FOR TWELVE YEARS?
BBRBLE...
REALLY?
REALLY?
NO, OF COURSE I CAN TALK.
BELIEVE ME, THERE ARE NO SECURITY RISKS AROUND.
YEAH, OF COURSE. I'LL BE IN FOR BRIEFING IN A HALF-HOUR.
THERE YOU GO, MISS ANNA.
WELL, LORRAINE, WHAT DO YOU THINK?
OH, I THINK WE'RE GONNA HAVE A GOOD DAY, MR. CASS.
I MEANT ABOUT THIS CRAZY JOB OF MINE.
OH, I WASN'T EVEN PAYING ATTENTION.
YOU'RE SWEET TO PRETEND. HAVE A GOOD DAY, MISS LORRAINE.
LOVE YOU, MOM.

EVEN FOR... NEO-BUDDHISTS THE SECURITY IS REMARKABLY LAX.
THE ENTIRE EXERCISE IS MAKING ME HOMESICK FOR ANOTHER LIFE.
TZA!
RUBY EQUIPPED ME WITH BIOELECTROMAGNETIC PULSE GLOVES. MY WHOLE SUIT SHIELDS ME, BUT ANY LIVING THING WITHIN 200 YARDS GETS THEIR RESET SWITCH FLIPPED.
IT'S A GENTLE NAP, NOT WHOLLY UNLIKE MEDITATION.
HOPEFULLY X'S APOSTLES WILL GO RIGHT BACK INTO THEIR ZEN TRIPS AND NOT EVEN REALIZE HE'S GONE.
IT TAKES A STEADY
H
A
N
D.
OH
SHIT.

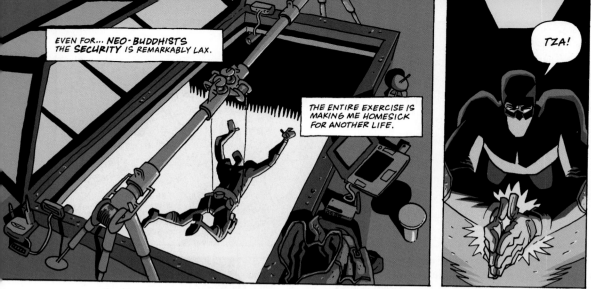

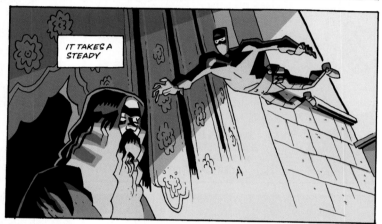

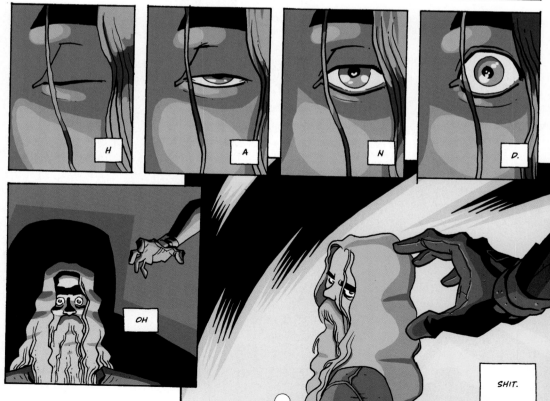

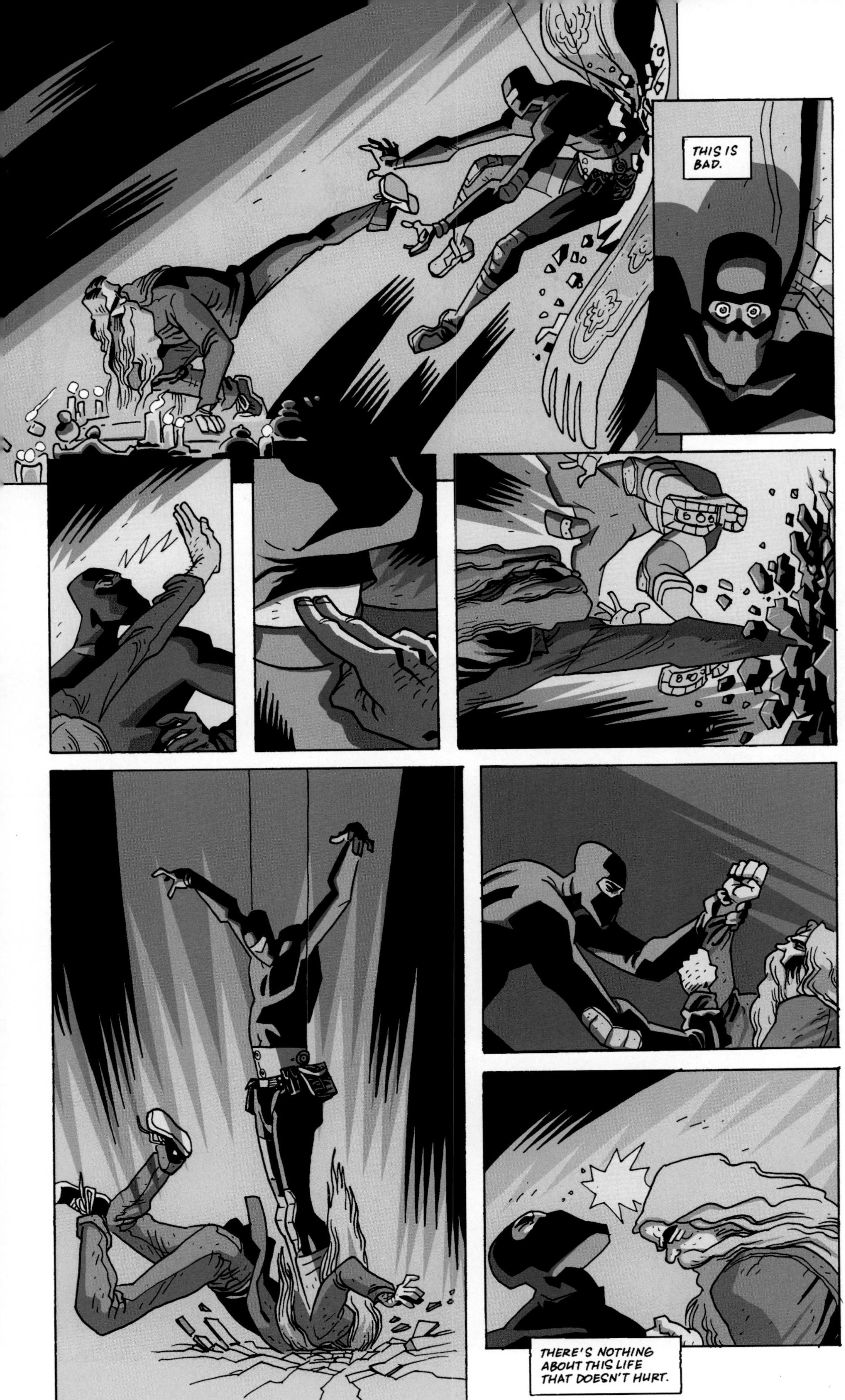
THIS IS BAD.
THERE'S NOTHING ABOUT THIS LIFE THAT DOESN'T HURT.

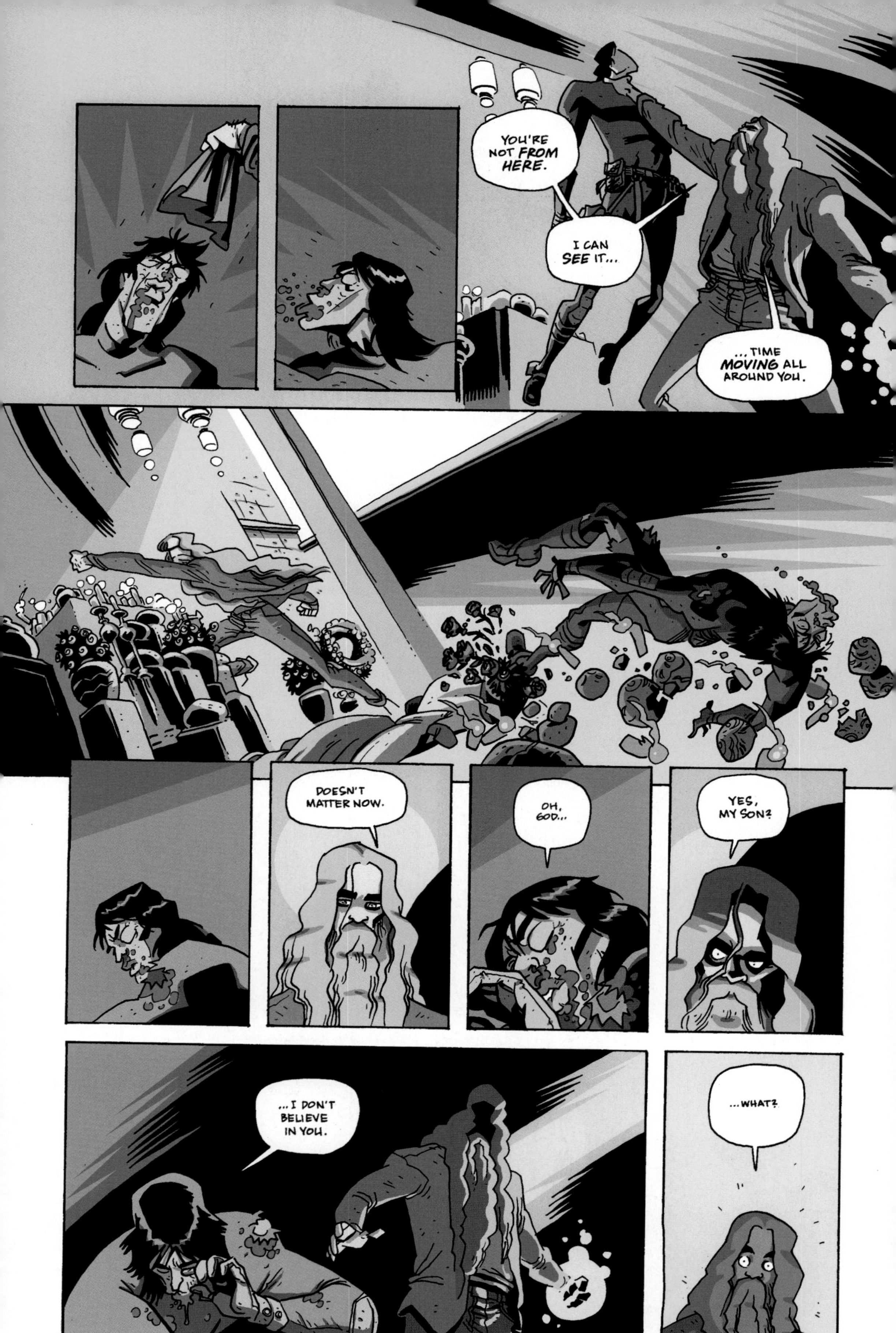

YOU'RE NOT FROM HERE.
I CAN SEE IT...
...TIME MOVING ALL AROUND YOU.
DOESN'T MATTER NOW.
OH, GOD...
YES, MY SON?
...I DON'T BELIEVE IN YOU.
...WHAT?

I...

... I DON'T UNDERSTAND.

YOU'RE A SCAM.

YOUR PEOPLE SNUCK YOU FOOD AND WATER. NO MEDICAL STAFF WAS EVER ALLOWED TO EXAMINE YOU.

THERE WERE TIMES WHEN THE PUBLIC WEREN'T ALLOWED IN THE FACILITY.

...

AND *I CALL BULLSHIT.*

AFTER PUNCHING GOD IN THE [R]AIN, I SMUGGLED THE VICIOUS [LIT]TLE BASTARD BACK TO E.M.P.I.R.E.

[I] HAVE NO IDEA WHAT THEY'LL *DO* [WI]TH A *HOSTAGE GOD*, BUT THE [WI]ND REELS, AND I HOPE IT HURTS.

[S]O WITH ONE *MASTER* APPEASED [A]ND MY BUZZ VERY THOROUGHLY [G]ON, I WENT TO APPEASE MY *OTHER MASTER...*

THERE WAS NO *TIME*, XENO. IT CAME UP AND AN HOUR LATER I WAS ON A PLANE.

NO NO NO! THIS WILL NEVER DO.

I RATHER *LIKE* THE IDEA OF A LITTLE *ZEN CHAOS.* YOU'LL JUST HAVE TO *REPLACE* HIM IN TIME FOR HIM TO *WAKE UP.*

THERE'S *NO WAY* I'D BE ABLE TO GET HIM OUT OF WHEREVER E.M.P.I.R.E. HAS HIM.

"THEN I SUGGEST *YOU TWO* FIND A *RINGER.* FAST."

SABINE SEYCHELLE.

WE NEED A MAN OF YOUR *UNIQUE TALENTS* AND *RESOURCES* TO SYN-THESIZE A HUMAN MALE IN THE NEXT TWELVE HOURS.

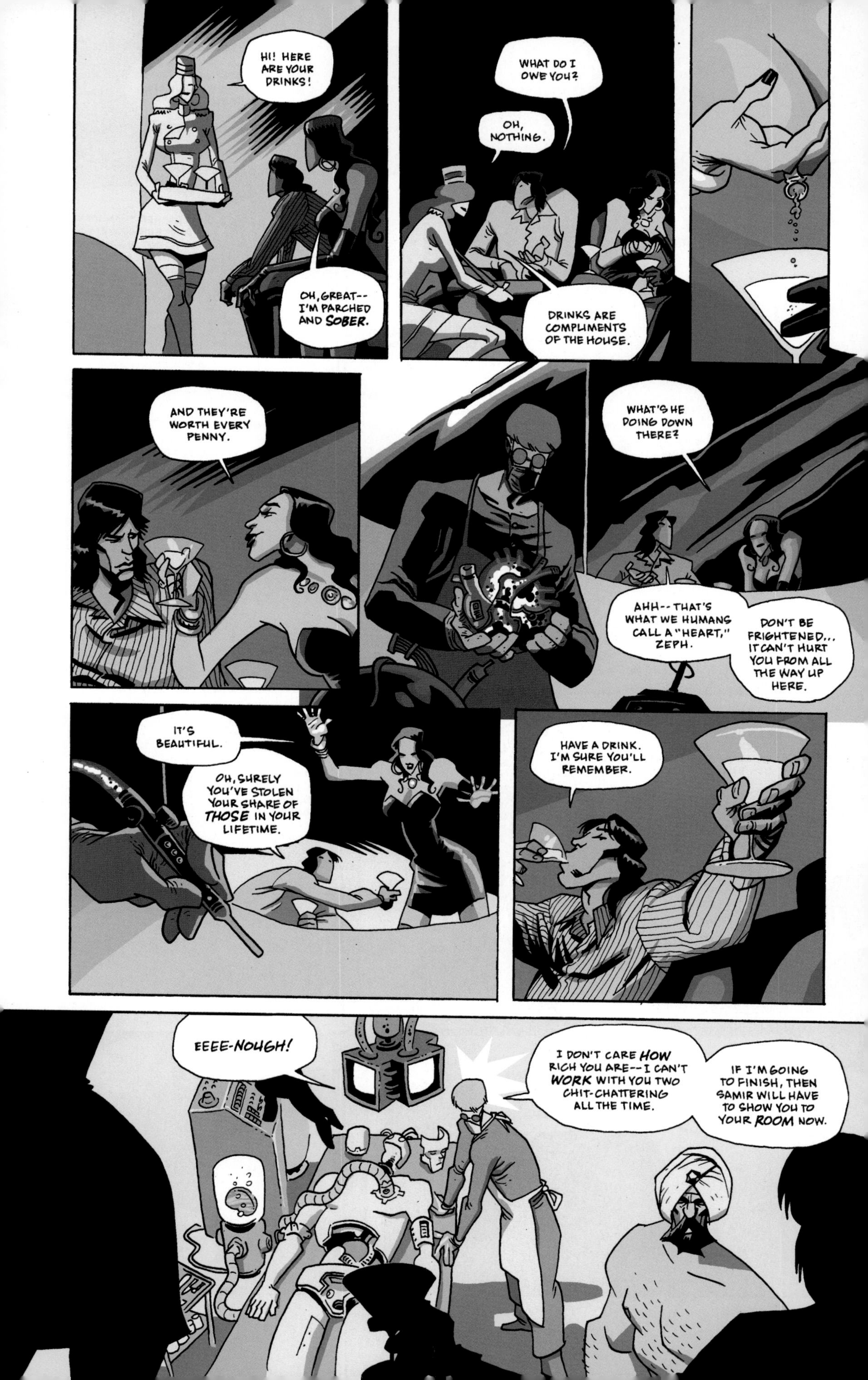

HI! HERE ARE YOUR DRINKS!
OH, GREAT-- I'M PARCHED AND SOBER.
WHAT DO I OWE YOU?
OH, NOTHING.
DRINKS ARE COMPLIMENTS OF THE HOUSE.
AND THEY'RE WORTH EVERY PENNY.
WHAT'S HE DOING DOWN THERE?
AHH-- THAT'S WHAT WE HUMANS CALL A "HEART," ZEPH.
DON'T BE FRIGHTENED... IT CAN'T HURT YOU FROM ALL THE WAY UP HERE.
IT'S BEAUTIFUL.
OH, SURELY YOU'VE STOLEN YOUR SHARE OF THOSE IN YOUR LIFETIME.
HAVE A DRINK. I'M SURE YOU'LL REMEMBER.
EEEE-NOUGH!
I DON'T CARE HOW RICH YOU ARE-- I CAN'T WORK WITH YOU TWO CHIT-CHATTERING ALL THE TIME.
IF I'M GOING TO FINISH, THEN SAMIR WILL HAVE TO SHOW YOU TO YOUR ROOM NOW.

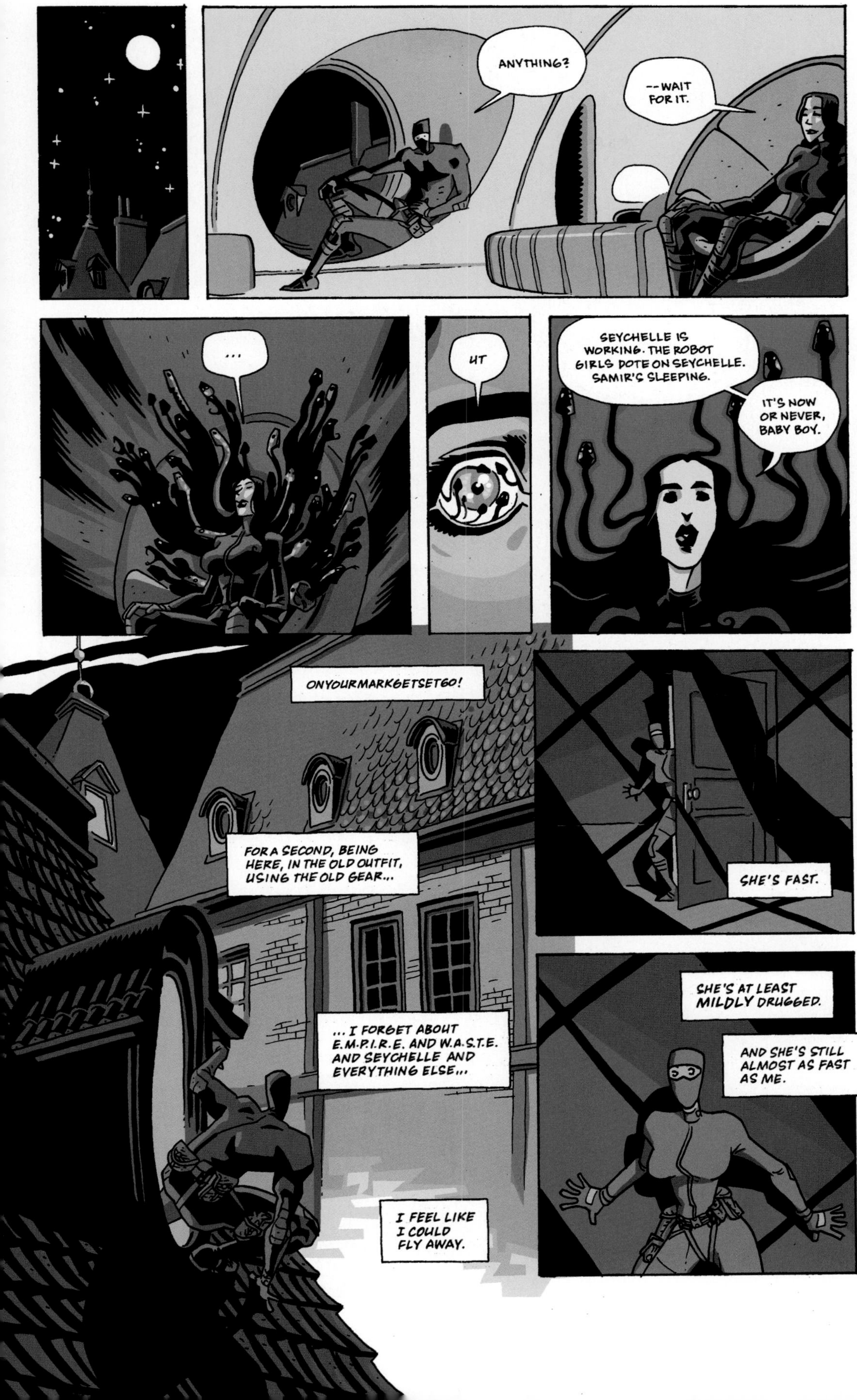

ANYTHING?
--WAIT FOR IT.
...
UT
SEYCHELLE IS WORKING. THE ROBOT GIRLS DOTE ON SEYCHELLE. SAMIR'S SLEEPING.
IT'S NOW OR NEVER, BABY BOY.
ONYOURMARKGETSETGO!
FOR A SECOND, BEING HERE, IN THE OLD OUTFIT, USING THE OLD GEAR...
...I FORGET ABOUT E.M.P.I.R.E. AND W.A.S.T.E. AND SEYCHELLE AND EVERYTHING ELSE...
I FEEL LIKE I COULD FLY AWAY.
SHE'S FAST.
SHE'S AT LEAST MILDLY DRUGGED.
AND SHE'S STILL ALMOST AS FAST AS ME.

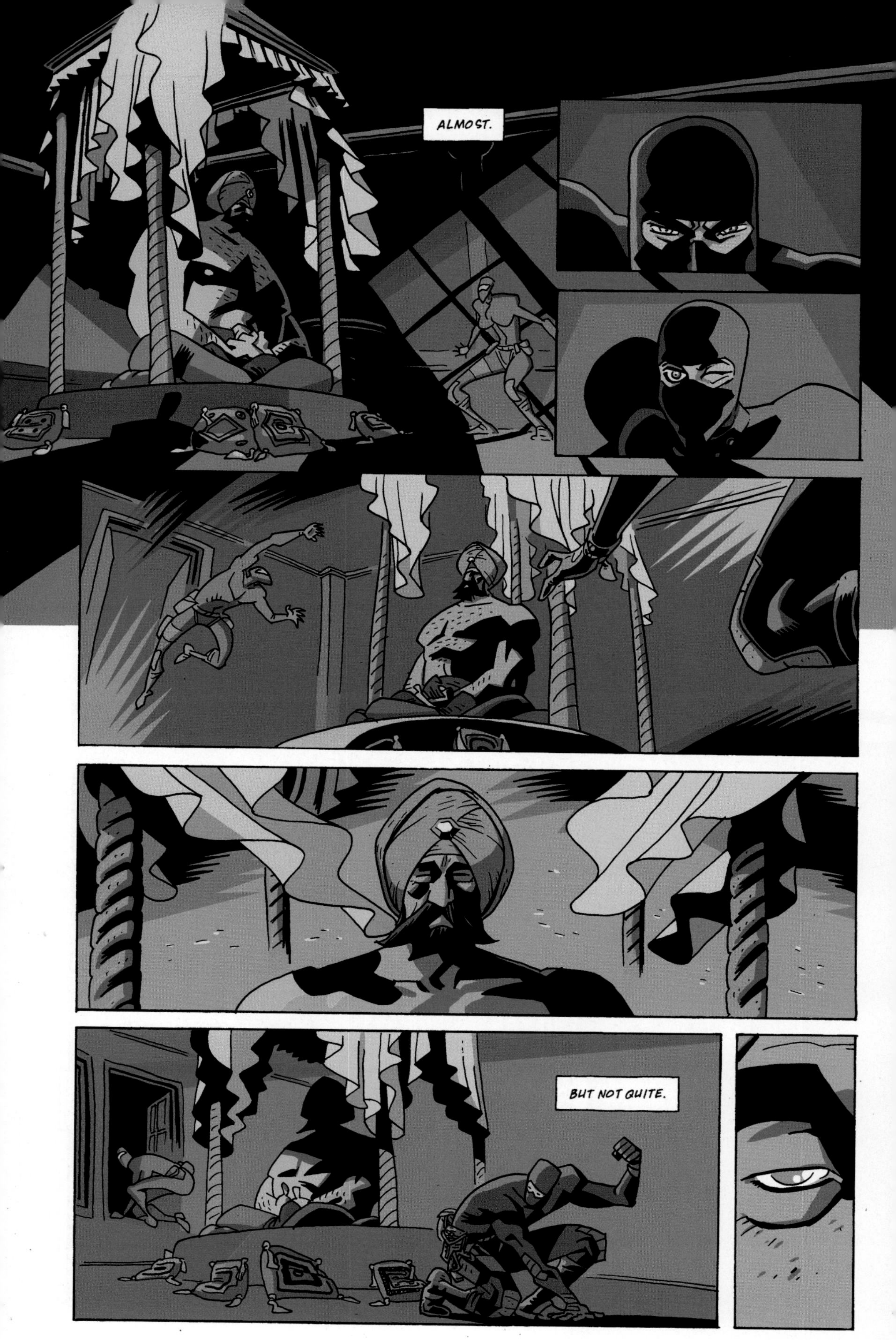
ALMOST.
BUT NOT QUITE.

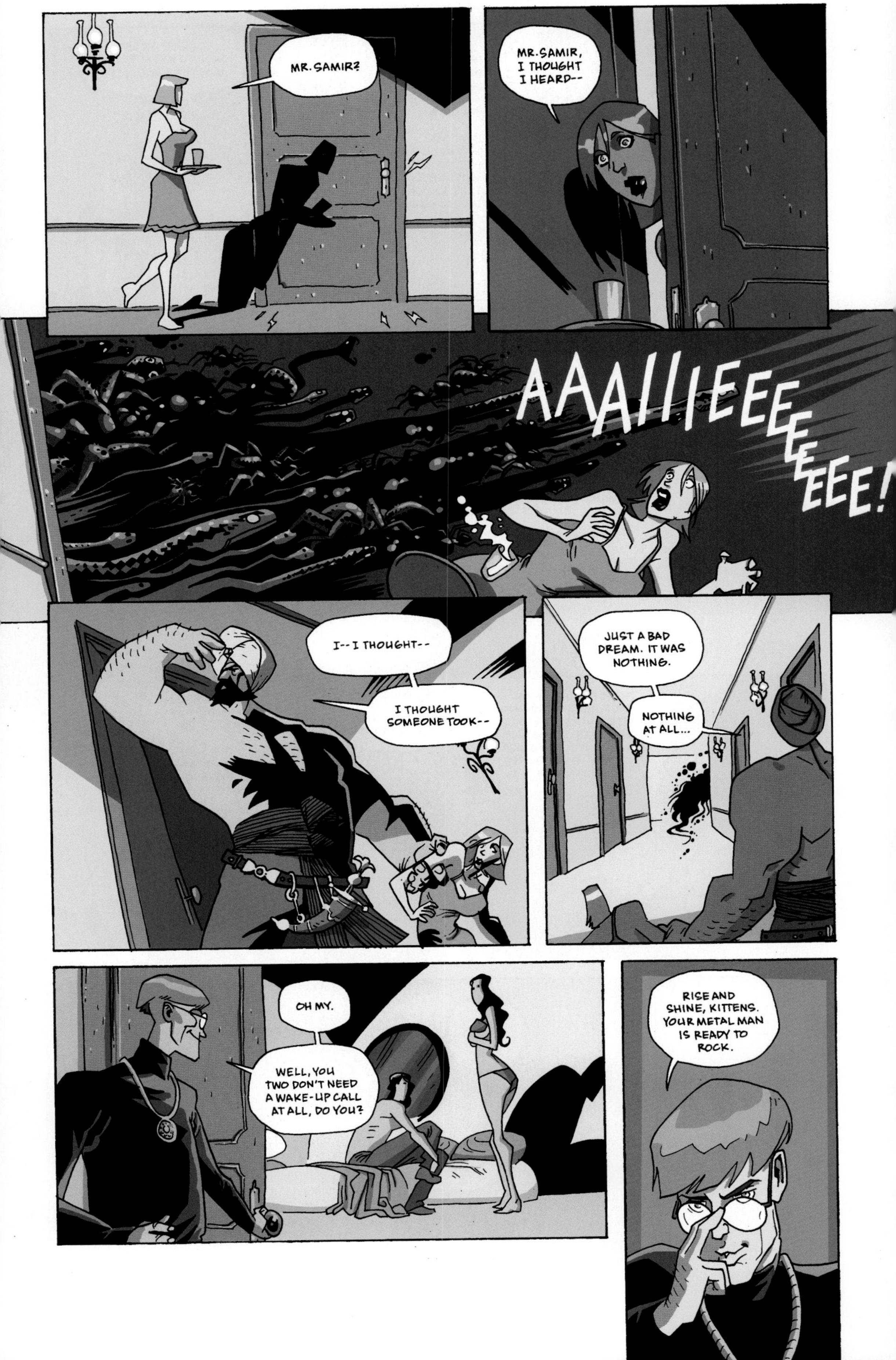
MR. SAMIR?
MR. SAMIR, I THOUGHT I HEARD--
AAAIIIEEEEEEEE!
I-- I THOUGHT--
I THOUGHT SOMEONE TOOK--
JUST A BAD DREAM. IT WAS NOTHING.
NOTHING AT ALL...
OH MY.
WELL, YOU TWO DON'T NEED A WAKE-UP CALL AT ALL, DO YOU?
RISE AND SHINE, KITTENS. YOUR METAL MAN IS READY TO ROCK.

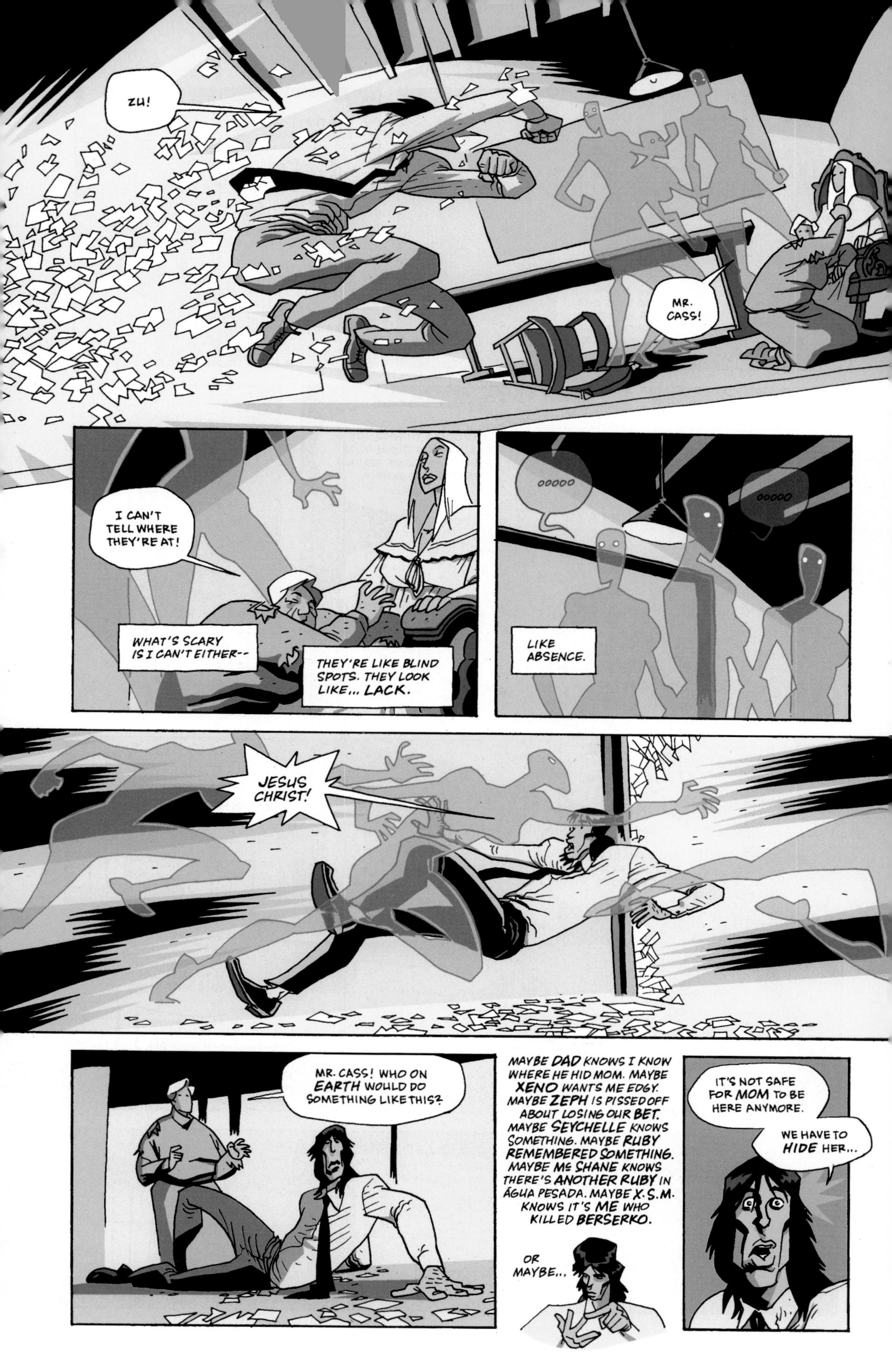
ZU!
MR. CASS!
I CAN'T TELL WHERE THEY'RE AT!
WHAT'S SCARY IS I CAN'T EITHER--
THEY'RE LIKE BLIND SPOTS. THEY LOOK LIKE... LACK.
OOOOO
OOOOO
LIKE ABSENCE.
JESUS CHRIST!
MR. CASS! WHO ON EARTH WOULD DO SOMETHING LIKE THIS?
MAYBE DAD KNOWS I KNOW WHERE HE HID MOM. MAYBE XENO WANTS ME EDGY. MAYBE ZEPH IS PISSED OFF ABOUT LOSING OUR BET. MAYBE SEYCHELLE KNOWS SOMETHING. MAYBE RUBY REMEMBERED SOMETHING. MAYBE MS SHANE KNOWS THERE'S ANOTHER RUBY IN ÁGUA PESADA. MAYBE X.S.M. KNOWS IT'S ME WHO KILLED BERSERKO.
OR MAYBE...
IT'S NOT SAFE FOR MOM TO BE HERE ANYMORE.
WE HAVE TO HIDE HER...

# CHAPTER 5
# COLDHEART

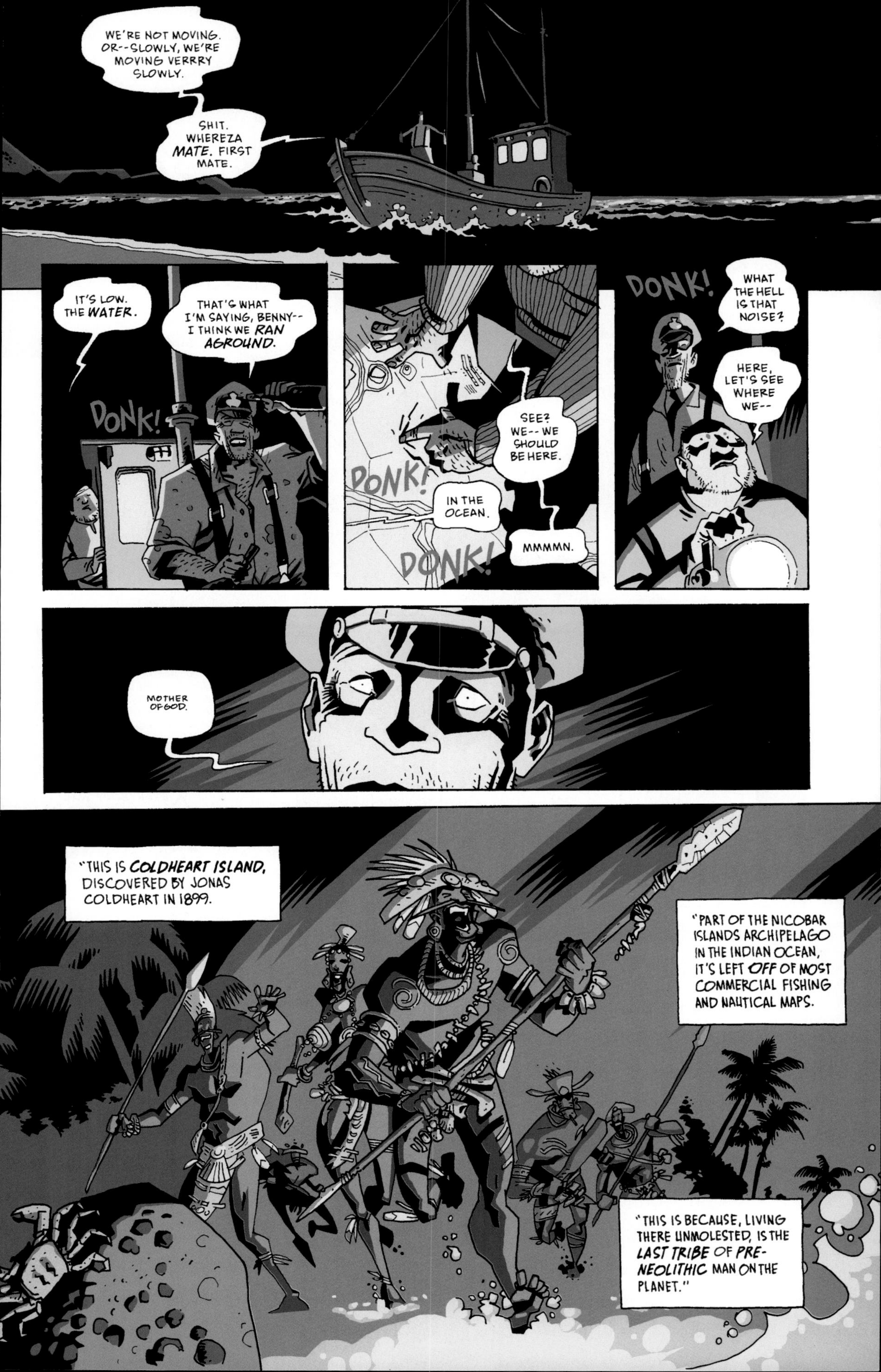
WE'RE NOT MOVING. OR--SLOWLY, WE'RE MOVING VERRRY SLOWLY.
SHIT. WHEREZA MATE. FIRST MATE.
IT'S LOW. THE WATER.
THAT'S WHAT I'M SAYING, BENNY-- I THINK WE RAN AGROUND.
DONK!
DONK!
SEE? WE-- WE SHOULD BE HERE.
IN THE OCEAN.
DONK!
MMMMN.
DONK!
WHAT THE HELL IS THAT NOISE?
HERE, LET'S SEE WHERE WE--
MOTHER OF GOD.
"THIS IS COLDHEART ISLAND, DISCOVERED BY JONAS COLDHEART IN 1899.
"PART OF THE NICOBAR ISLANDS ARCHIPELAGO IN THE INDIAN OCEAN, IT'S LEFT OFF OF MOST COMMERCIAL FISHING AND NAUTICAL MAPS.
"THIS IS BECAUSE, LIVING THERE UNMOLESTED, IS THE LAST TRIBE OF PRE-NEOLITHIC MAN ON THE PLANET."

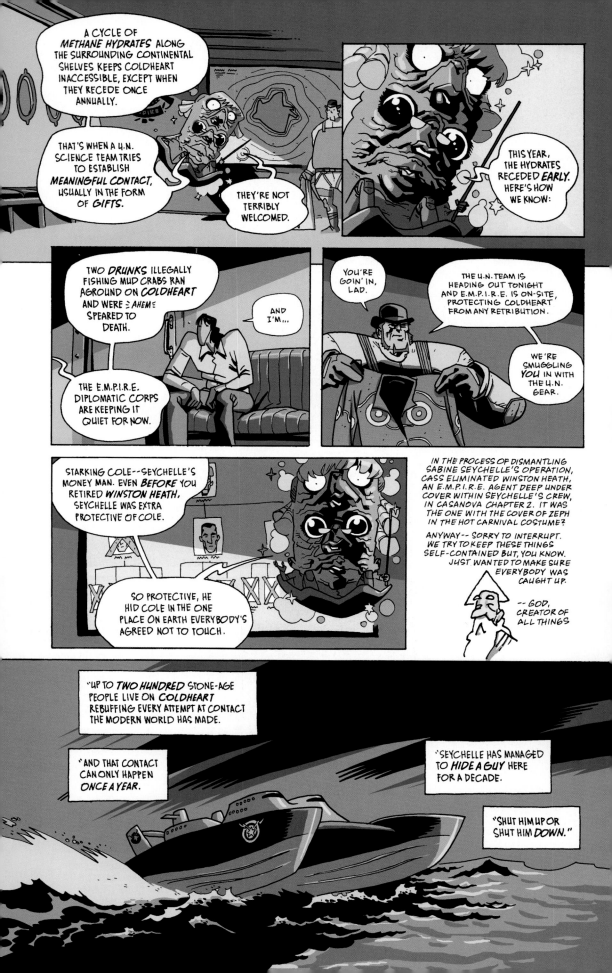

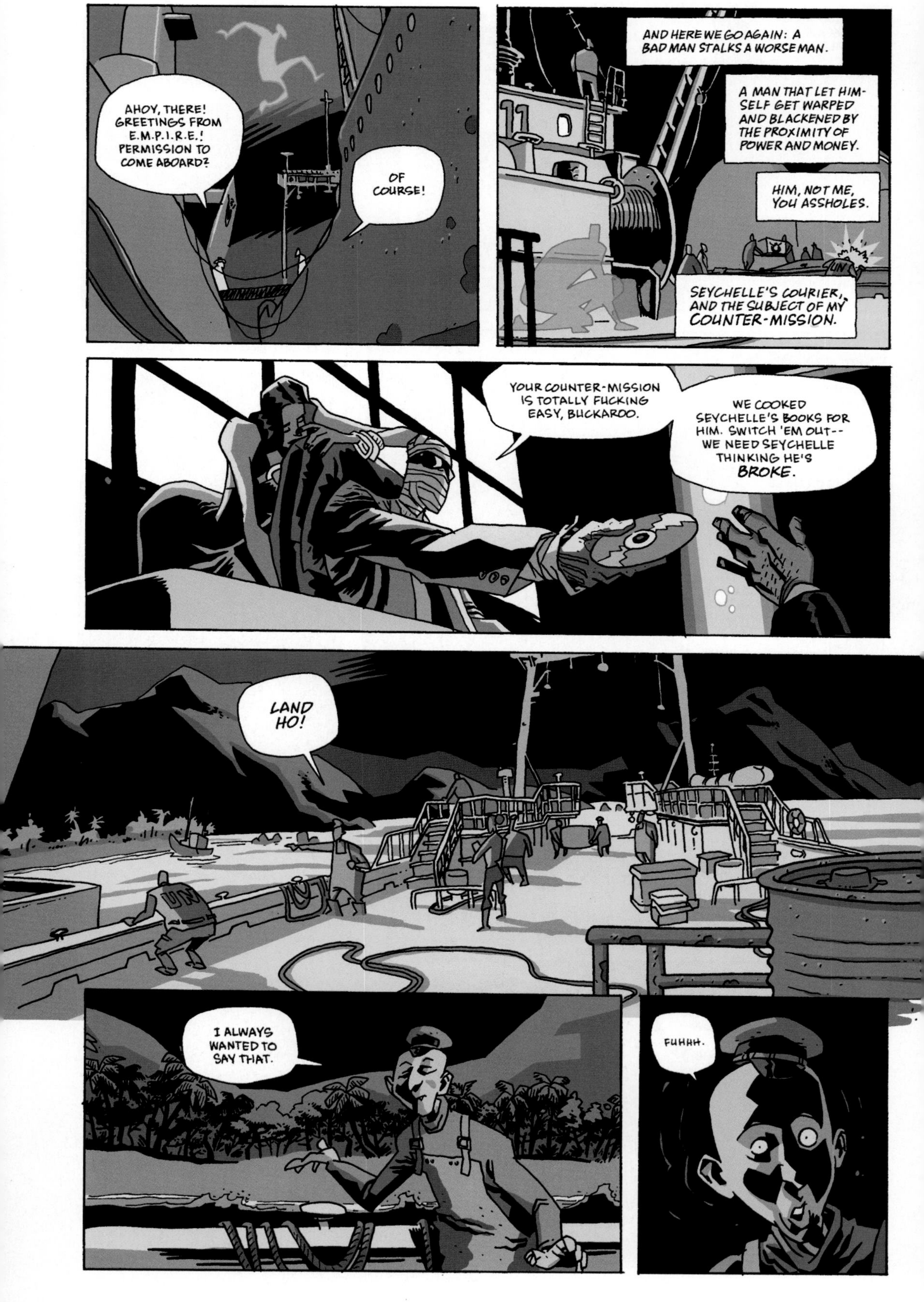
AHOY, THERE! GREETINGS FROM E.M.P.I.R.E.! PERMISSION TO COME ABOARD?
OF COURSE!
AND HERE WE GO AGAIN: A BAD MAN STALKS A WORSE MAN.
A MAN THAT LET HIMSELF GET WARPED AND BLACKENED BY THE PROXIMITY OF POWER AND MONEY.
HIM, NOT ME, YOU ASSHOLES.
SEYCHELLE'S COURIER, AND THE SUBJECT OF MY COUNTER-MISSION.
YOUR COUNTER-MISSION IS TOTALLY FUCKING EASY, BUCKAROO.
WE COOKED SEYCHELLE'S BOOKS FOR HIM. SWITCH 'EM OUT-- WE NEED SEYCHELLE THINKING HE'S BROKE.
LAND HO!
I ALWAYS WANTED TO SAY THAT.
FUHHH.

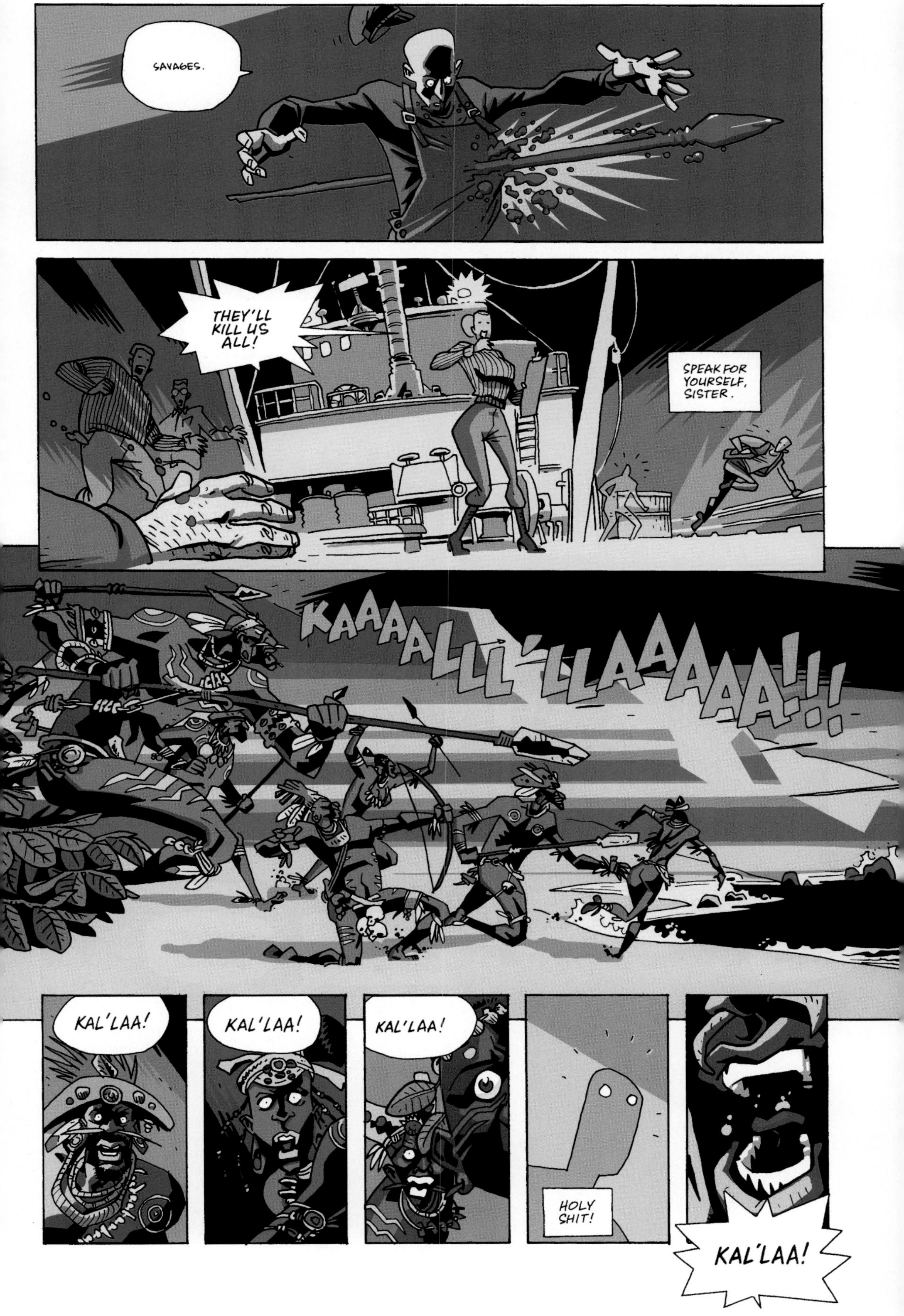
SAVAGES.
THEY'LL KILL US ALL!
SPEAK FOR YOURSELF, SISTER.
KAAAALLL'LLAAAAAA!!!
KAL'LAA!
KAL'LAA!
KAL'LAA!
HOLY SHIT!
KAL'LAA!

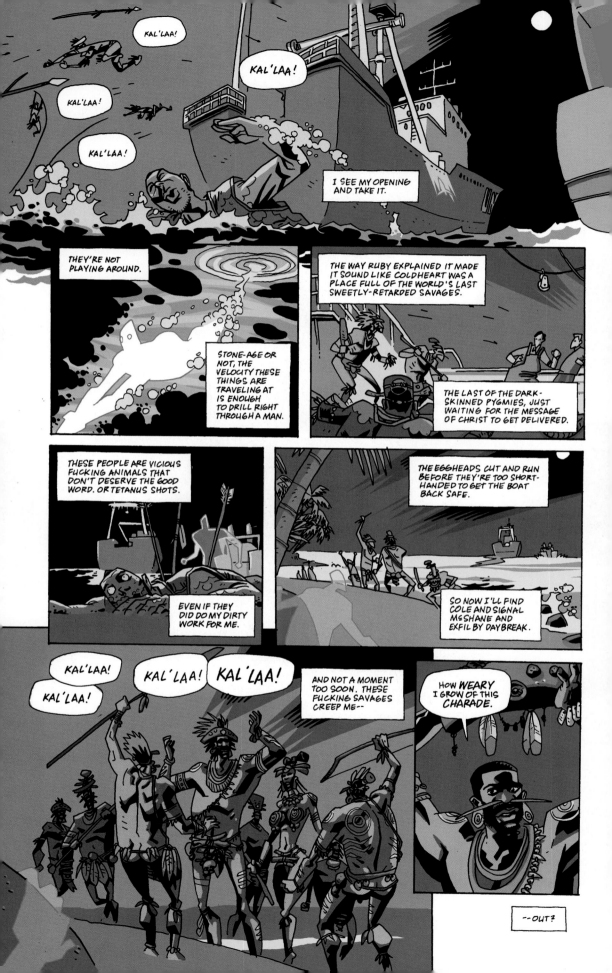

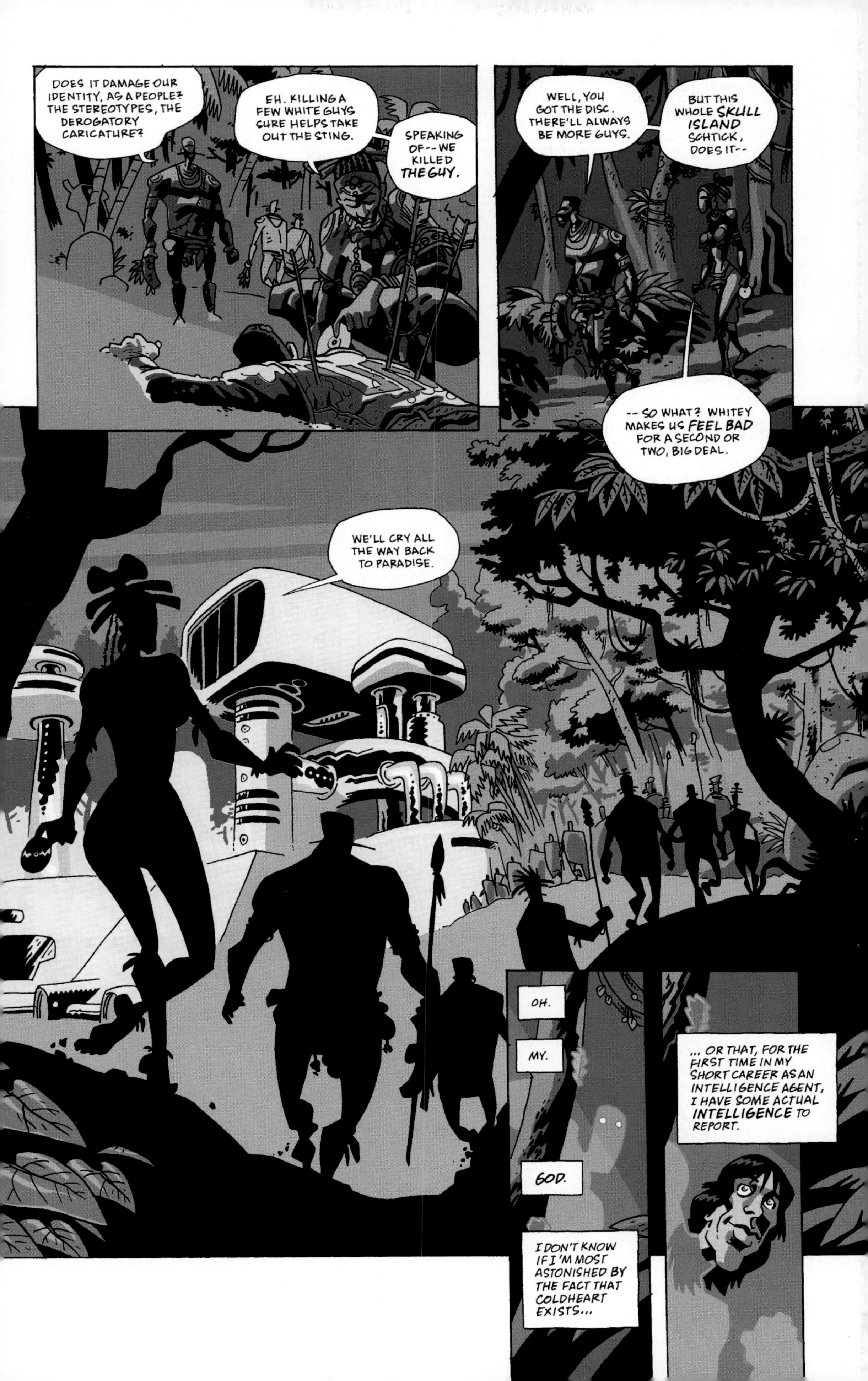
DOES IT DAMAGE OUR IDENTITY, AS A PEOPLE? THE STEREOTYPES, THE DEROGATORY CARICATURE?
EH. KILLING A FEW WHITE GUYS SURE HELPS TAKE OUT THE STING.
SPEAKING OF--WE KILLED THE GUY.
WELL, YOU GOT THE DISC. THERE'LL ALWAYS BE MORE GUYS.
BUT THIS WHOLE SKULL ISLAND SCHTICK, DOES IT--
--SO WHAT? WHITEY MAKES US FEEL BAD FOR A SECOND OR TWO, BIG DEAL.
WE'LL CRY ALL THE WAY BACK TO PARADISE.
OH.
MY.
GOD.
I DON'T KNOW IF I'M MOST ASTONISHED BY THE FACT THAT COLDHEART EXISTS...
... OR THAT, FOR THE FIRST TIME IN MY SHORT CAREER AS AN INTELLIGENCE AGENT, I HAVE SOME ACTUAL INTELLIGENCE TO REPORT.

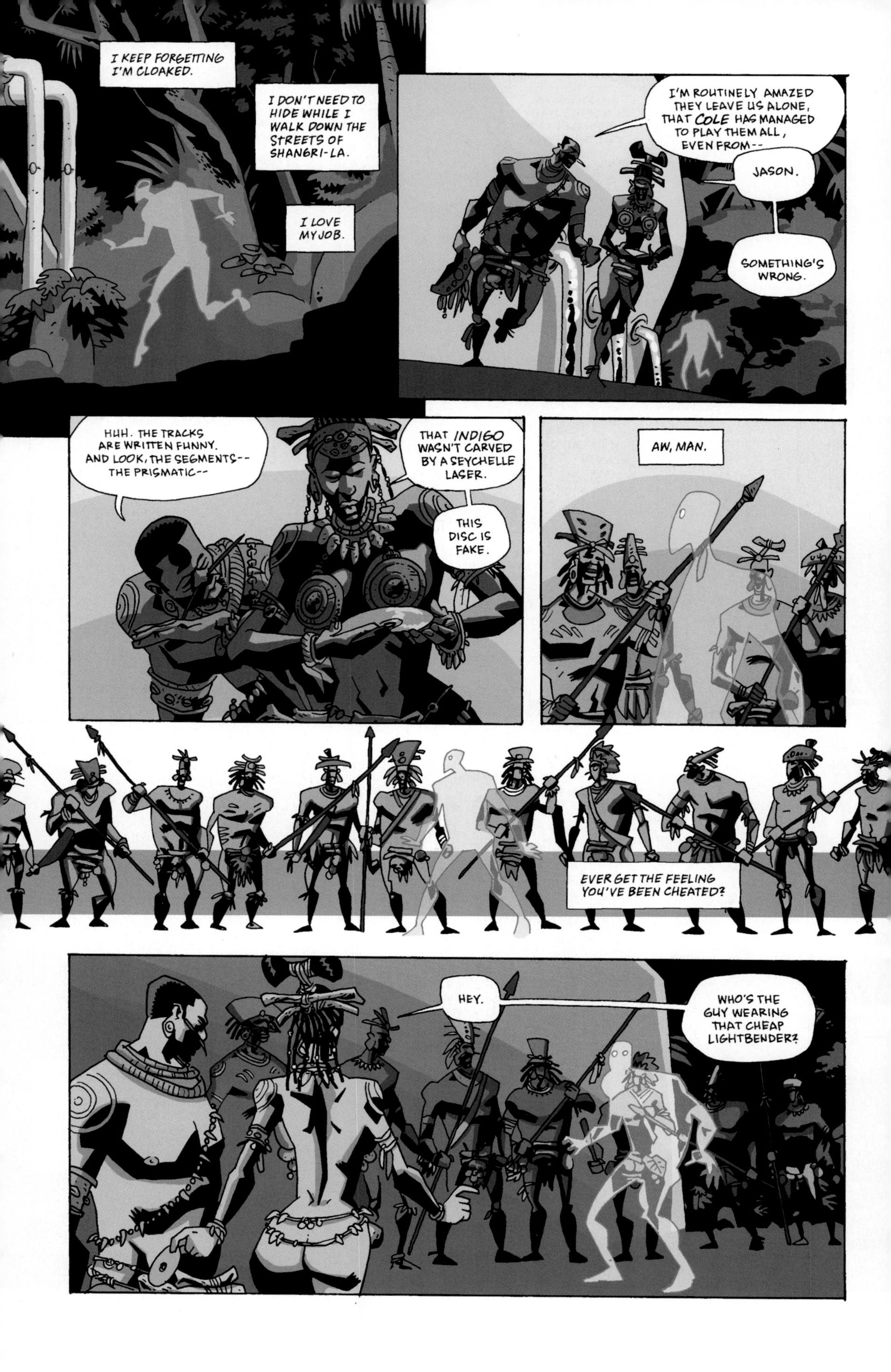
I KEEP FORGETTING I'M CLOAKED.
I DON'T NEED TO HIDE WHILE I WALK DOWN THE STREETS OF SHANGRI-LA.
I LOVE MY JOB.
I'M ROUTINELY AMAZED THEY LEAVE US ALONE, THAT COLE HAS MANAGED TO PLAY THEM ALL, EVEN FROM--
JASON.
SOMETHING'S WRONG.
HUH. THE TRACKS ARE WRITTEN FUNNY. AND LOOK, THE SEGMENTS-- THE PRISMATIC--
THAT INDIGO WASN'T CARVED BY A SEYCHELLE LASER.
THIS DISC IS FAKE.
AW, MAN.
EVER GET THE FEELING YOU'VE BEEN CHEATED?
HEY.
WHO'S THE GUY WEARING THAT CHEAP LIGHTBENDER?

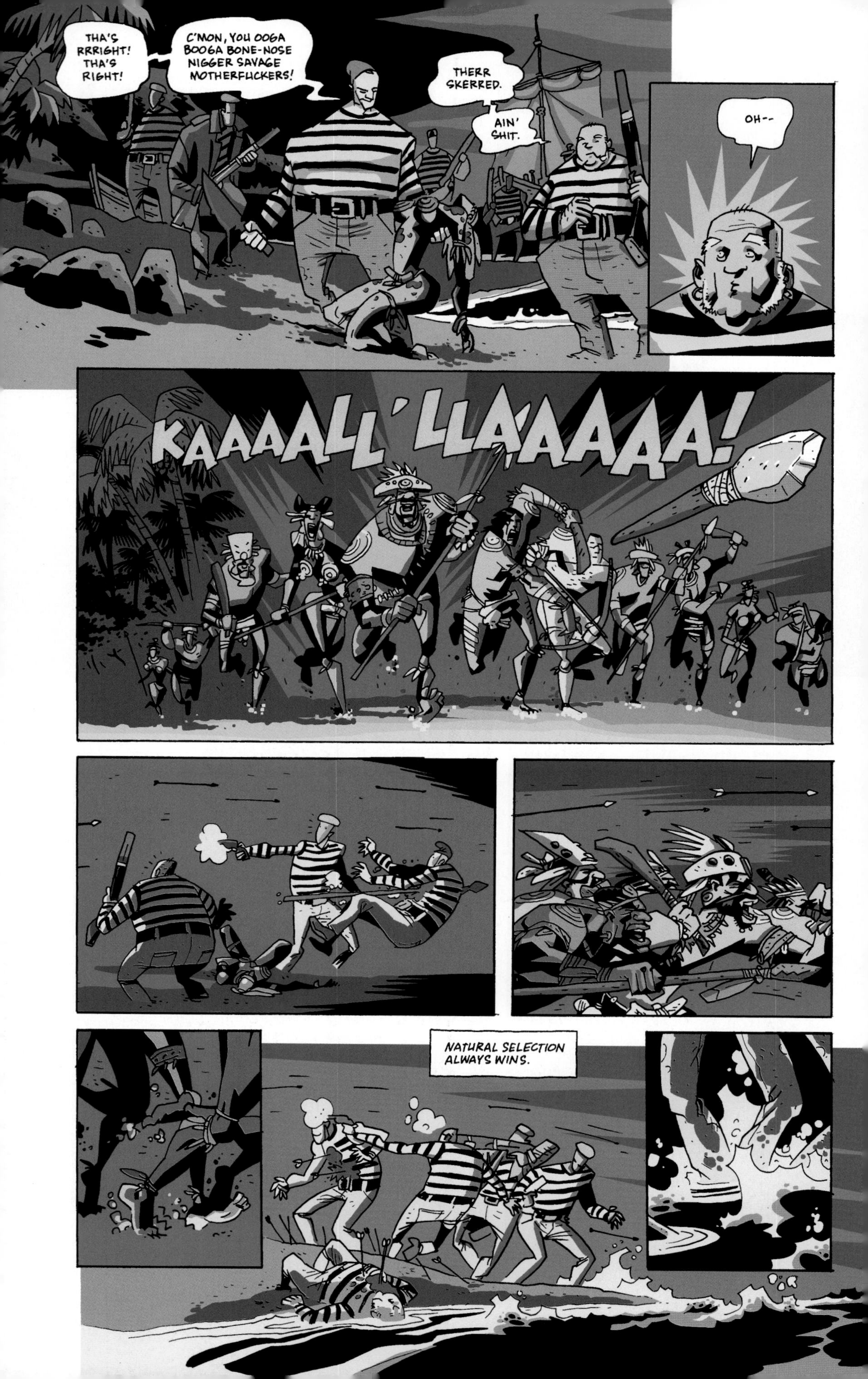

THA'S RRRIGHT! THA'S RIGHT!
C'MON, YOU OOGA BOOGA BONE-NOSE NIGGER SAVAGE MOTHERFUCKERS!
THERR SKERRED.
AIN' SHIT.
OH--
KAAAALL' LLAAAAAA!
NATURAL SELECTION ALWAYS WINS.

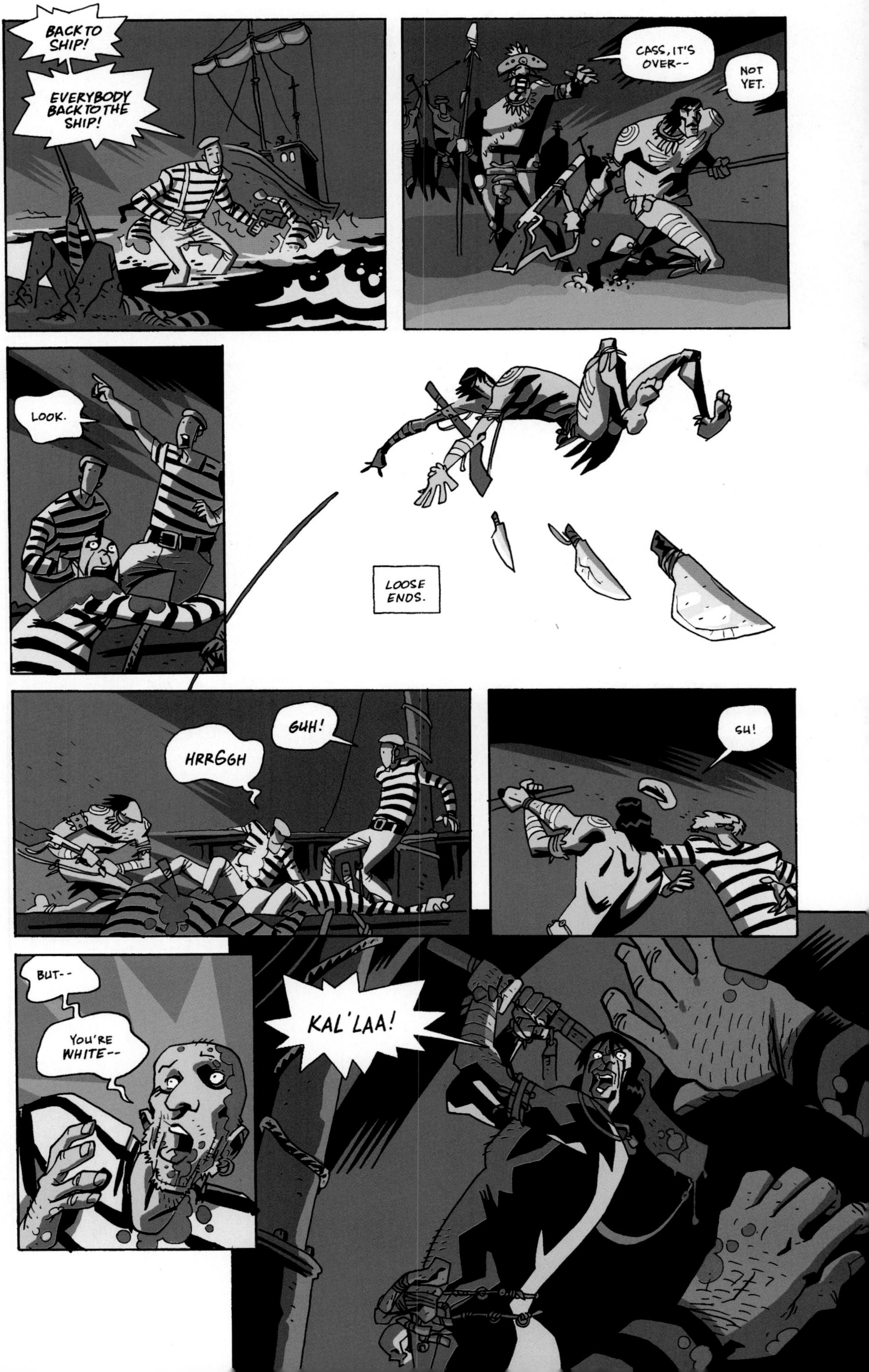
BACK TO SHIP!
EVERYBODY BACK TO THE SHIP!
CASS, IT'S OVER--
NOT YET.
LOOK.
LOOSE ENDS.
HRRGGH
GUH!
GU!
BUT--
YOU'RE WHITE--
KAL'LAA!

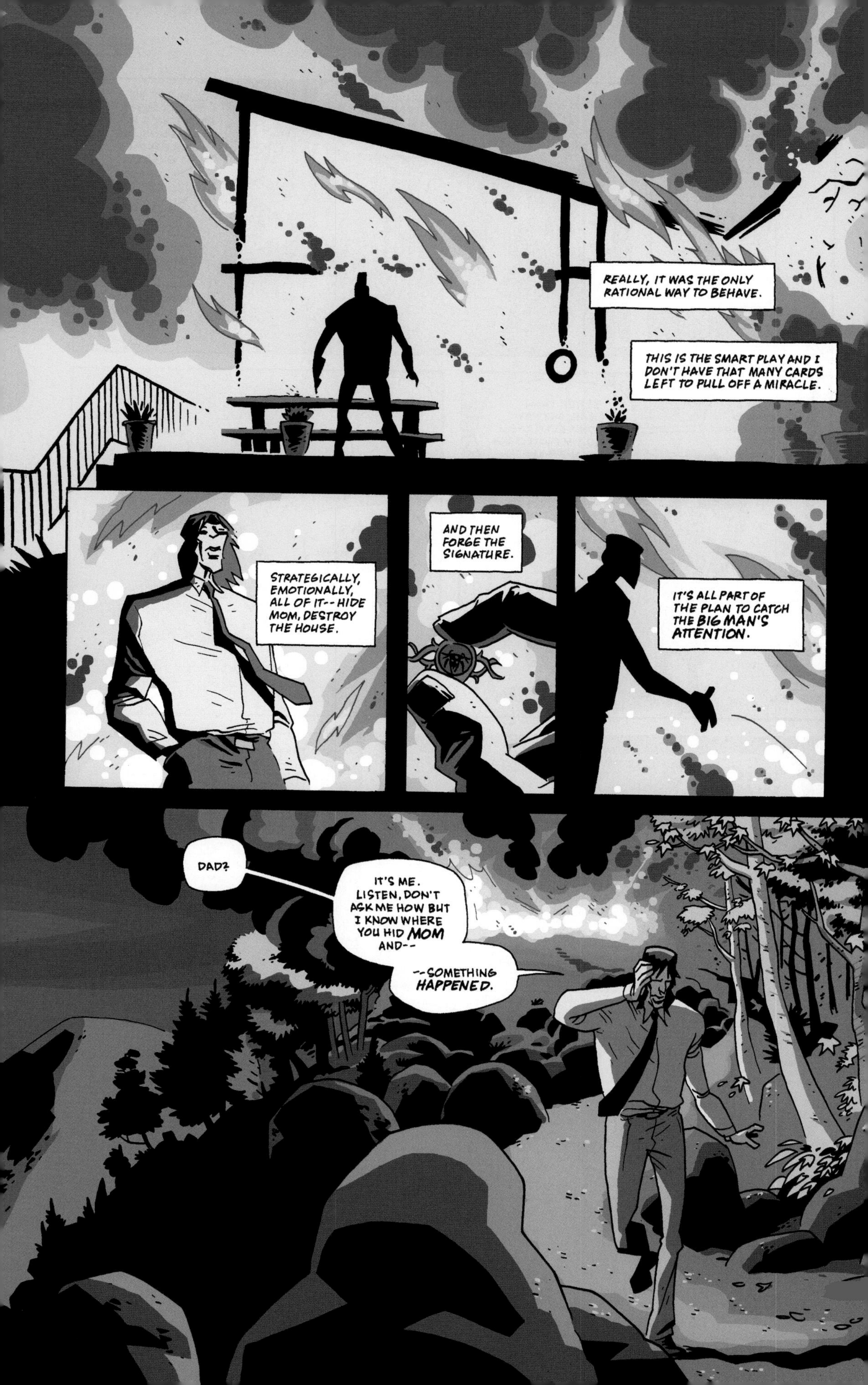
REALLY, IT WAS THE ONLY RATIONAL WAY TO BEHAVE.
THIS IS THE SMART PLAY AND I DON'T HAVE THAT MANY CARDS LEFT TO PULL OFF A MIRACLE.
STRATEGICALLY, EMOTIONALLY, ALL OF IT-- HIDE MOM, DESTROY THE HOUSE.
AND THEN FORGE THE SIGNATURE.
IT'S ALL PART OF THE PLAN TO CATCH THE BIG MAN'S ATTENTION.
DAD?
IT'S ME. LISTEN, DON'T ASK ME HOW BUT I KNOW WHERE YOU HID MOM AND--
--SOMETHING HAPPENED.

# CHAPTER 6
# WOMEN AND MEN
## (PART ONE)

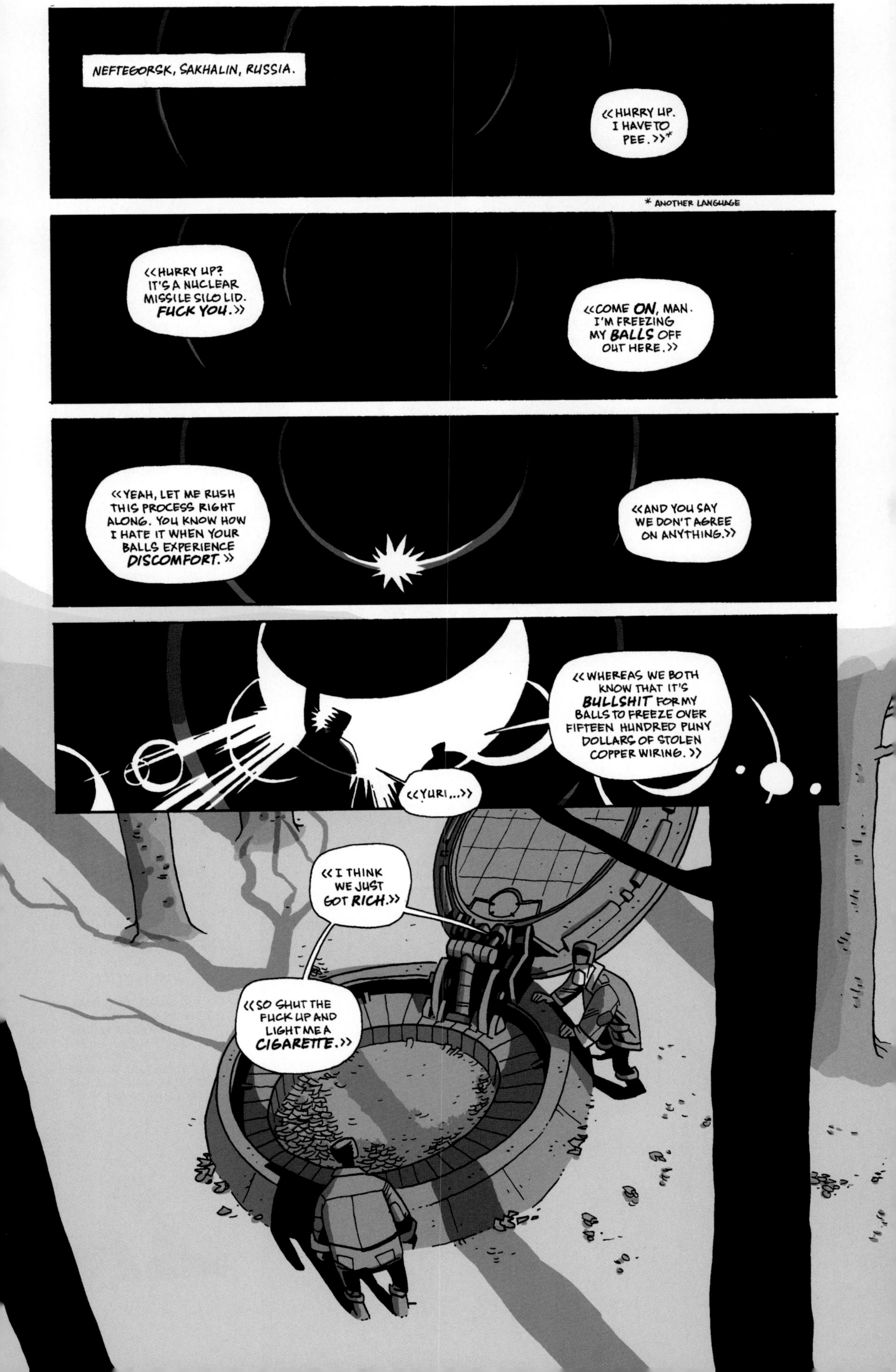
NEFTEGORSK, SAKHALIN, RUSSIA.
<<HURRY UP. I HAVE TO PEE.>>*
* ANOTHER LANGUAGE
<<HURRY UP? IT'S A NUCLEAR MISSILE SILO LID. FUCK YOU.>>
<<COME ON, MAN. I'M FREEZING MY BALLS OFF OUT HERE.>>
<<YEAH, LET ME RUSH THIS PROCESS RIGHT ALONG. YOU KNOW HOW I HATE IT WHEN YOUR BALLS EXPERIENCE DISCOMFORT.>>
<<AND YOU SAY WE DON'T AGREE ON ANYTHING.>>
<<WHEREAS WE BOTH KNOW THAT IT'S BULLSHIT FOR MY BALLS TO FREEZE OVER FIFTEEN HUNDRED PUNY DOLLARS OF STOLEN COPPER WIRING.>>
<<YURI...>>
<<I THINK WE JUST GOT RICH.>>
<<SO SHUT THE FUCK UP AND LIGHT ME A CIGARETTE.>>

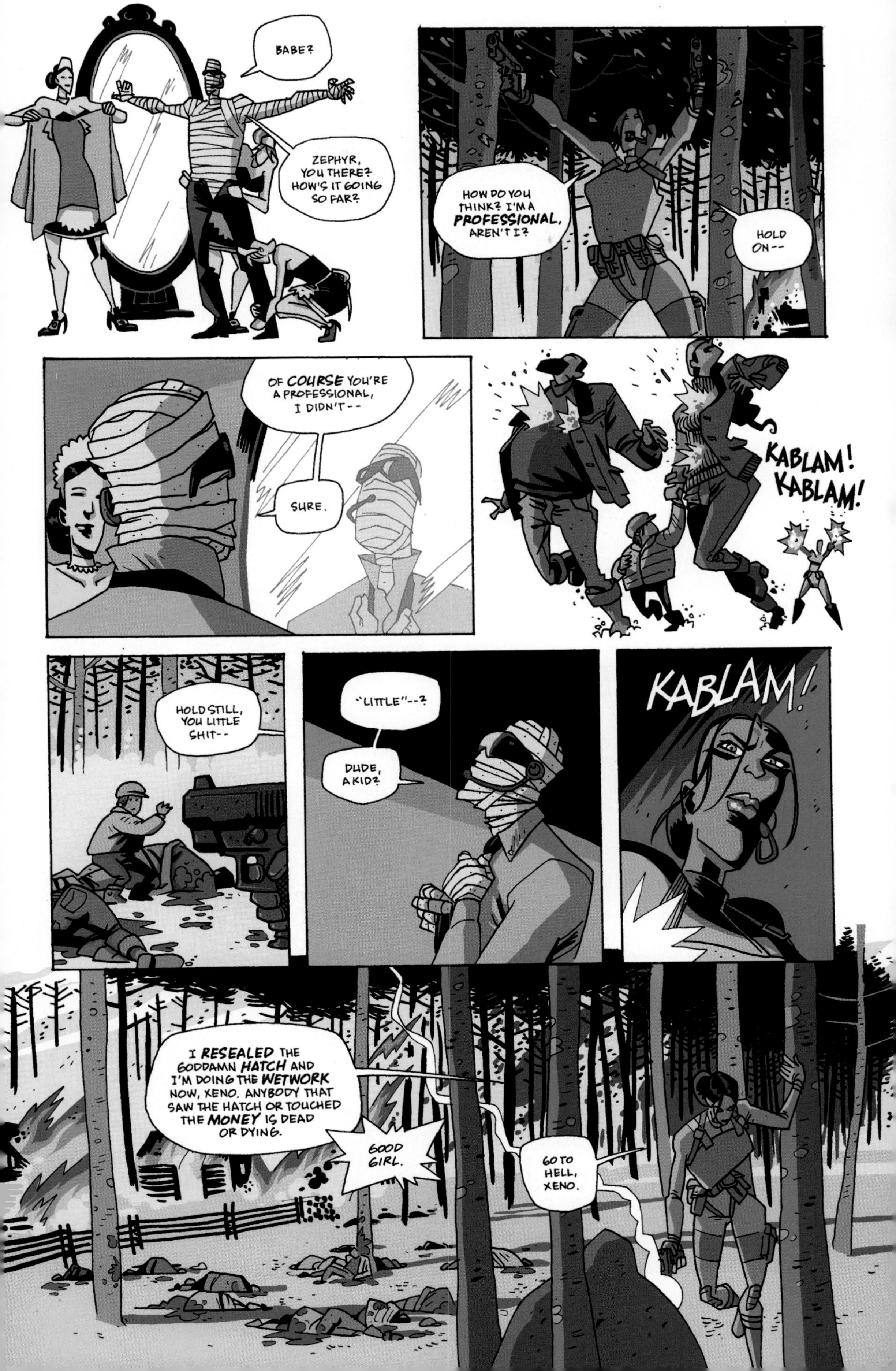
BABE?
ZEPHYR, YOU THERE? HOW'S IT GOING SO FAR?
HOW DO YOU THINK? I'M A PROFESSIONAL, AREN'T I?
HOLD ON--
OF COURSE YOU'RE A PROFESSIONAL, I DIDN'T--
SURE.
KABLAM! KABLAM!
HOLD STILL, YOU LITTLE SHIT--
"LITTLE"--?
DUDE, A KID?
KABLAM!
I RESEALED THE GODDAMN HATCH AND I'M DOING THE WETWORK NOW, XENO. ANYBODY THAT SAW THE HATCH OR TOUCHED THE MONEY IS DEAD OR DYING.
GOOD GIRL.
GO TO HELL, XENO.

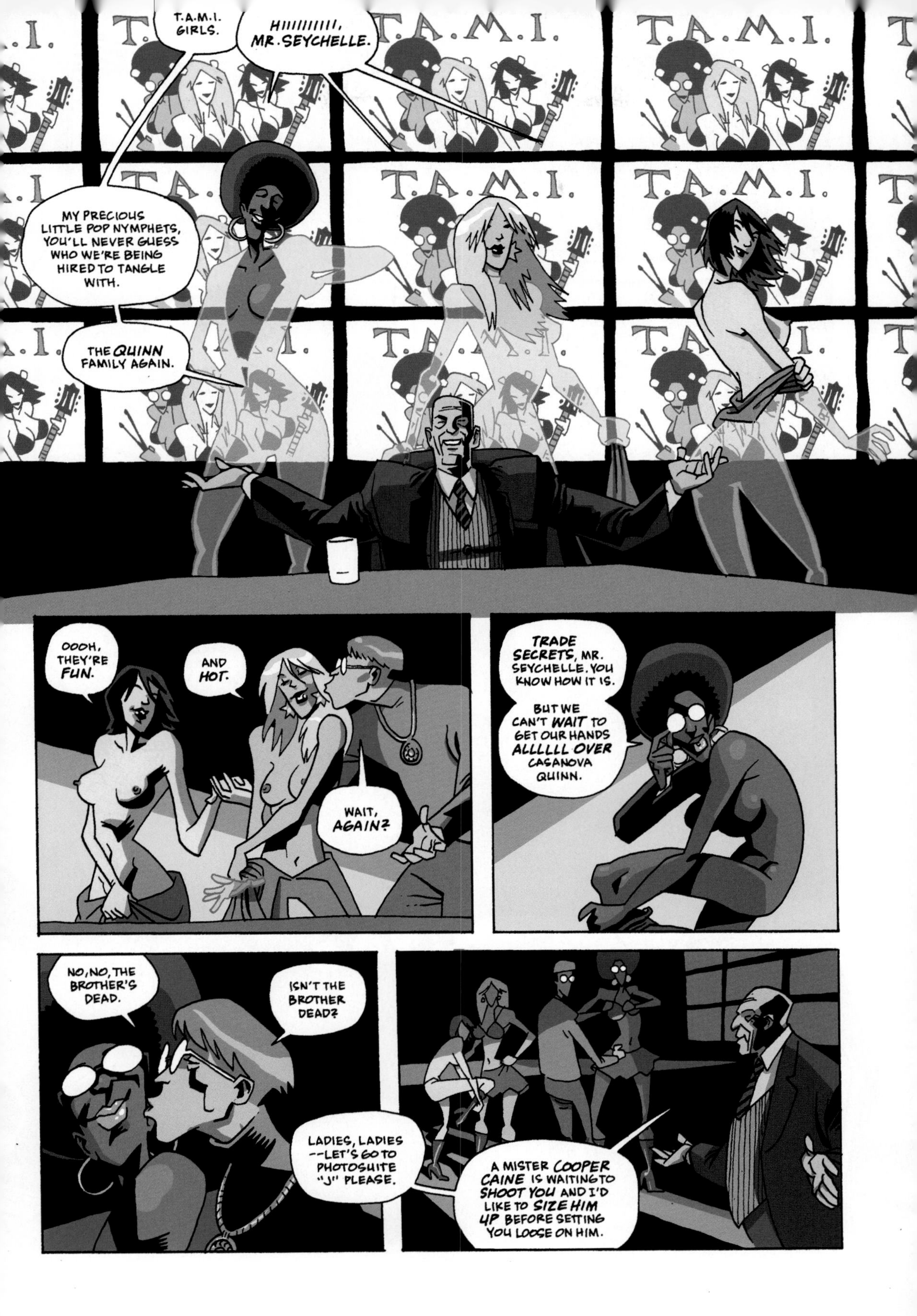
T.A.M.I.
T.A.M.I. GIRLS.
HIIIIIIIIII, MR. SEYCHELLE.
MY PRECIOUS LITTLE POP NYMPHETS, YOU'LL NEVER GUESS WHO WE'RE BEING HIRED TO TANGLE WITH.
THE QUINN FAMILY AGAIN.
OOOH, THEY'RE FUN.
AND HOT.
WAIT, AGAIN?
TRADE SECRETS, MR. SEYCHELLE. YOU KNOW HOW IT IS.
BUT WE CAN'T WAIT TO GET OUR HANDS ALLLLLL OVER CASANOVA QUINN.
NO, NO, THE BROTHER'S DEAD.
ISN'T THE BROTHER DEAD?
LADIES, LADIES --LET'S GO TO PHOTOSUITE "J" PLEASE.
A MISTER COOPER CAINE IS WAITING TO SHOOT YOU AND I'D LIKE TO SIZE HIM UP BEFORE SETTING YOU LOOSE ON HIM.

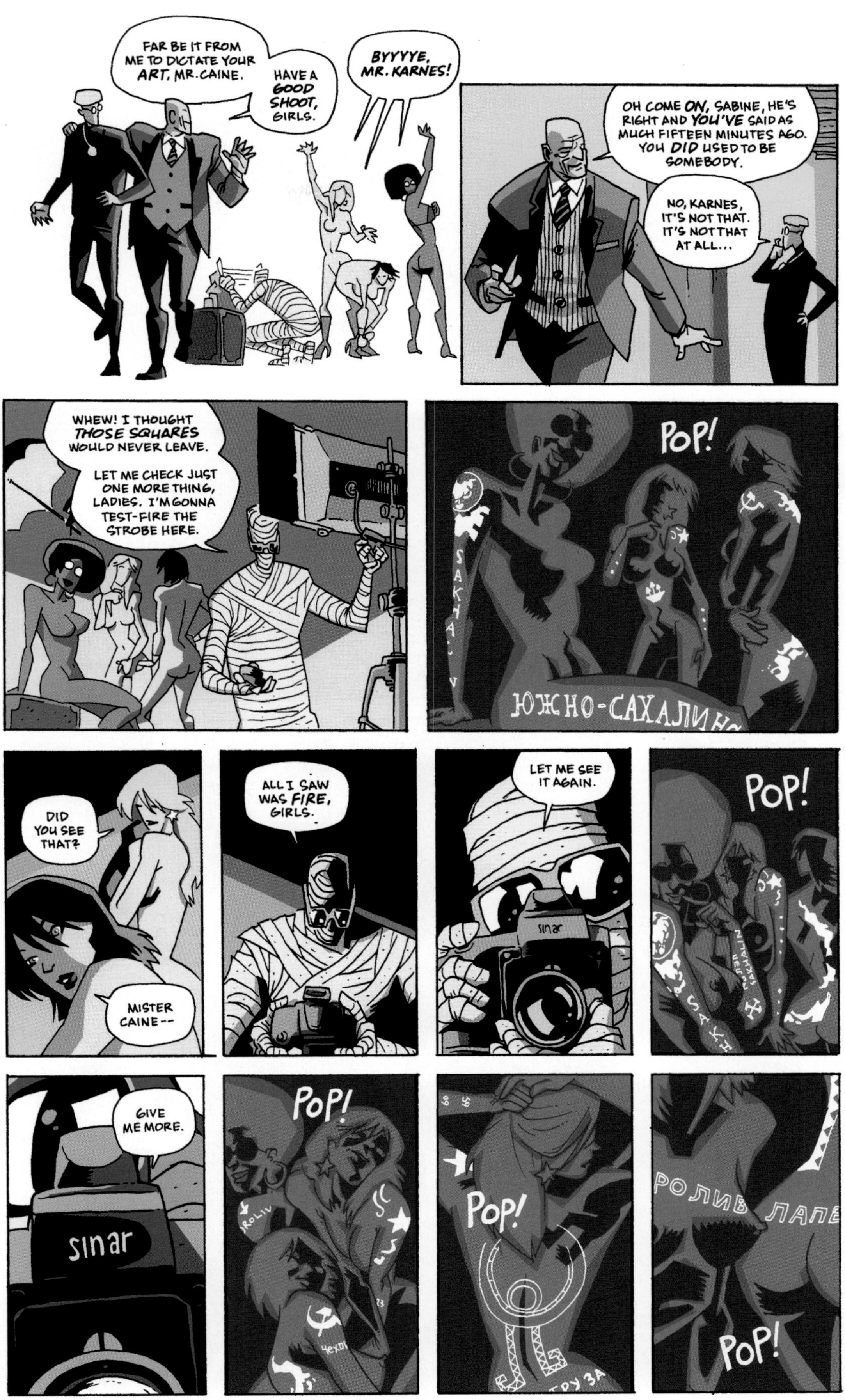
FAR BE IT FROM ME TO DICTATE YOUR ART, MR. CAINE.
HAVE A GOOD SHOOT, GIRLS.
BYYYYE, MR. KARNES!
OH COME ON, SABINE, HE'S RIGHT AND YOU'VE SAID AS MUCH FIFTEEN MINUTES AGO. YOU DID USED TO BE SOMEBODY.
NO, KARNES, IT'S NOT THAT. IT'S NOT THAT AT ALL...
WHEW! I THOUGHT THOSE SQUARES WOULD NEVER LEAVE.
LET ME CHECK JUST ONE MORE THING, LADIES. I'M GONNA TEST-FIRE THE STROBE HERE.
POP!
ЮЖНО-САХАЛИНС
DID YOU SEE THAT?
MISTER CAINE--
ALL I SAW WAS FIRE, GIRLS.
LET ME SEE IT AGAIN.
sinar
POP!
GIVE ME MORE.
sinar
POP!
POP!
ТРУЗА
РОЛИВ ЛАПЕ
POP!

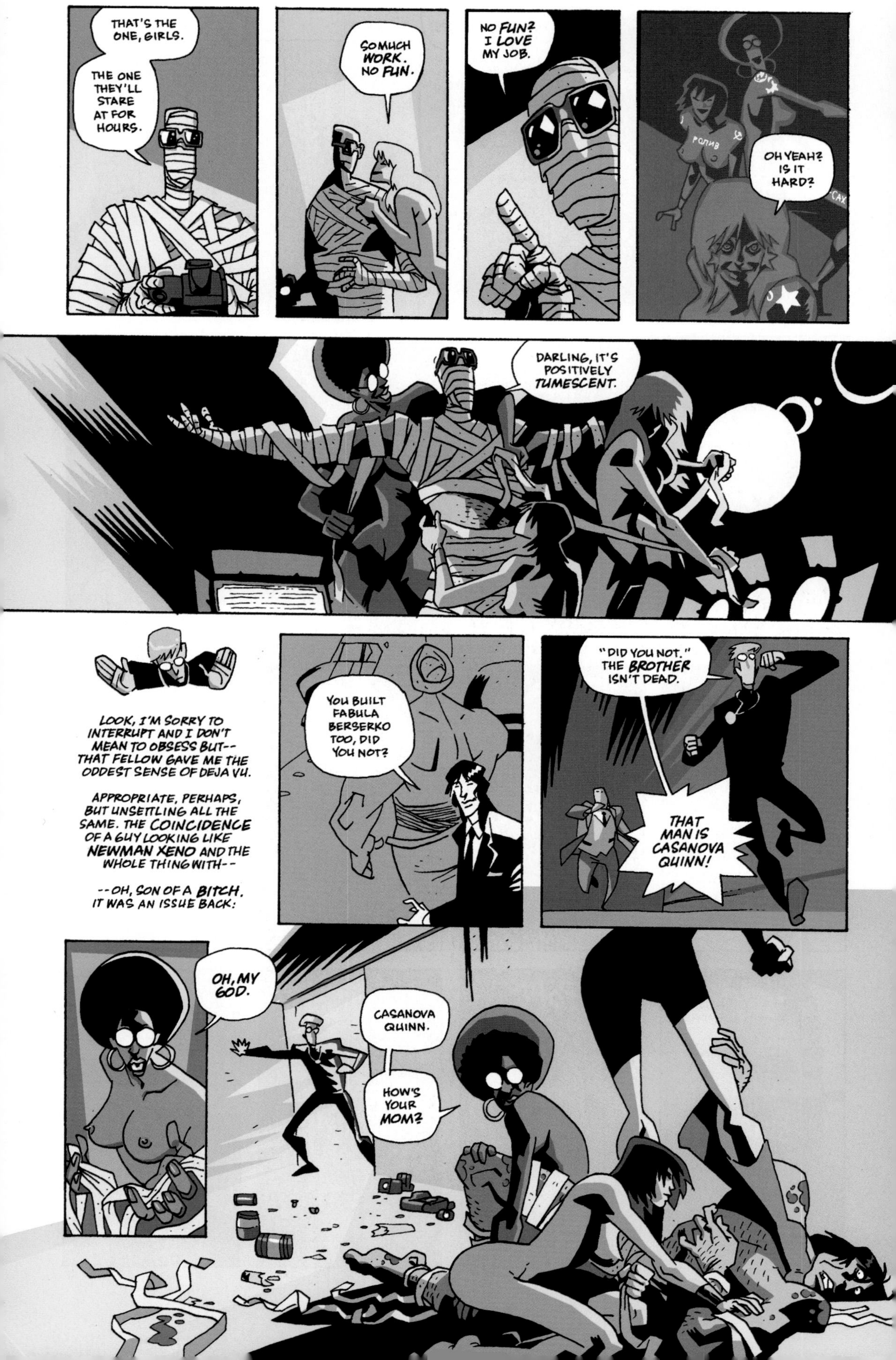
THAT'S THE ONE, GIRLS.
THE ONE THEY'LL STARE AT FOR HOURS.
SO MUCH WORK. NO FUN.
NO FUN? I LOVE MY JOB.
OH YEAH? IS IT HARD?
DARLING, IT'S POSITIVELY TUMESCENT.
LOOK, I'M SORRY TO INTERRUPT AND I DON'T MEAN TO OBSESS BUT-- THAT FELLOW GAVE ME THE ODDEST SENSE OF DEJA VU.
APPROPRIATE, PERHAPS, BUT UNSETTLING ALL THE SAME. THE COINCIDENCE OF A GUY LOOKING LIKE NEWMAN XENO AND THE WHOLE THING WITH--
--OH, SON OF A BITCH. IT WAS AN ISSUE BACK:
YOU BUILT FABULA BERSERKO TOO, DID YOU NOT?
"DID YOU NOT." THE BROTHER ISN'T DEAD.
THAT MAN IS CASANOVA QUINN!
OH, MY GOD.
CASANOVA QUINN.
HOW'S YOUR MOM?

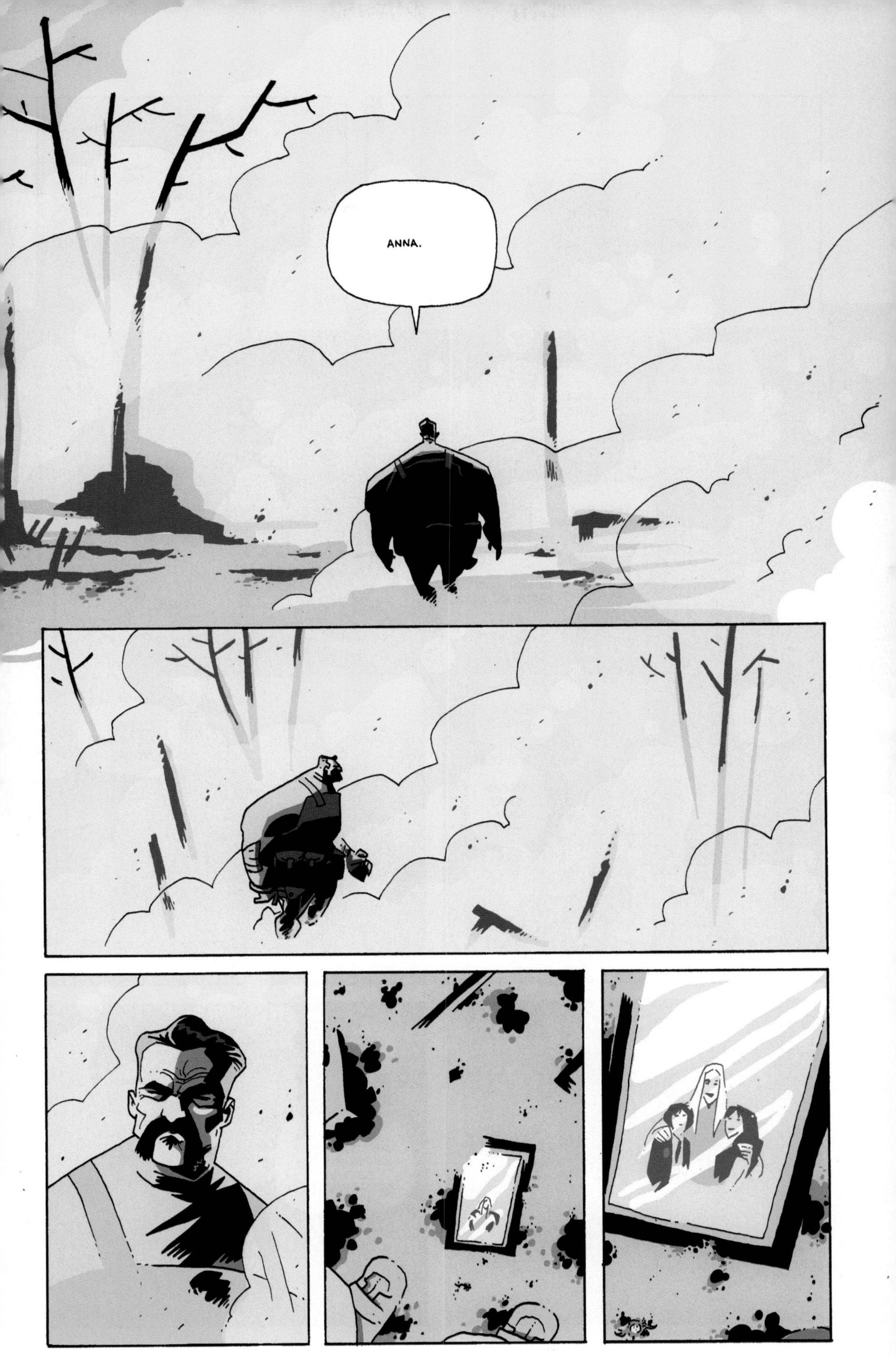
ANNA.

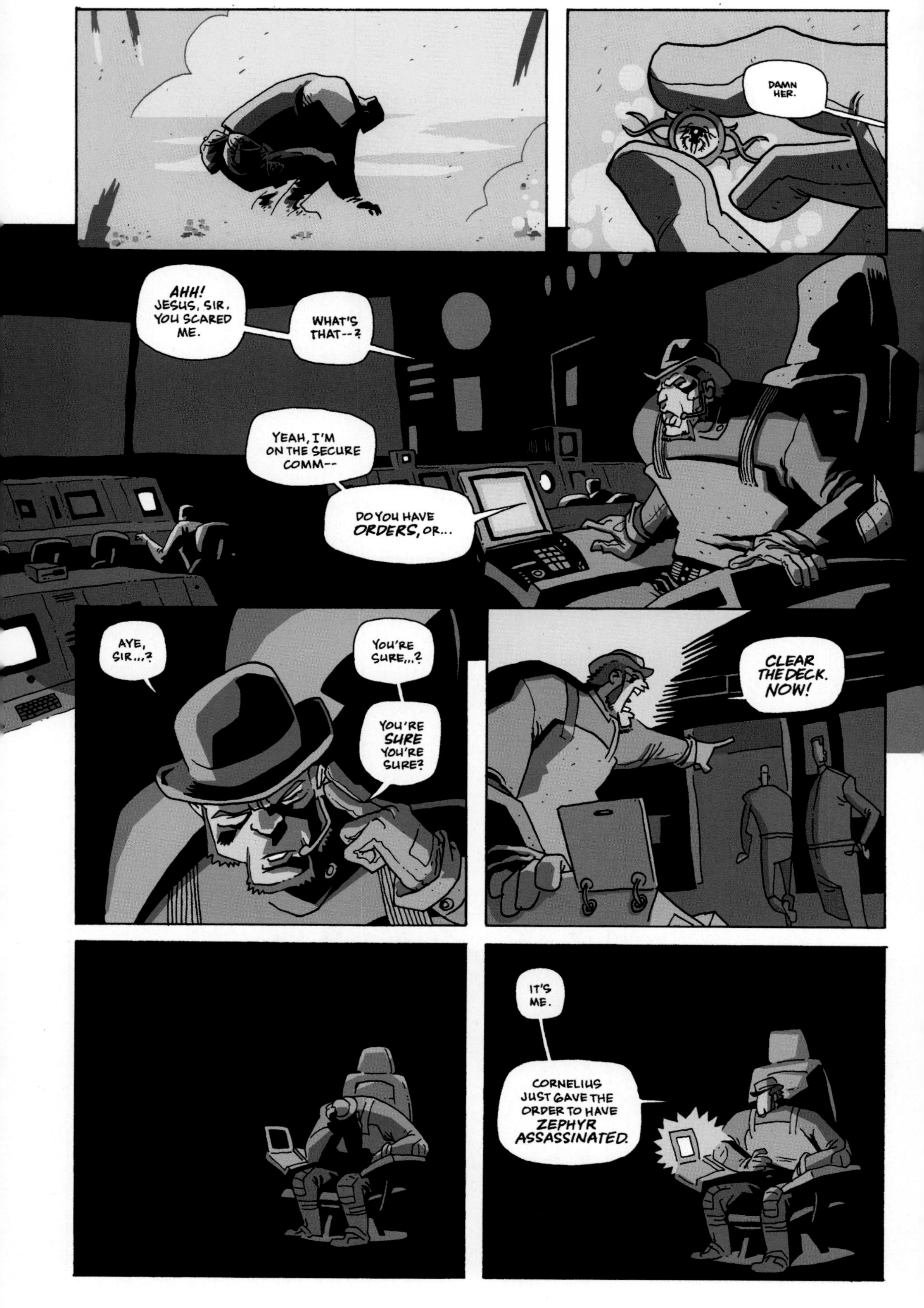
DAMN HER.
AHH! JESUS, SIR. YOU SCARED ME.
WHAT'S THAT--?
YEAH, I'M ON THE SECURE COMM--
DO YOU HAVE ORDERS, OR...
AYE, SIR...?
YOU'RE SURE...?
YOU'RE SURE YOU'RE SURE?
CLEAR THE DECK. NOW!
IT'S ME.
CORNELIUS JUST GAVE THE ORDER TO HAVE ZEPHYR ASSASSINATED.

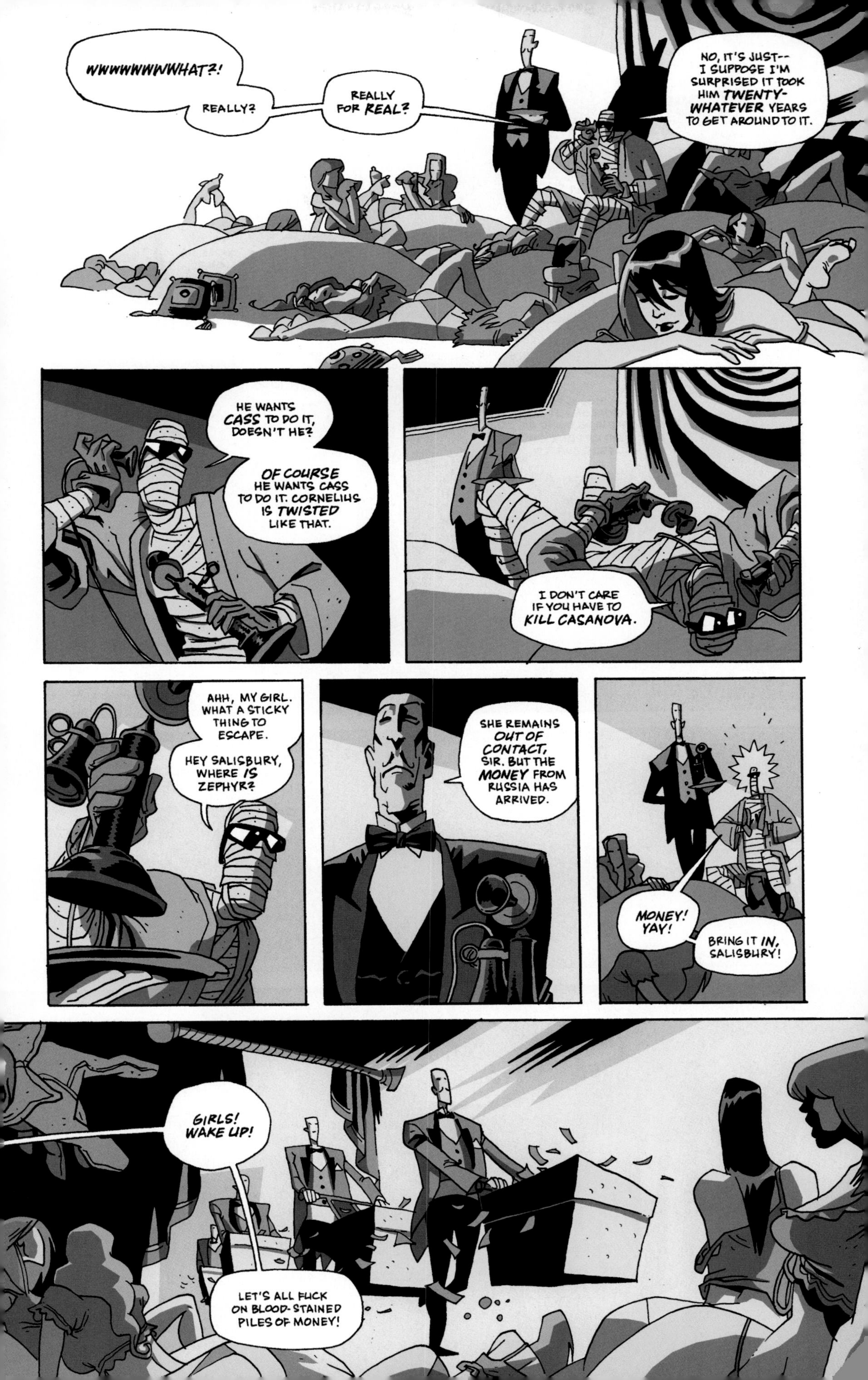
WWWWWWWWHAT?!
REALLY?
REALLY FOR REAL?
NO, IT'S JUST-- I SUPPOSE I'M SURPRISED IT TOOK HIM TWENTY-WHATEVER YEARS TO GET AROUND TO IT.
HE WANTS CASS TO DO IT, DOESN'T HE?
OF COURSE HE WANTS CASS TO DO IT. CORNELIUS IS TWISTED LIKE THAT.
I DON'T CARE IF YOU HAVE TO KILL CASANOVA.
AHH, MY GIRL. WHAT A STICKY THING TO ESCAPE.
HEY SALISBURY, WHERE IS ZEPHYR?
SHE REMAINS OUT OF CONTACT, SIR. BUT THE MONEY FROM RUSSIA HAS ARRIVED.
MONEY! YAY!
BRING IT IN, SALISBURY!
GIRLS! WAKE UP!
LET'S ALL FUCK ON BLOOD-STAINED PILES OF MONEY!

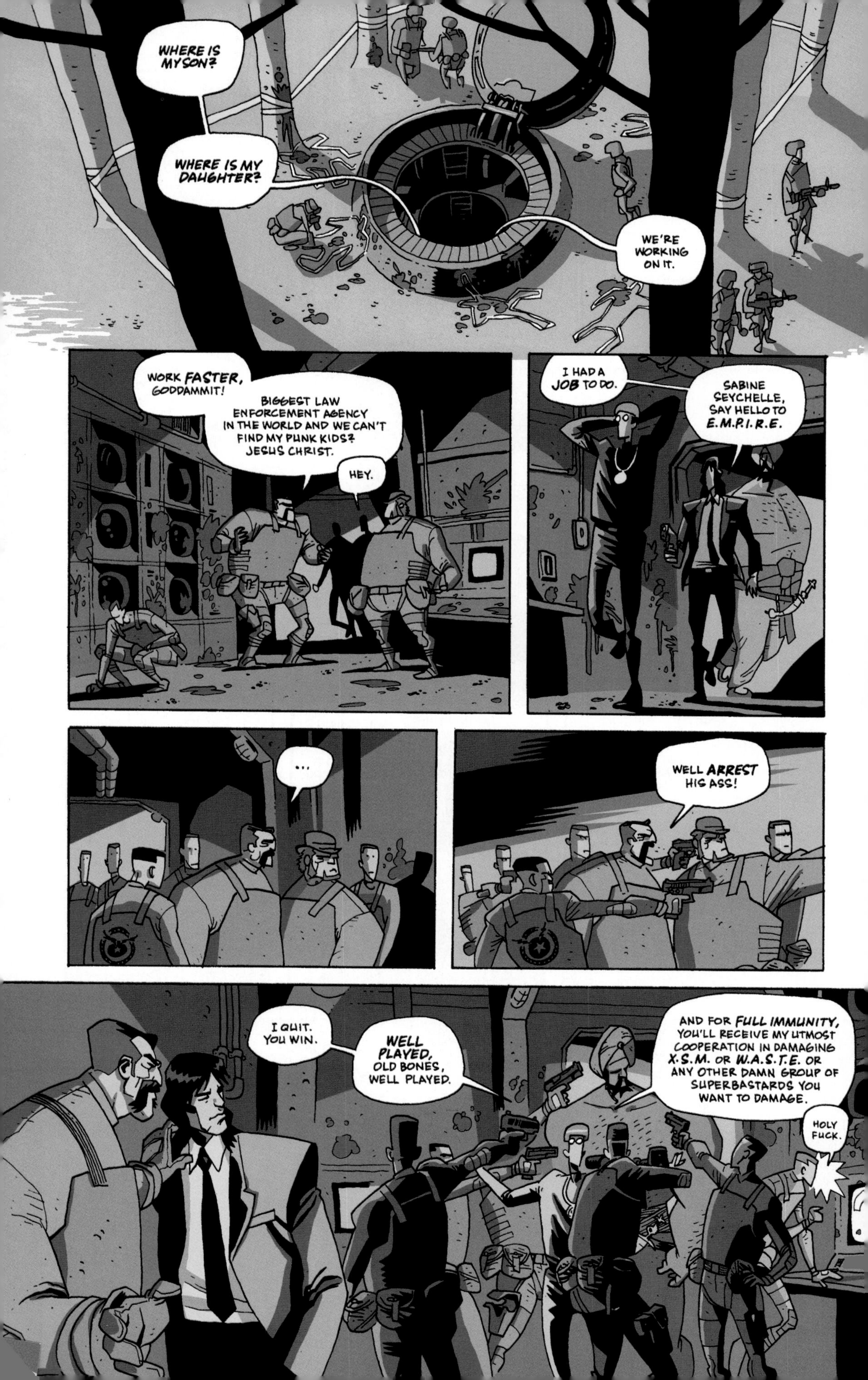

WHERE IS MY SON?
WHERE IS MY DAUGHTER?
WE'RE WORKING ON IT.
WORK FASTER, GODDAMMIT!
BIGGEST LAW ENFORCEMENT AGENCY IN THE WORLD AND WE CAN'T FIND MY PUNK KIDS? JESUS CHRIST.
HEY.
I HAD A JOB TO DO.
SABINE SEYCHELLE, SAY HELLO TO E.M.P.I.R.E.
...
WELL ARREST HIS ASS!
I QUIT. YOU WIN.
WELL PLAYED, OLD BONES, WELL PLAYED.
AND FOR FULL IMMUNITY, YOU'LL RECEIVE MY UTMOST COOPERATION IN DAMAGING X.S.M. OR W.A.S.T.E. OR ANY OTHER DAMN GROUP OF SUPERBASTARDS YOU WANT TO DAMAGE.
HOLY FUCK.

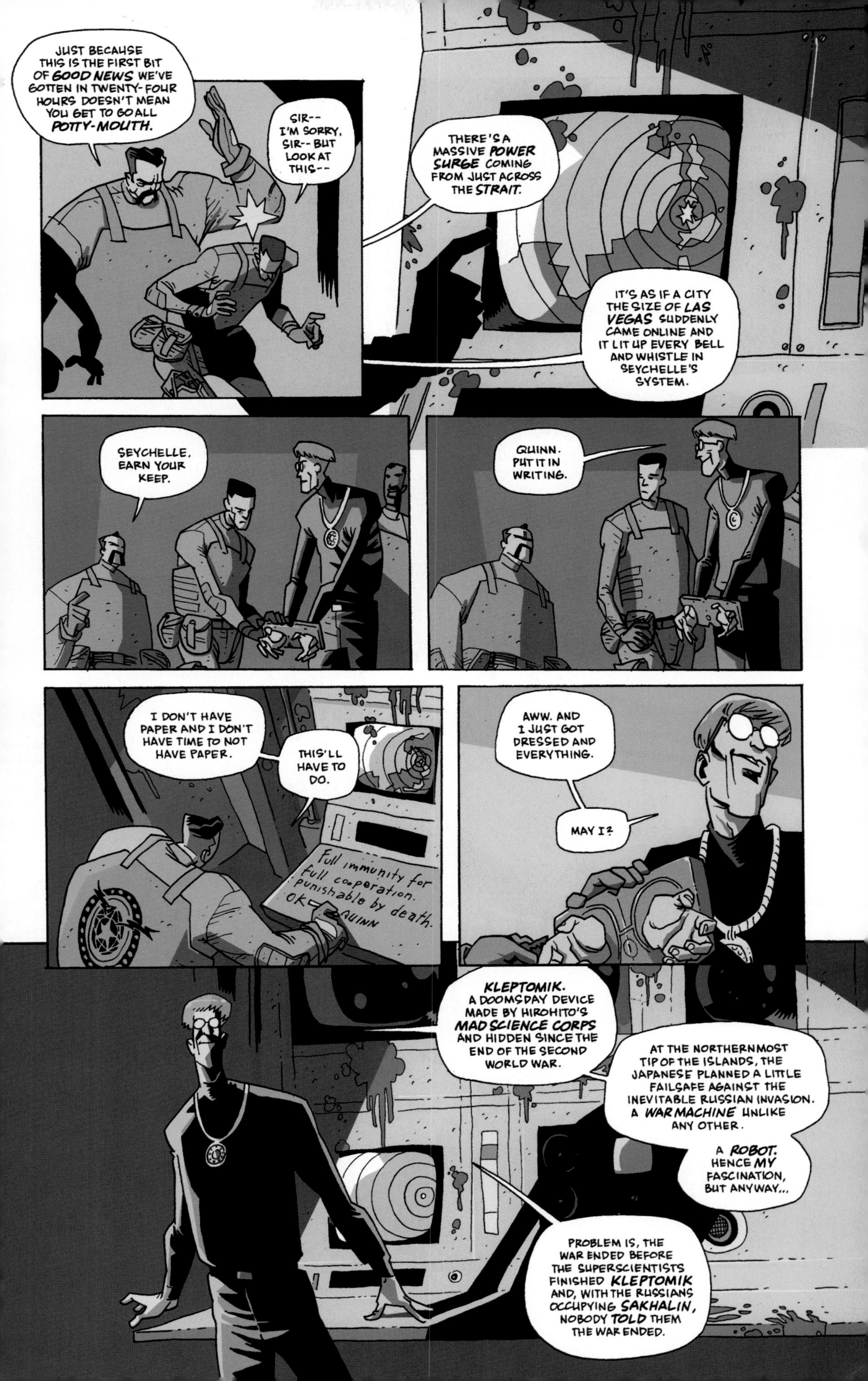
JUST BECAUSE THIS IS THE FIRST BIT OF GOOD NEWS WE'VE GOTTEN IN TWENTY-FOUR HOURS DOESN'T MEAN YOU GET TO GO ALL POTTY-MOUTH.
SIR-- I'M SORRY, SIR-- BUT LOOK AT THIS--
THERE'S A MASSIVE POWER SURGE COMING FROM JUST ACROSS THE STRAIT.
IT'S AS IF A CITY THE SIZE OF LAS VEGAS SUDDENLY CAME ONLINE AND IT LIT UP EVERY BELL AND WHISTLE IN SEYCHELLE'S SYSTEM.
SEYCHELLE. EARN YOUR KEEP.
QUINN. PUT IT IN WRITING.
I DON'T HAVE PAPER AND I DON'T HAVE TIME TO NOT HAVE PAPER.
THIS'LL HAVE TO DO.
Full immunity for full cooperation. punishable by death.
OK-QUINN
AWW. AND I JUST GOT DRESSED AND EVERYTHING.
MAY I?
KLEPTOMIK. A DOOMSDAY DEVICE MADE BY HIROHITO'S MAD SCIENCE CORPS AND HIDDEN SINCE THE END OF THE SECOND WORLD WAR.
AT THE NORTHERNMOST TIP OF THE ISLANDS, THE JAPANESE PLANNED A LITTLE FAILSAFE AGAINST THE INEVITABLE RUSSIAN INVASION. A WAR MACHINE UNLIKE ANY OTHER.
A ROBOT. HENCE MY FASCINATION, BUT ANYWAY...
PROBLEM IS, THE WAR ENDED BEFORE THE SUPERSCIENTISTS FINISHED KLEPTOMIK AND, WITH THE RUSSIANS OCCUPYING SAKHALIN, NOBODY TOLD THEM THE WAR ENDED.

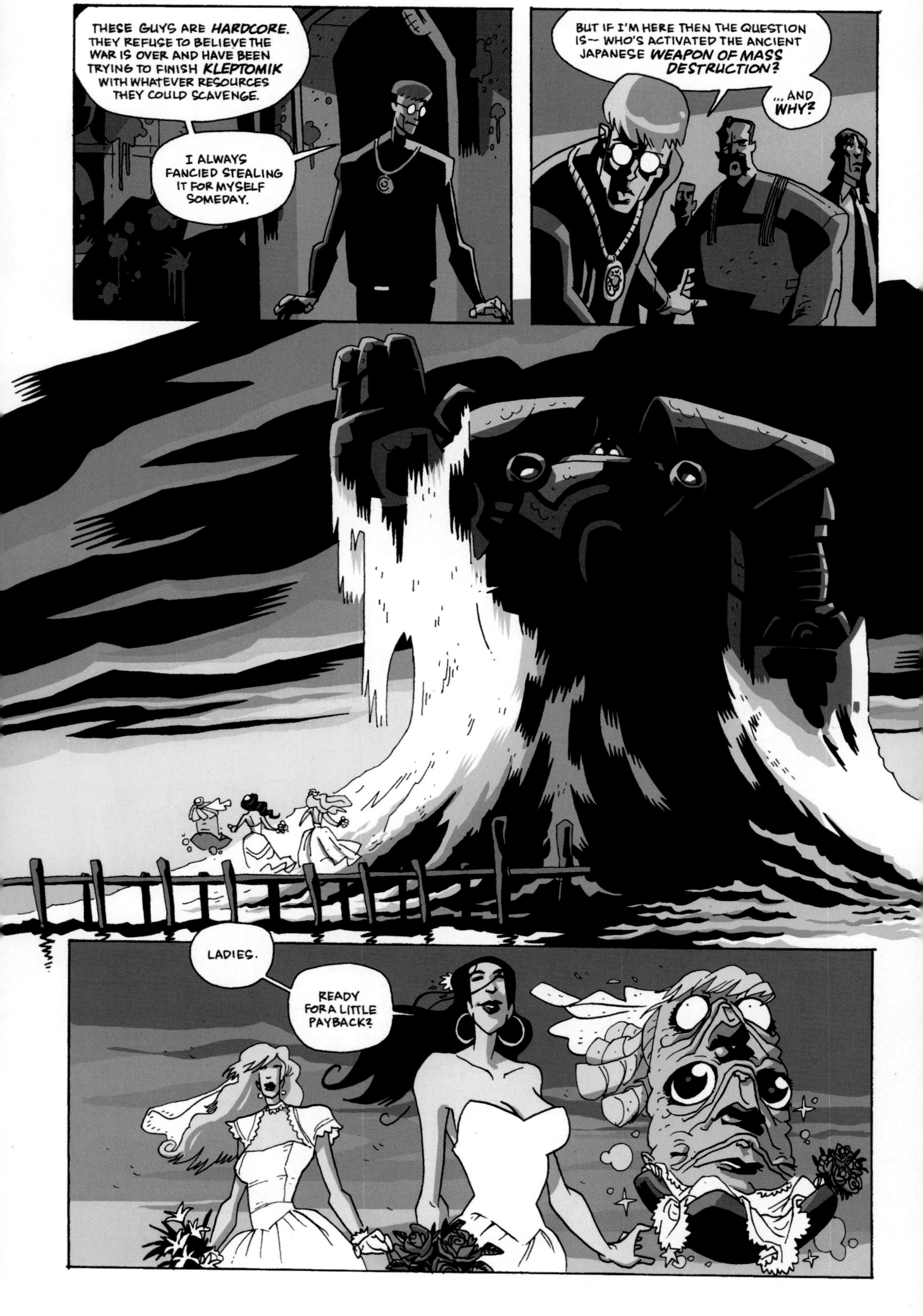
THESE GUYS ARE HARDCORE. THEY REFUSE TO BELIEVE THE WAR IS OVER AND HAVE BEEN TRYING TO FINISH KLEPTOMIK WITH WHATEVER RESOURCES THEY COULD SCAVENGE.
I ALWAYS FANCIED STEALING IT FOR MYSELF SOMEDAY.
BUT IF I'M HERE THEN THE QUESTION IS-- WHO'S ACTIVATED THE ANCIENT JAPANESE WEAPON OF MASS DESTRUCTION?
...AND WHY?
LADIES.
READY FOR A LITTLE PAYBACK?

# CHAPTER 7

# WOMEN AND MEN
## (PART TWO)

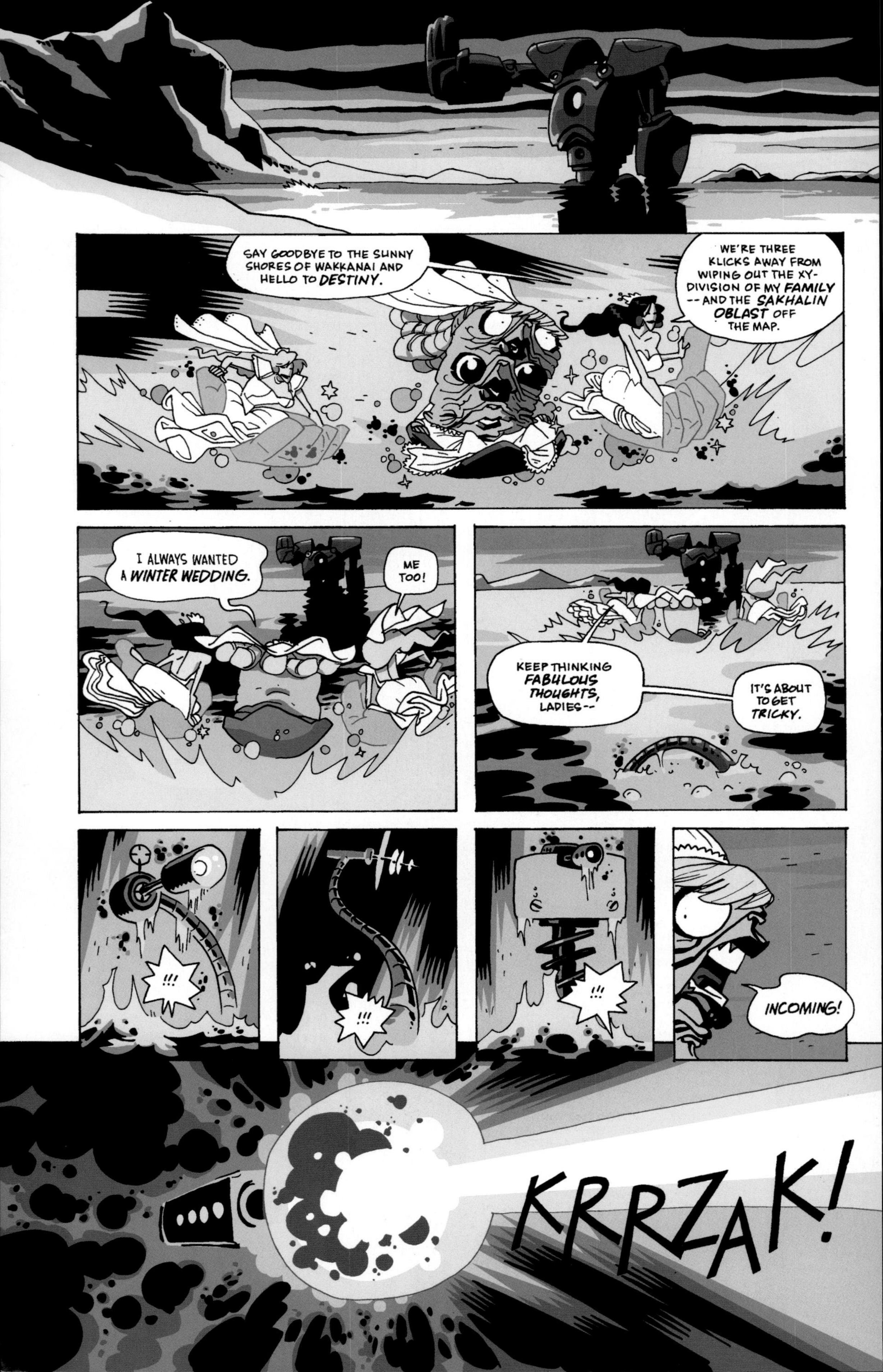
SAY GOODBYE TO THE SUNNY SHORES OF WAKKANAI AND HELLO TO DESTINY.
WE'RE THREE KLICKS AWAY FROM WIPING OUT THE XY-DIVISION OF MY FAMILY --AND THE SAKHALIN OBLAST OFF THE MAP.
I ALWAYS WANTED A WINTER WEDDING.
ME TOO!
KEEP THINKING FABULOUS THOUGHTS, LADIES--
IT'S ABOUT TO GET TRICKY.
!!!
!!!
!!!
INCOMING!
KRRZAK!

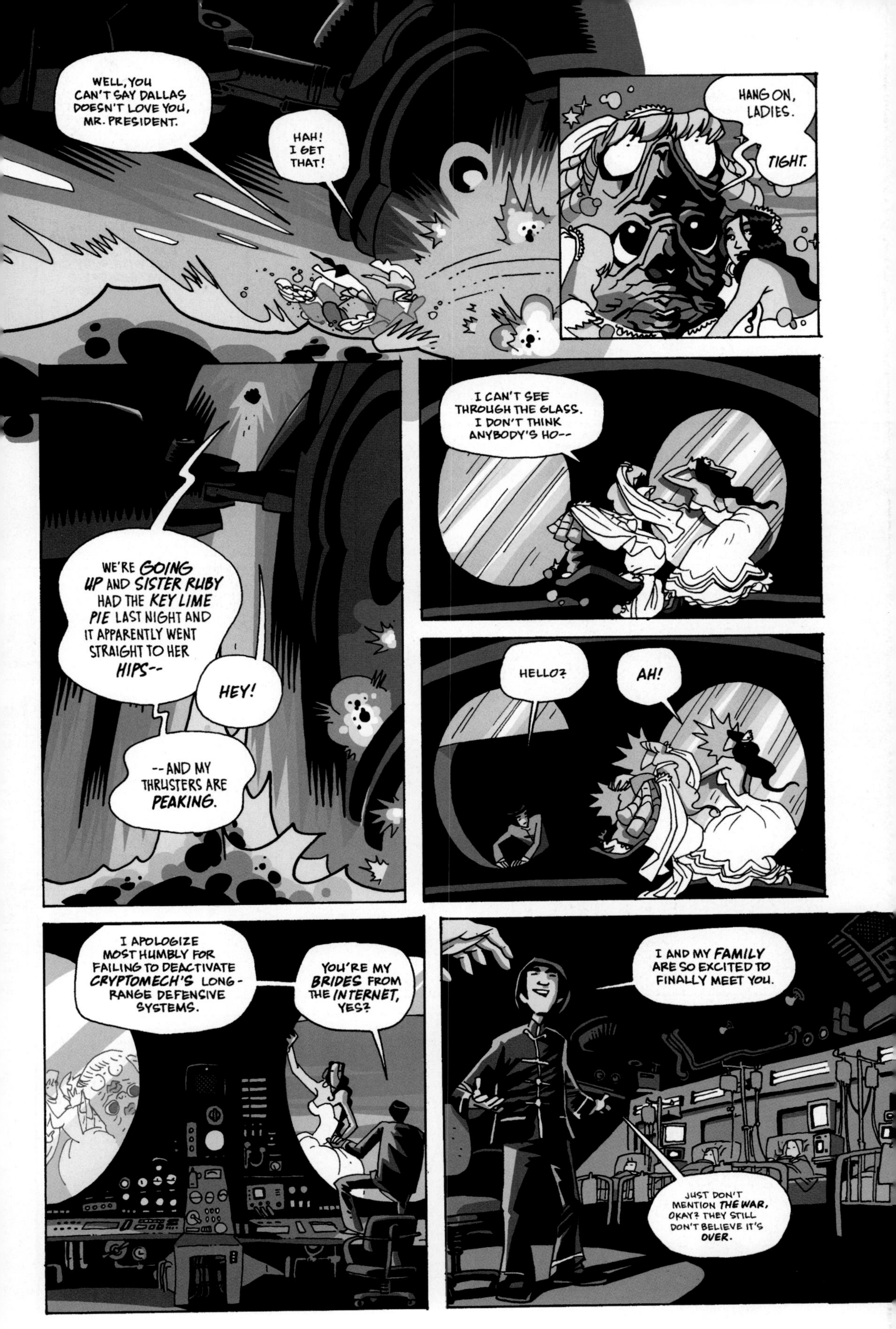
WELL, YOU CAN'T SAY DALLAS DOESN'T LOVE YOU, MR. PRESIDENT.
HAH! I GET THAT!
HANG ON, LADIES.
TIGHT.
WE'RE GOING UP AND SISTER RUBY HAD THE KEY LIME PIE LAST NIGHT AND IT APPARENTLY WENT STRAIGHT TO HER HIPS--
HEY!
--AND MY THRUSTERS ARE PEAKING.
I CAN'T SEE THROUGH THE GLASS. I DON'T THINK ANYBODY'S HO--
HELLO?
AH!
I APOLOGIZE MOST HUMBLY FOR FAILING TO DEACTIVATE CRYPTOMECH'S LONG-RANGE DEFENSIVE SYSTEMS.
YOU'RE MY BRIDES FROM THE INTERNET, YES?
I AND MY FAMILY ARE SO EXCITED TO FINALLY MEET YOU.
JUST DON'T MENTION THE WAR, OKAY? THEY STILL DON'T BELIEVE IT'S OVER.

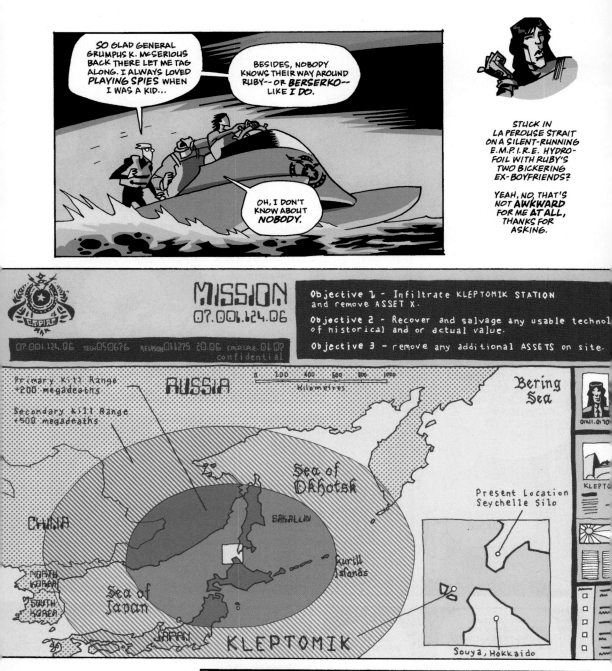

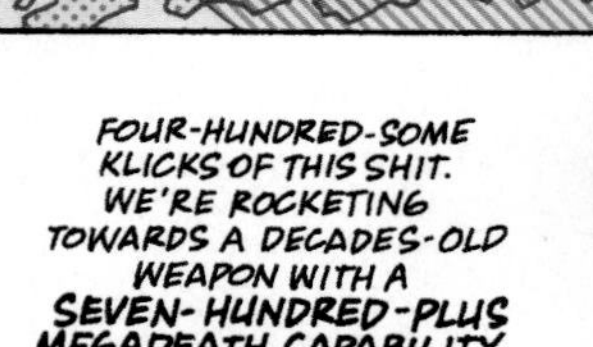

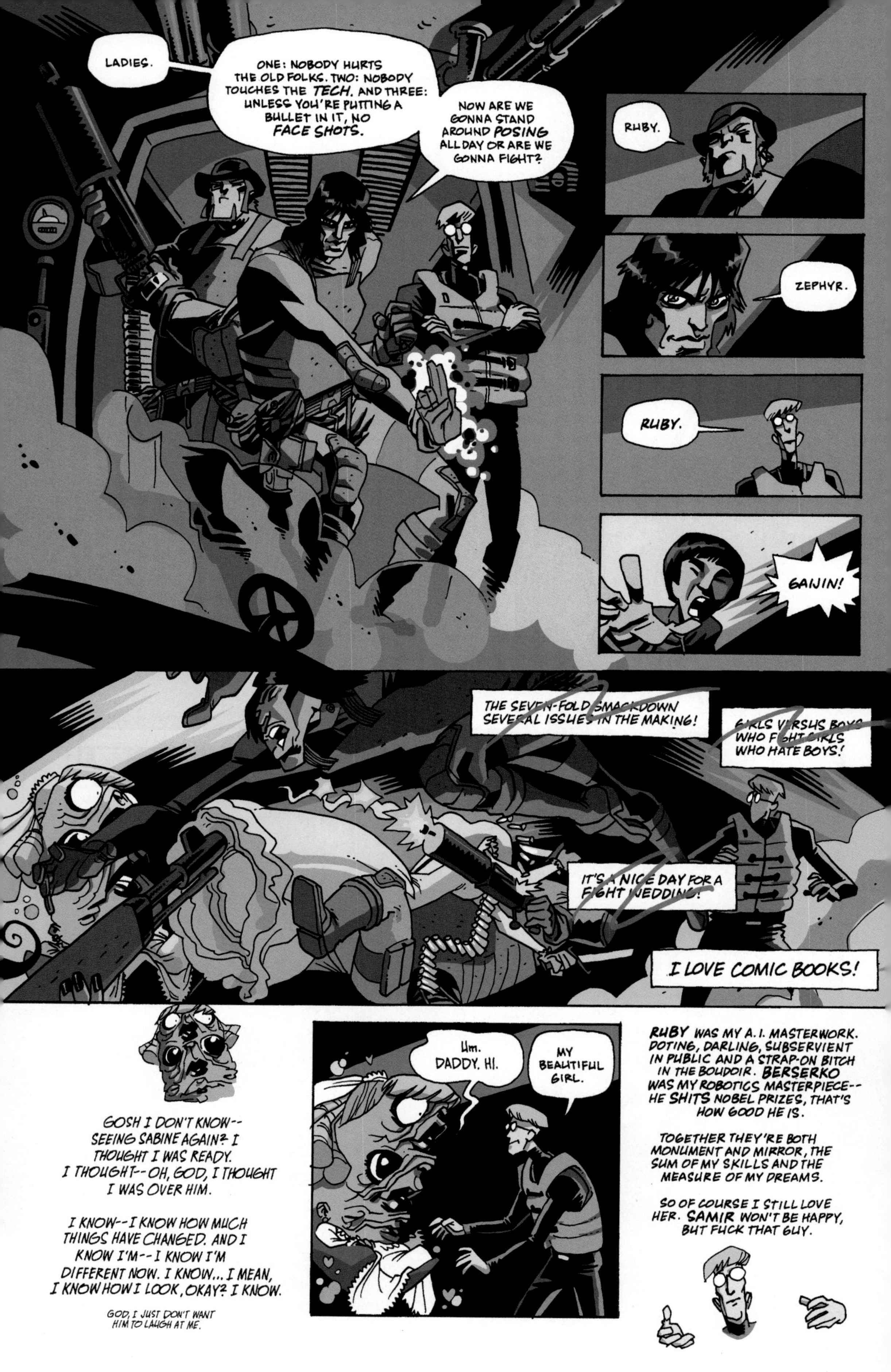

LADIES.
ONE: NOBODY HURTS THE OLD FOLKS. TWO: NOBODY TOUCHES THE TECH. AND THREE: UNLESS YOU'RE PUTTING A BULLET IN IT, NO FACE SHOTS.
NOW ARE WE GONNA STAND AROUND POSING ALL DAY OR ARE WE GONNA FIGHT?
RUBY.
ZEPHYR.
RUBY.
GAIJIN!
THE SEVEN-FOLD SMACKDOWN SEVERAL ISSUES IN THE MAKING!
GIRLS VERSUS BOYS WHO FIGHT GIRLS WHO HATE BOYS!
IT'S A NICE DAY FOR A FIGHT WEDDING!
I LOVE COMIC BOOKS!
GOSH I DON'T KNOW-- SEEING SABINE AGAIN? I THOUGHT I WAS READY. I THOUGHT--OH, GOD, I THOUGHT I WAS OVER HIM.
I KNOW--I KNOW HOW MUCH THINGS HAVE CHANGED. AND I KNOW I'M--I KNOW I'M DIFFERENT NOW. I KNOW... I MEAN, I KNOW HOW I LOOK, OKAY? I KNOW.
GOD, I JUST DON'T WANT HIM TO LAUGH AT ME.
Um. DADDY. HI.
MY BEAUTIFUL GIRL.
RUBY WAS MY A.I. MASTERWORK. DOTING, DARLING, SUBSERVIENT IN PUBLIC AND A STRAP-ON BITCH IN THE BOUDOIR. BERSERKO WAS MY ROBOTICS MASTERPIECE-- HE SHITS NOBEL PRIZES, THAT'S HOW GOOD HE IS.
TOGETHER THEY'RE BOTH MONUMENT AND MIRROR, THE SUM OF MY SKILLS AND THE MEASURE OF MY DREAMS.
SO OF COURSE I STILL LOVE HER. SAMIR WON'T BE HAPPY, BUT FUCK THAT GUY.

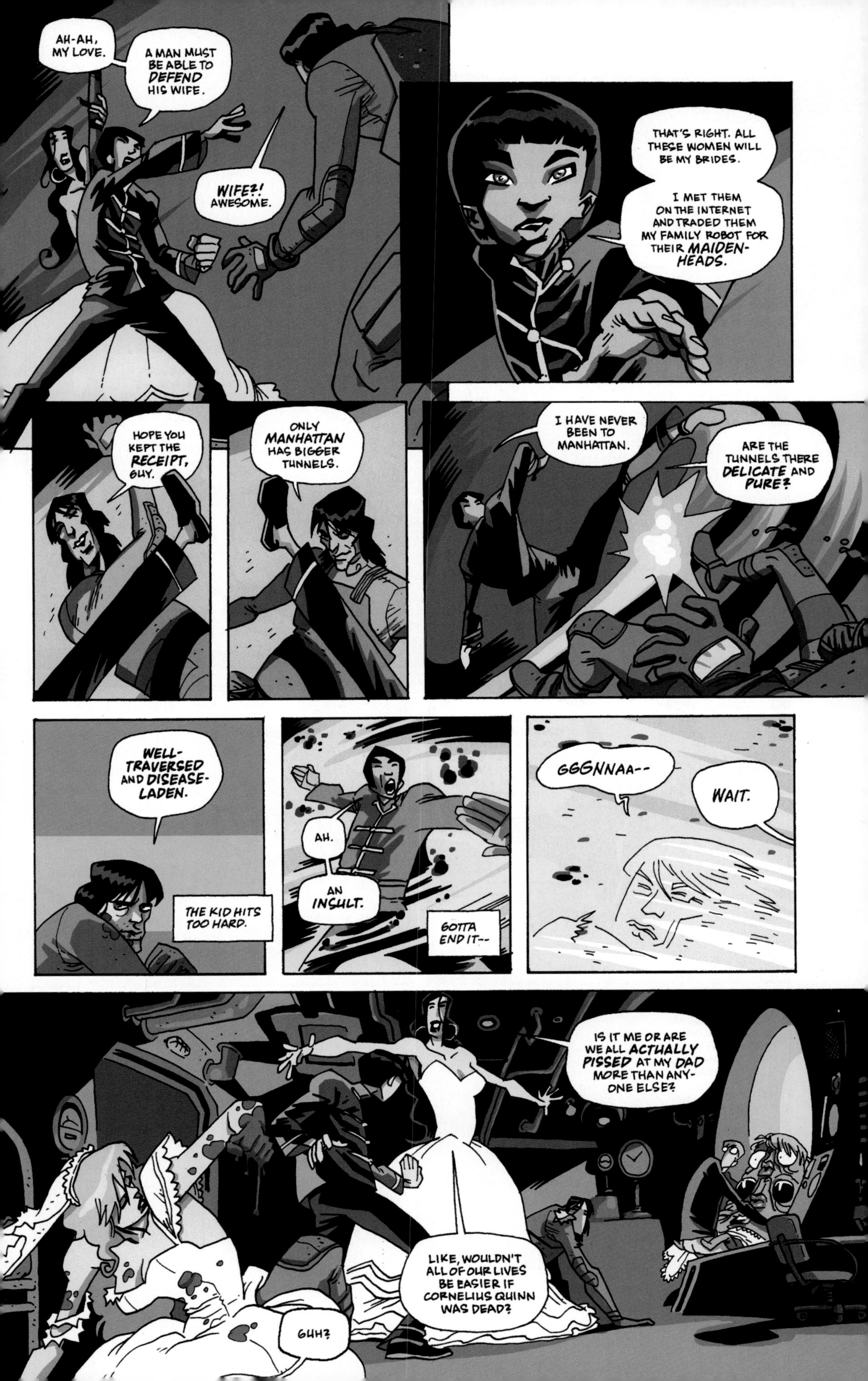

AH-AH, MY LOVE.
A MAN MUST BE ABLE TO DEFEND HIS WIFE.
WIFE?! AWESOME.
THAT'S RIGHT. ALL THESE WOMEN WILL BE MY BRIDES.
I MET THEM ON THE INTERNET AND TRADED THEM MY FAMILY ROBOT FOR THEIR MAIDEN-HEADS.
HOPE YOU KEPT THE RECEIPT, GUY.
ONLY MANHATTAN HAS BIGGER TUNNELS.
I HAVE NEVER BEEN TO MANHATTAN.
ARE THE TUNNELS THERE DELICATE AND PURE?
WELL-TRAVERSED AND DISEASE-LADEN.
THE KID HITS TOO HARD.
AH.
AN INSULT.
GOTTA END IT--
GGGNNAA--
WAIT.
IS IT ME OR ARE WE ALL ACTUALLY PISSED AT MY DAD MORE THAN ANY-ONE ELSE?
LIKE, WOULDN'T ALL OF OUR LIVES BE EASIER IF CORNELIUS QUINN WAS DEAD?
GUH?

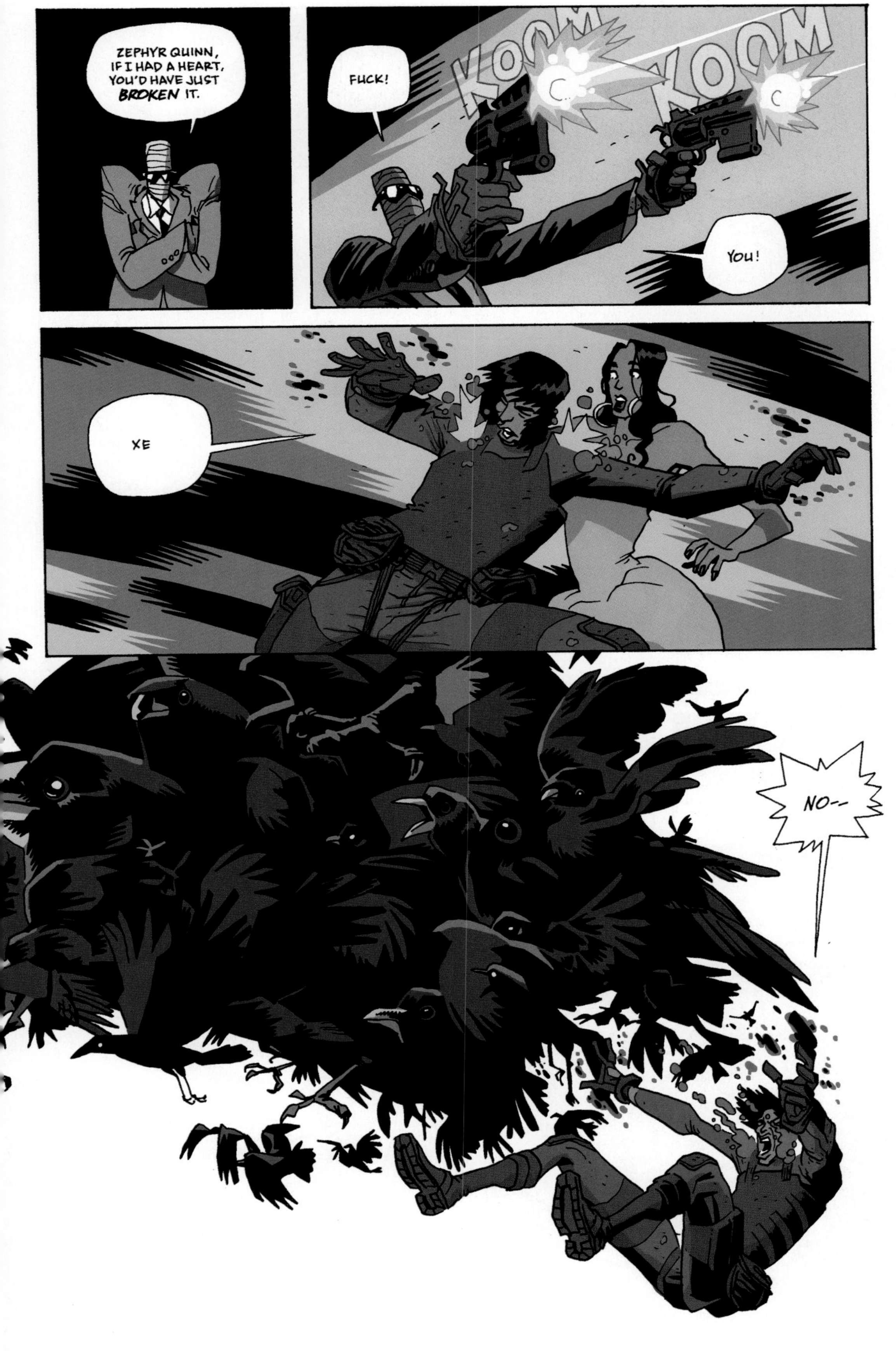
ZEPHYR QUINN, IF I HAD A HEART, YOU'D HAVE JUST BROKEN IT.
FUCK!
KOOM
KOOM
YOU!
XE
NO--

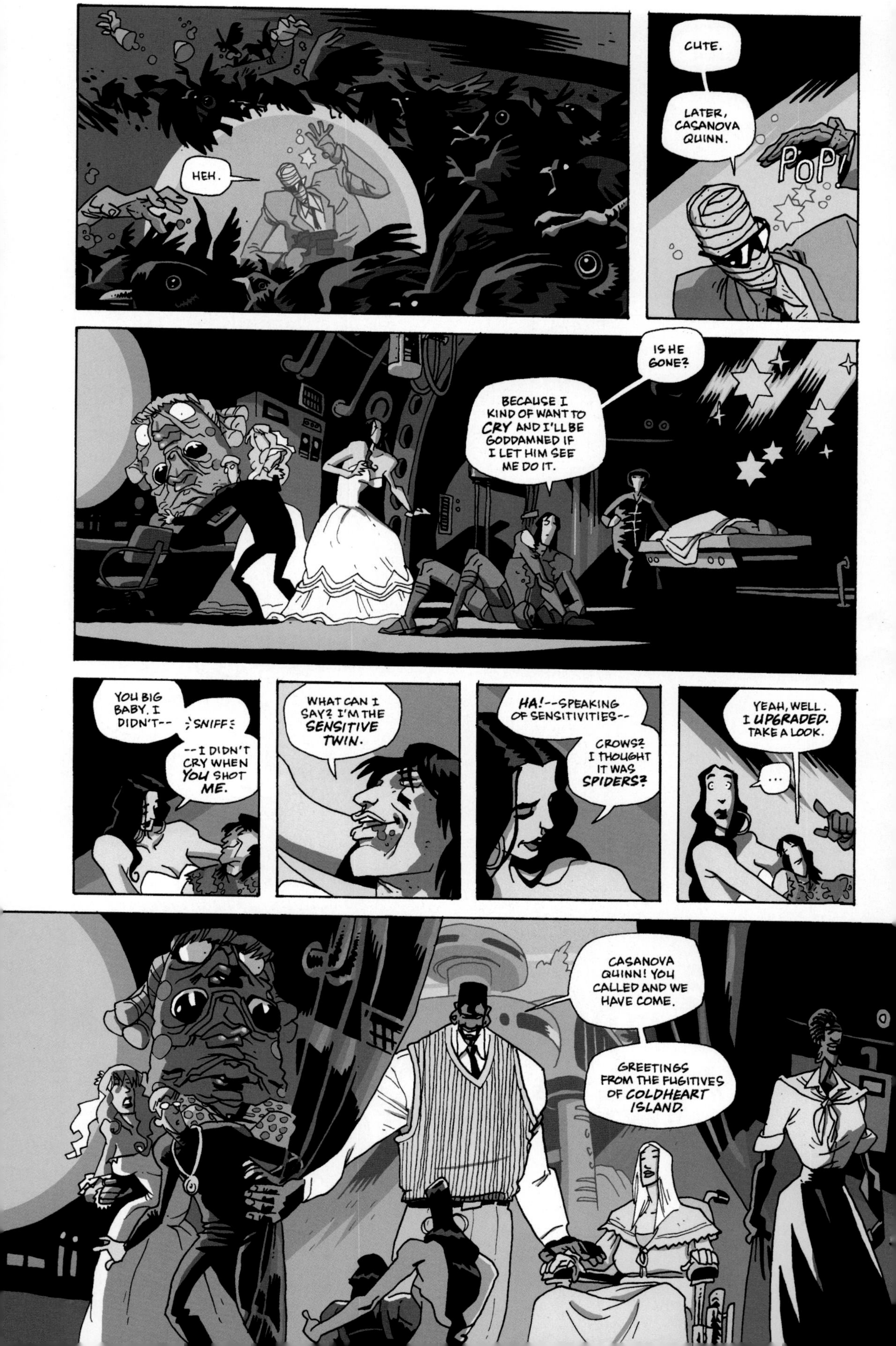
HEH.
CUTE.
LATER, CASANOVA QUINN.
POP!
IS HE GONE?
BECAUSE I KIND OF WANT TO CRY AND I'LL BE GODDAMNED IF I LET HIM SEE ME DO IT.
YOU BIG BABY. I DIDN'T--
SNIFF
--I DIDN'T CRY WHEN YOU SHOT ME.
WHAT CAN I SAY? I'M THE SENSITIVE TWIN.
HA!--SPEAKING OF SENSITIVITIES--
CROWS? I THOUGHT IT WAS SPIDERS?
YEAH, WELL. I UPGRADED. TAKE A LOOK.
...
CASANOVA QUINN! YOU CALLED AND WE HAVE COME.
GREETINGS FROM THE FUGITIVES OF COLDHEART ISLAND.

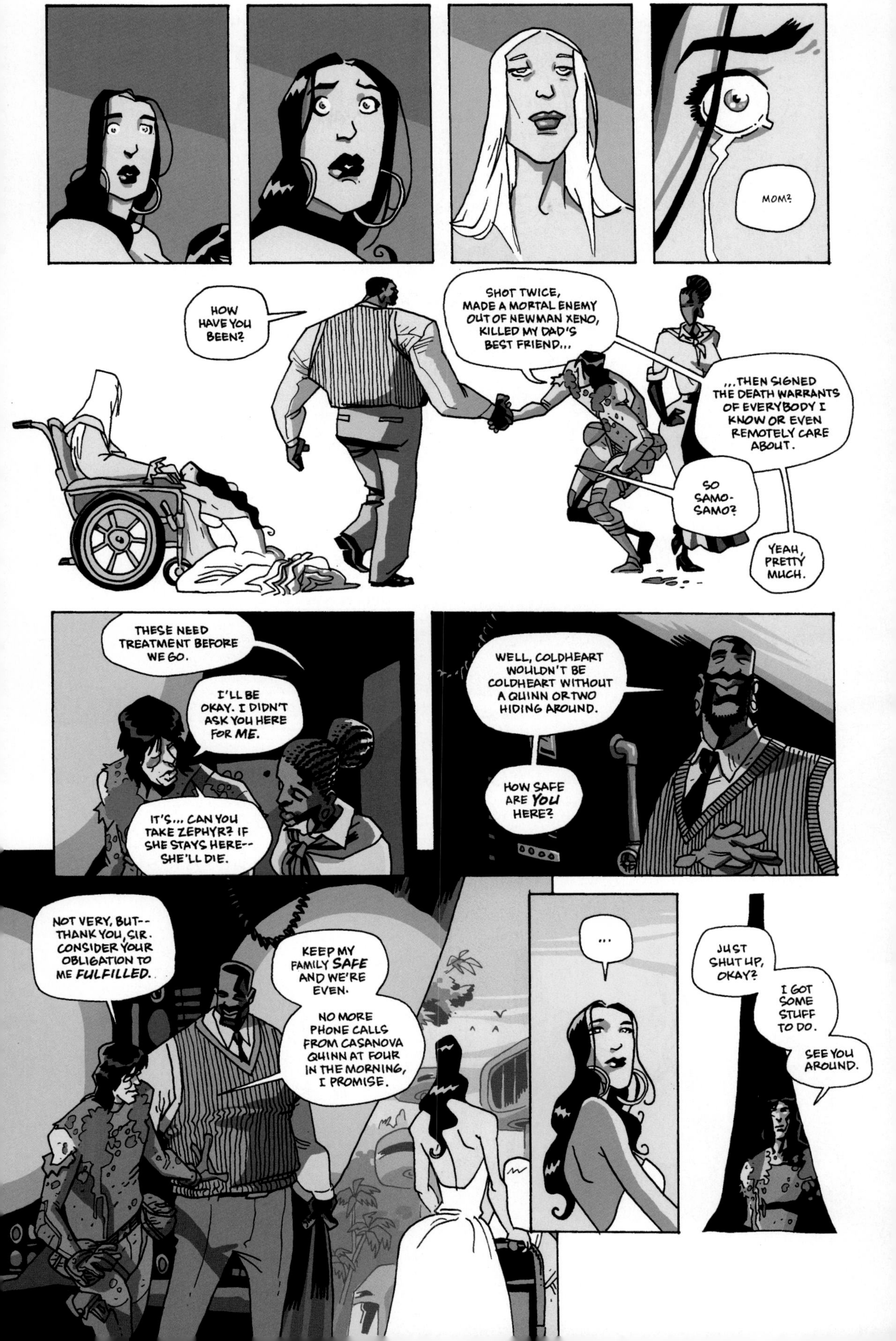
MOM?
HOW HAVE YOU BEEN?
SHOT TWICE, MADE A MORTAL ENEMY OUT OF NEWMAN XENO, KILLED MY DAD'S BEST FRIEND...
...THEN SIGNED THE DEATH WARRANTS OF EVERYBODY I KNOW OR EVEN REMOTELY CARE ABOUT.
SO SAMO-SAMO?
YEAH, PRETTY MUCH.
THESE NEED TREATMENT BEFORE WE GO.
I'LL BE OKAY. I DIDN'T ASK YOU HERE FOR ME.
IT'S... CAN YOU TAKE ZEPHYR? IF SHE STAYS HERE--SHE'LL DIE.
WELL, COLDHEART WOULDN'T BE COLDHEART WITHOUT A QUINN OR TWO HIDING AROUND.
HOW SAFE ARE YOU HERE?
NOT VERY, BUT--THANK YOU, SIR. CONSIDER YOUR OBLIGATION TO ME FULFILLED.
KEEP MY FAMILY SAFE AND WE'RE EVEN.
NO MORE PHONE CALLS FROM CASANOVA QUINN AT FOUR IN THE MORNING, I PROMISE.
...
JUST SHUT UP, OKAY?
I GOT SOME STUFF TO DO.
SEE YOU AROUND.

# BONUS STORY

# I THINK I ALMOST
# LOVED HIM

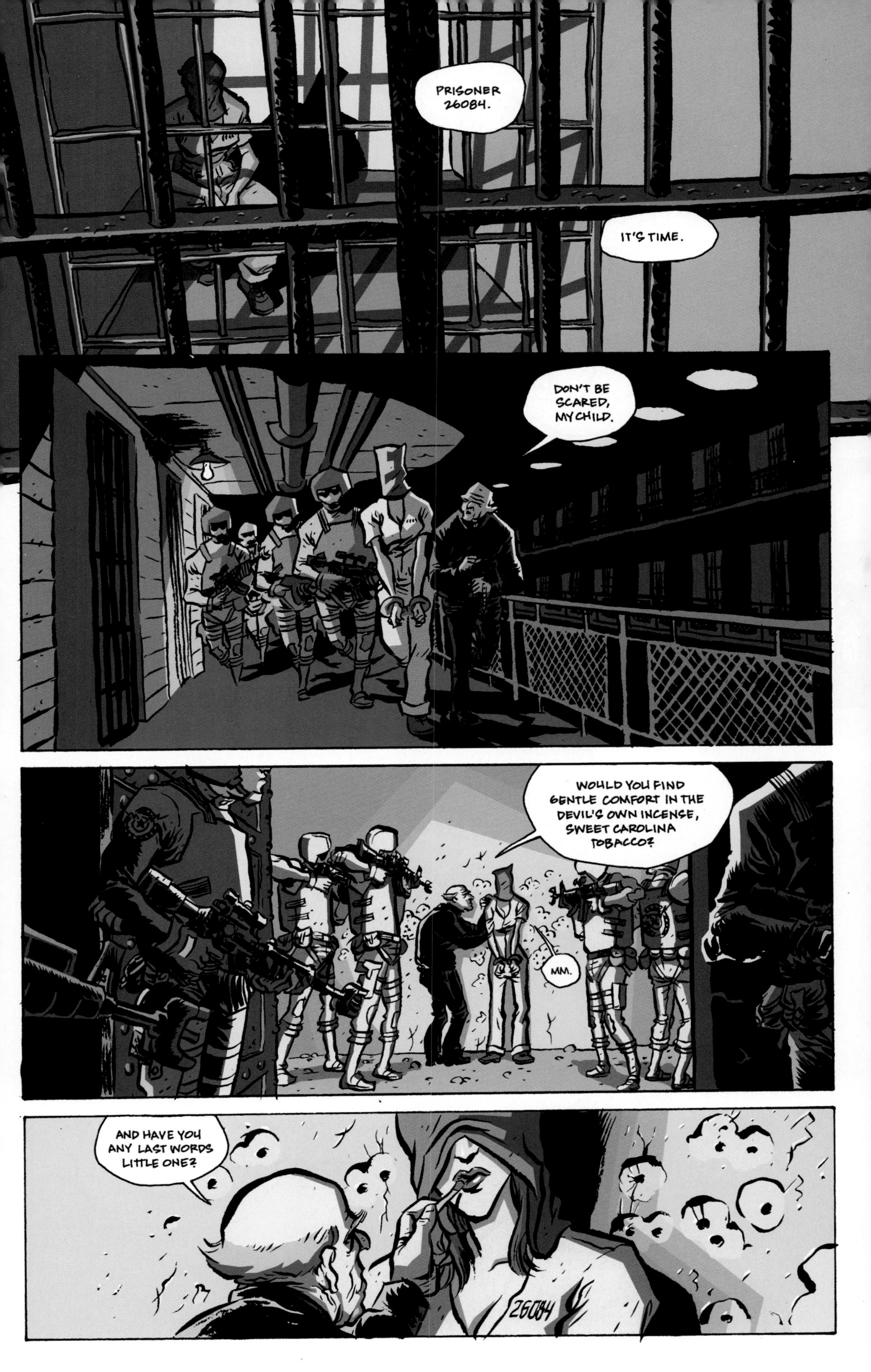
PRISONER 26084.
IT'S TIME.
DON'T BE SCARED, MY CHILD.
WOULD YOU FIND GENTLE COMFORT IN THE DEVIL'S OWN INCENSE, SWEET CAROLINA TOBACCO?
MM.
AND HAVE YOU ANY LAST WORDS LITTLE ONE?
26084

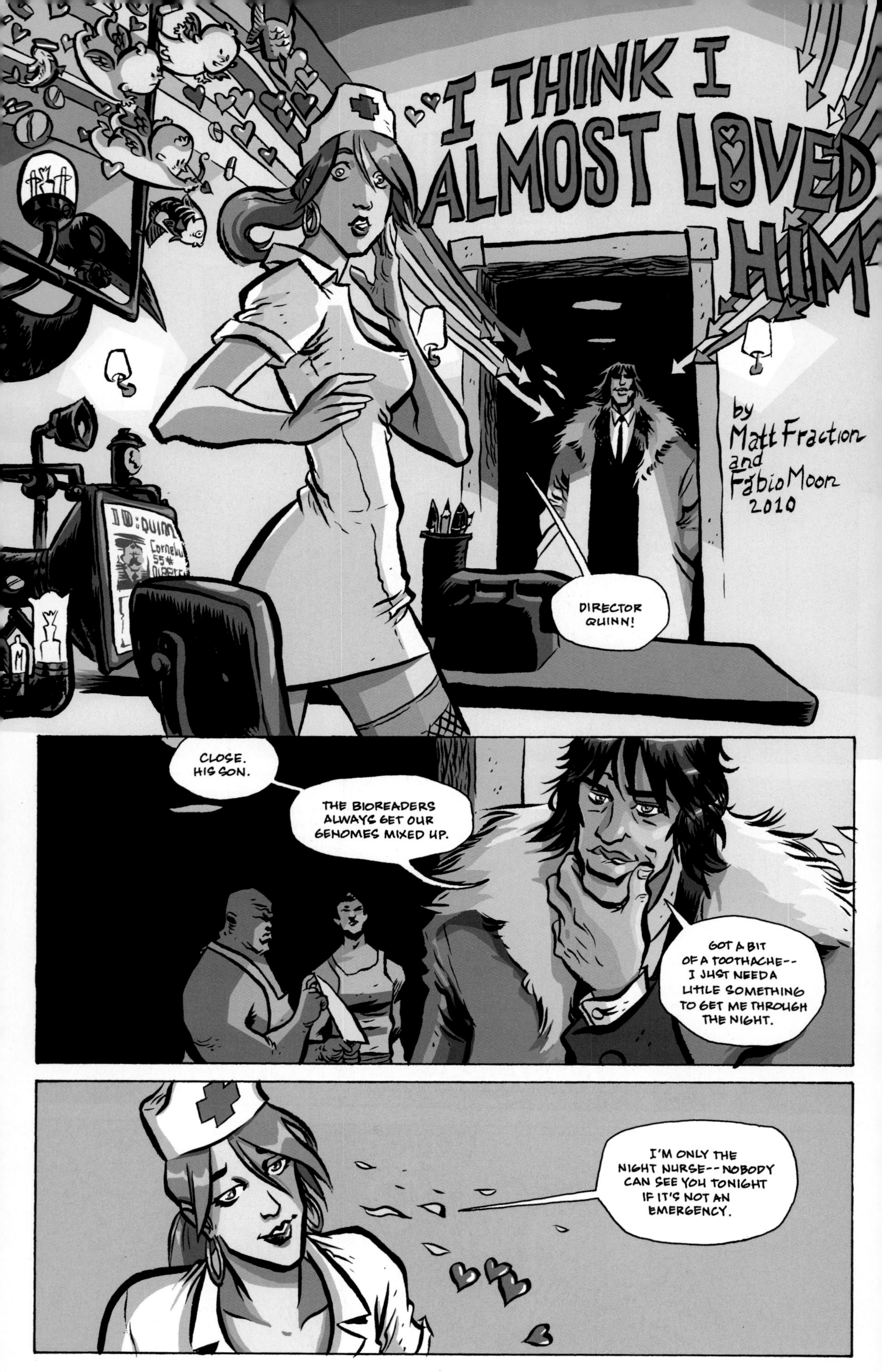
I THINK I ALMOST LOVED HIM
by Matt Fraction and Fábio Moon 2010
DIRECTOR QUINN!
CLOSE. HIS SON.
THE BIOREADERS ALWAYS GET OUR GENOMES MIXED UP.
GOT A BIT OF A TOOTHACHE-- I JUST NEED A LITTLE SOMETHING TO GET ME THROUGH THE NIGHT.
I'M ONLY THE NIGHT NURSE--NOBODY CAN SEE YOU TONIGHT IF IT'S NOT AN EMERGENCY.

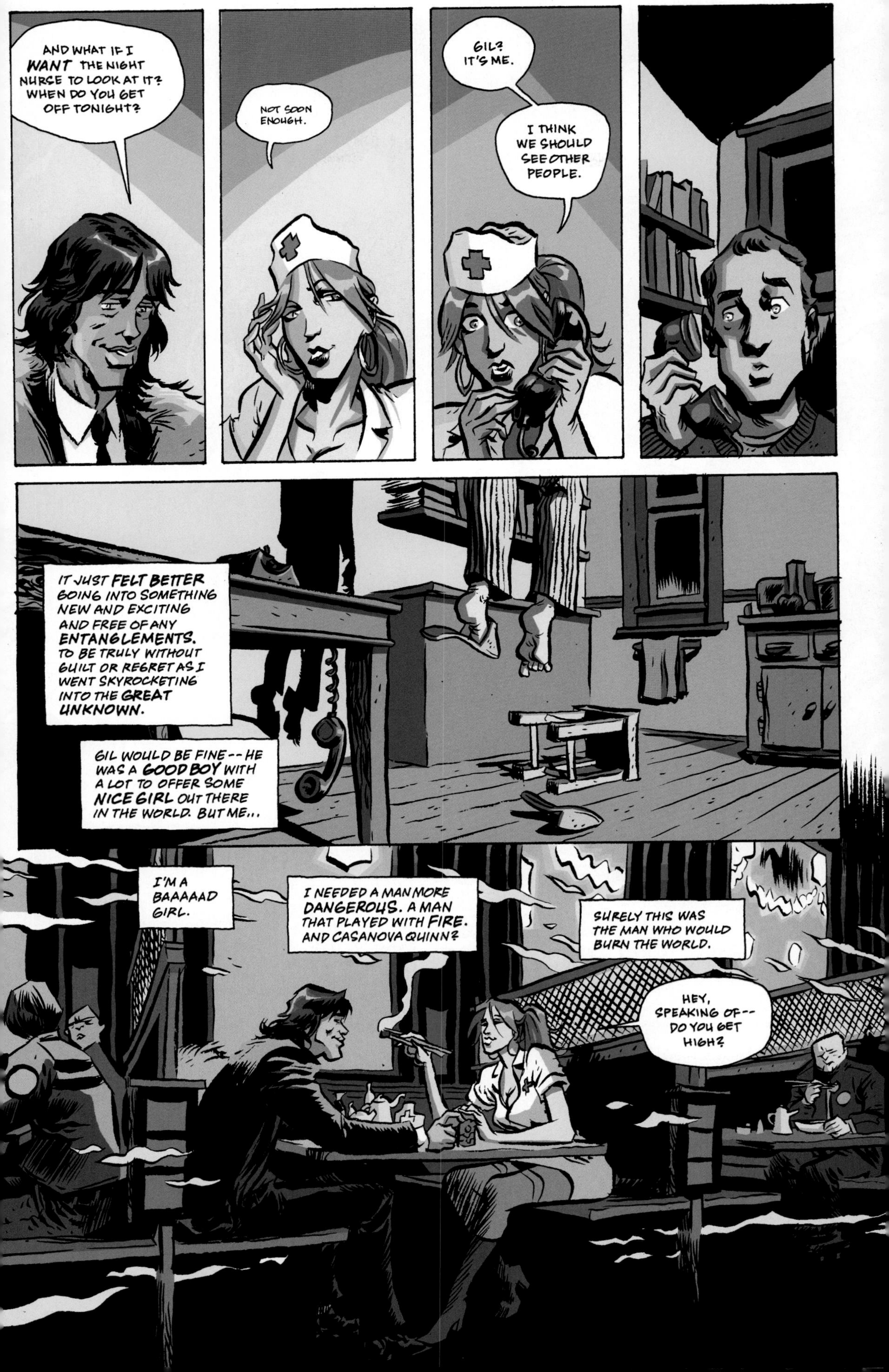
AND WHAT IF I WANT THE NIGHT NURSE TO LOOK AT IT? WHEN DO YOU GET OFF TONIGHT?
NOT SOON ENOUGH.
GIL? IT'S ME.
I THINK WE SHOULD SEE OTHER PEOPLE.
IT JUST FELT BETTER GOING INTO SOMETHING NEW AND EXCITING AND FREE OF ANY ENTANGLEMENTS. TO BE TRULY WITHOUT GUILT OR REGRET AS I WENT SKYROCKETING INTO THE GREAT UNKNOWN.
GIL WOULD BE FINE -- HE WAS A GOOD BOY WITH A LOT TO OFFER SOME NICE GIRL OUT THERE IN THE WORLD. BUT ME...
I'M A BAAAAAD GIRL.
I NEEDED A MAN MORE DANGEROUS. A MAN THAT PLAYED WITH FIRE. AND CASANOVA QUINN?
SURELY THIS WAS THE MAN WHO WOULD BURN THE WORLD.
HEY, SPEAKING OF -- DO YOU GET HIGH?

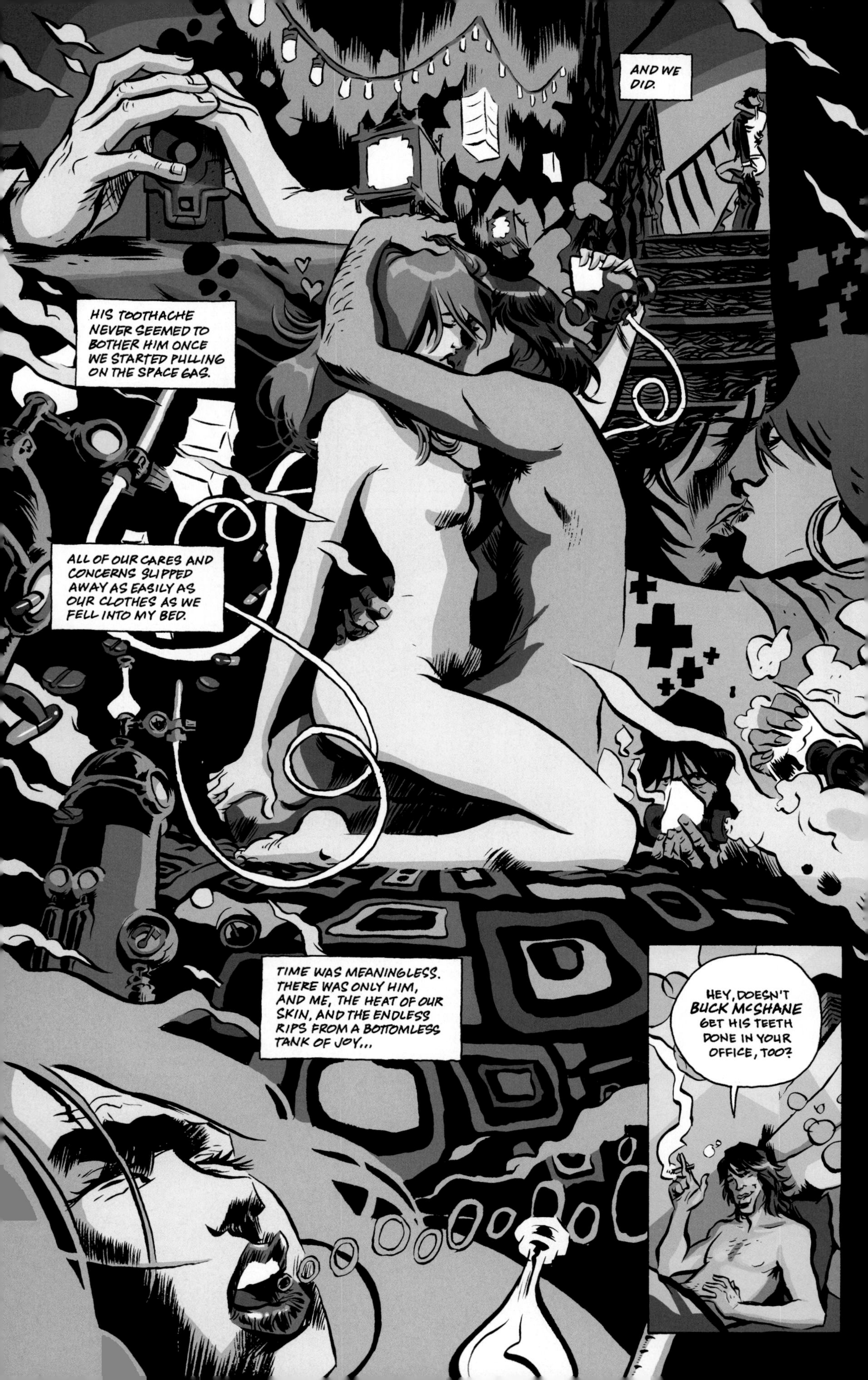
AND WE DID.
HIS TOOTHACHE NEVER SEEMED TO BOTHER HIM ONCE WE STARTED PULLING ON THE SPACE GAS.
ALL OF OUR CARES AND CONCERNS SLIPPED AWAY AS EASILY AS OUR CLOTHES AS WE FELL INTO MY BED.
TIME WAS MEANINGLESS. THERE WAS ONLY HIM, AND ME, THE HEAT OF OUR SKIN, AND THE ENDLESS RIPS FROM A BOTTOMLESS TANK OF JOY...
HEY, DOESN'T BUCK McSHANE GET HIS TEETH DONE IN YOUR OFFICE, TOO?

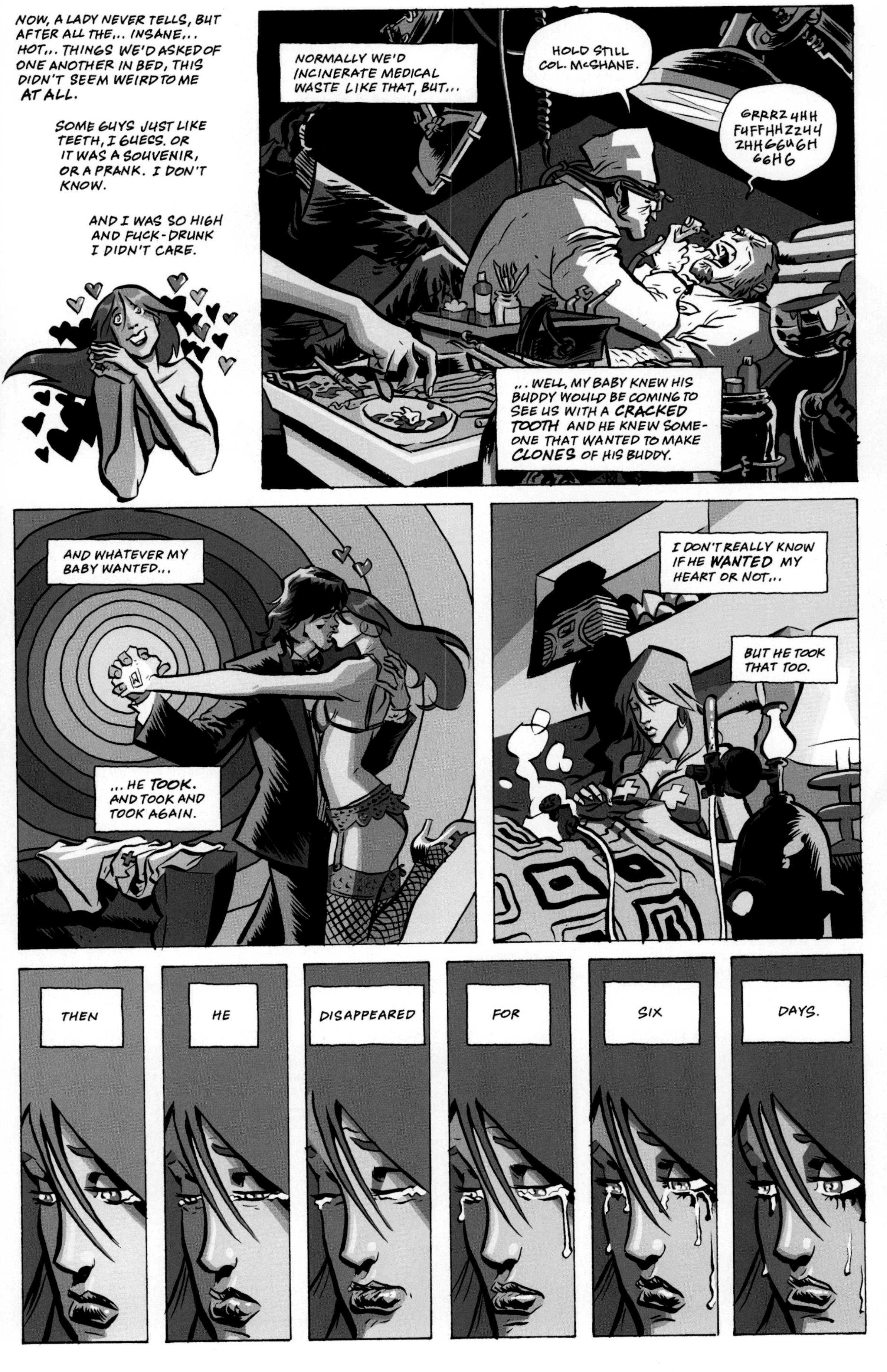
NOW, A LADY NEVER TELLS, BUT AFTER ALL THE... INSANE... HOT... THINGS WE'D ASKED OF ONE ANOTHER IN BED, THIS DIDN'T SEEM WEIRD TO ME AT ALL.
SOME GUYS JUST LIKE TEETH, I GUESS. OR IT WAS A SOUVENIR, OR A PRANK. I DON'T KNOW.
AND I WAS SO HIGH AND FUCK-DRUNK I DIDN'T CARE.
NORMALLY WE'D INCINERATE MEDICAL WASTE LIKE THAT, BUT...
HOLD STILL COL. McSHANE.
GRRRZ UHH FUFFHHZZUU ZHHGGUGH GGHG
...WELL, MY BABY KNEW HIS BUDDY WOULD BE COMING TO SEE US WITH A CRACKED TOOTH AND HE KNEW SOME-ONE THAT WANTED TO MAKE CLONES OF HIS BUDDY.
AND WHATEVER MY BABY WANTED...
...HE TOOK. AND TOOK AND TOOK AGAIN.
I DON'T REALLY KNOW IF HE WANTED MY HEART OR NOT...
BUT HE TOOK THAT TOO.
THEN
HE
DISAPPEARED
FOR
SIX
DAYS.

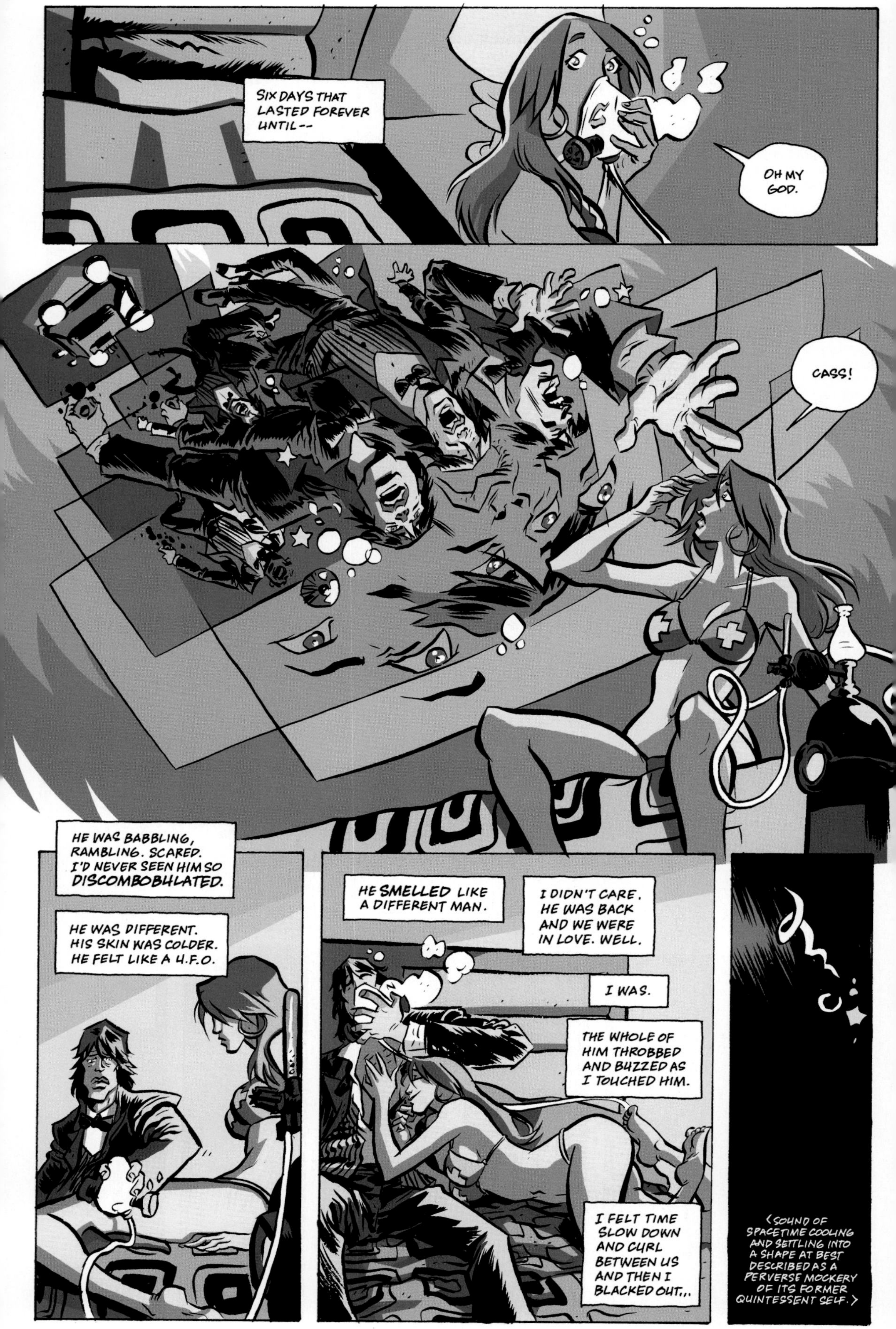
SIX DAYS THAT LASTED FOREVER UNTIL--
OH MY GOD.
CASS!
HE WAS BABBLING, RAMBLING. SCARED. I'D NEVER SEEN HIM SO DISCOMBOBULATED.
HE WAS DIFFERENT. HIS SKIN WAS COLDER. HE FELT LIKE A U.F.O.
HE SMELLED LIKE A DIFFERENT MAN.
I DIDN'T CARE. HE WAS BACK AND WE WERE IN LOVE. WELL.
I WAS.
THE WHOLE OF HIM THROBBED AND BUZZED AS I TOUCHED HIM.
I FELT TIME SLOW DOWN AND CURL BETWEEN US AND THEN I BLACKED OUT...
<SOUND OF SPACETIME COOLING AND SETTLING INTO A SHAPE AT BEST DESCRIBED AS A PERVERSE MOCKERY OF ITS FORMER QUINTESSENT SELF.>

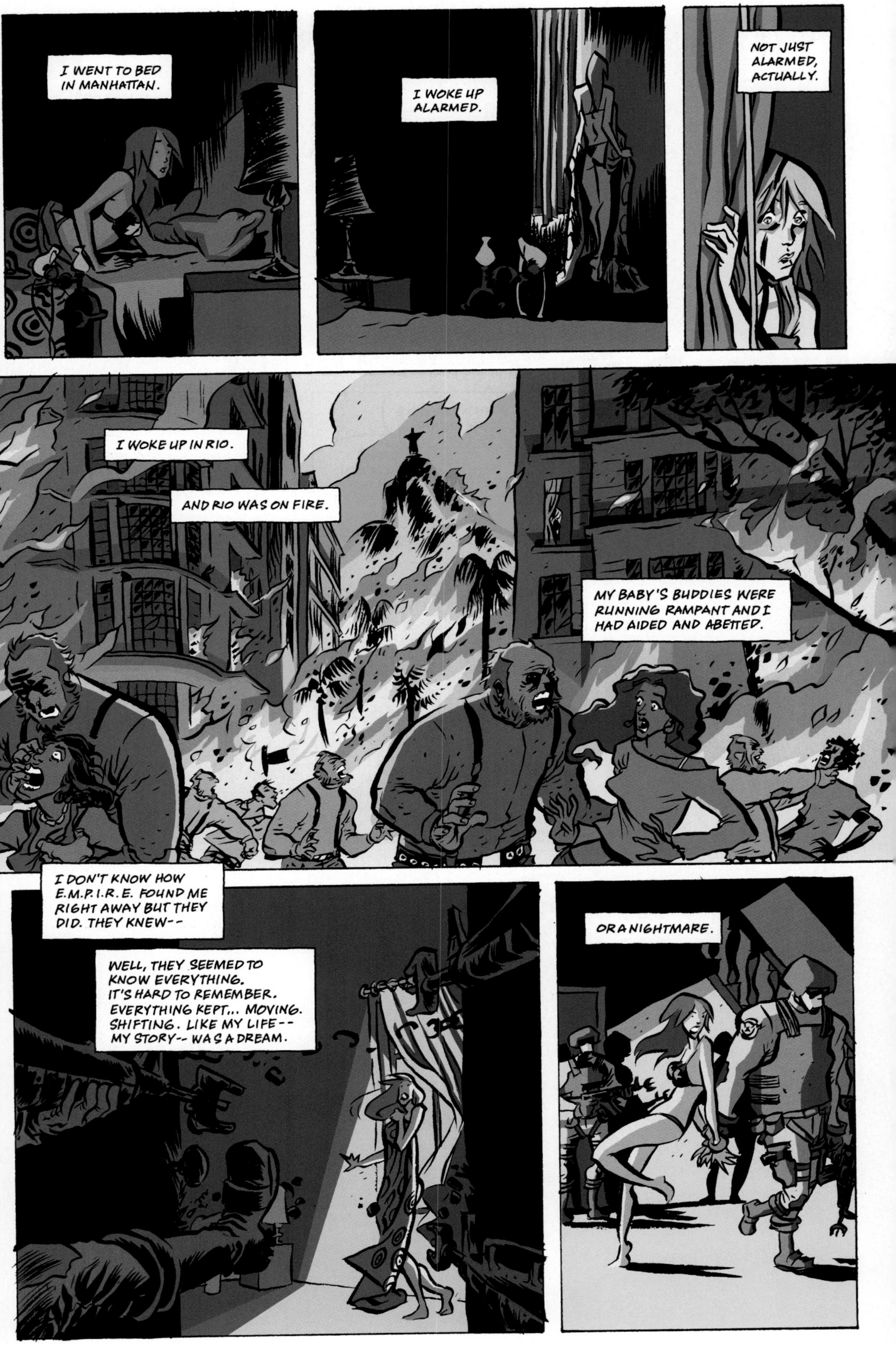
I WENT TO BED IN MANHATTAN.
I WOKE UP ALARMED.
NOT JUST ALARMED, ACTUALLY.
I WOKE UP IN RIO.
AND RIO WAS ON FIRE.
MY BABY'S BUDDIES WERE RUNNING RAMPANT AND I HAD AIDED AND ABETTED.
I DON'T KNOW HOW E.M.P.I.R.E. FOUND ME RIGHT AWAY BUT THEY DID. THEY KNEW--
WELL, THEY SEEMED TO KNOW EVERYTHING. IT'S HARD TO REMEMBER. EVERYTHING KEPT... MOVING. SHIFTING. LIKE MY LIFE-- MY STORY-- WAS A DREAM.
OR A NIGHTMARE.

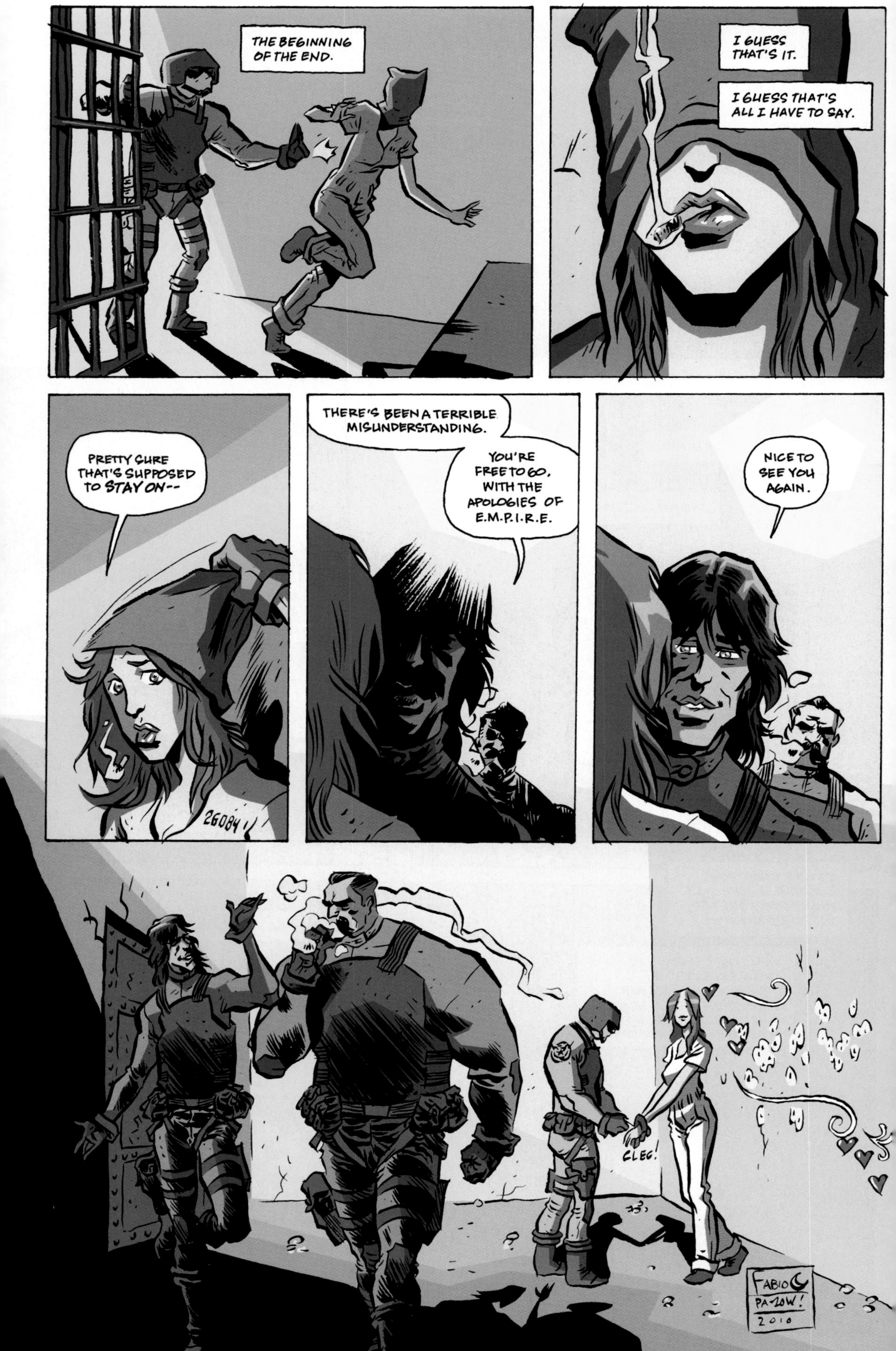
THE BEGINNING OF THE END.
I GUESS THAT'S IT.
I GUESS THAT'S ALL I HAVE TO SAY.
PRETTY SURE THAT'S SUPPOSED TO STAY ON--
26084
THERE'S BEEN A TERRIBLE MISUNDERSTANDING.
YOU'RE FREE TO GO, WITH THE APOLOGIES OF E.M.P.I.R.E.
NICE TO SEE YOU AGAIN.
CLEC!
FABIO PA-ZOW! 2010

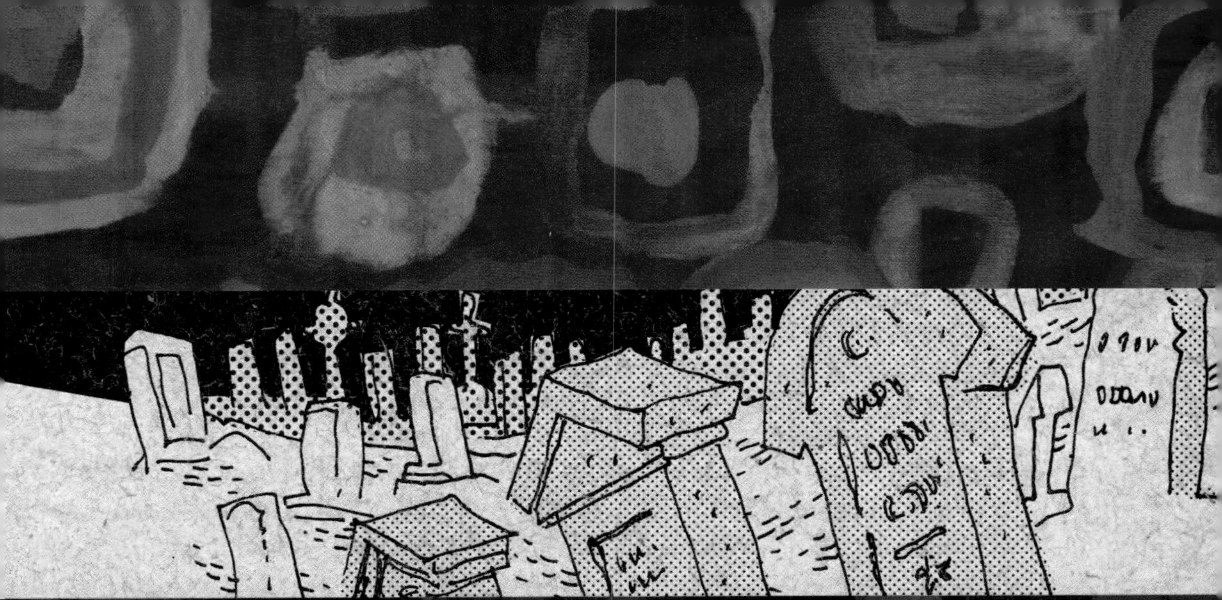

# IS THIS IT? (2:34)

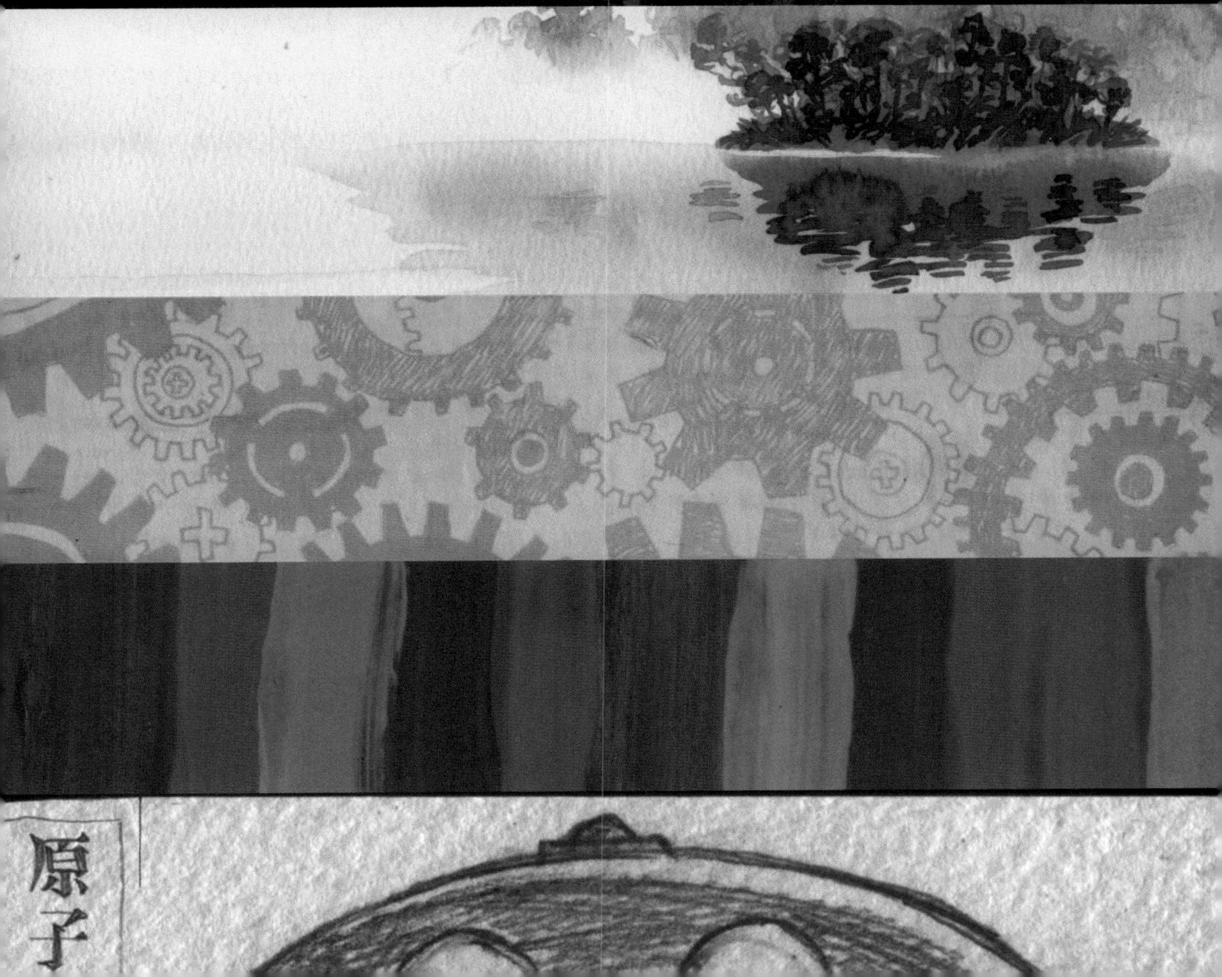
原子

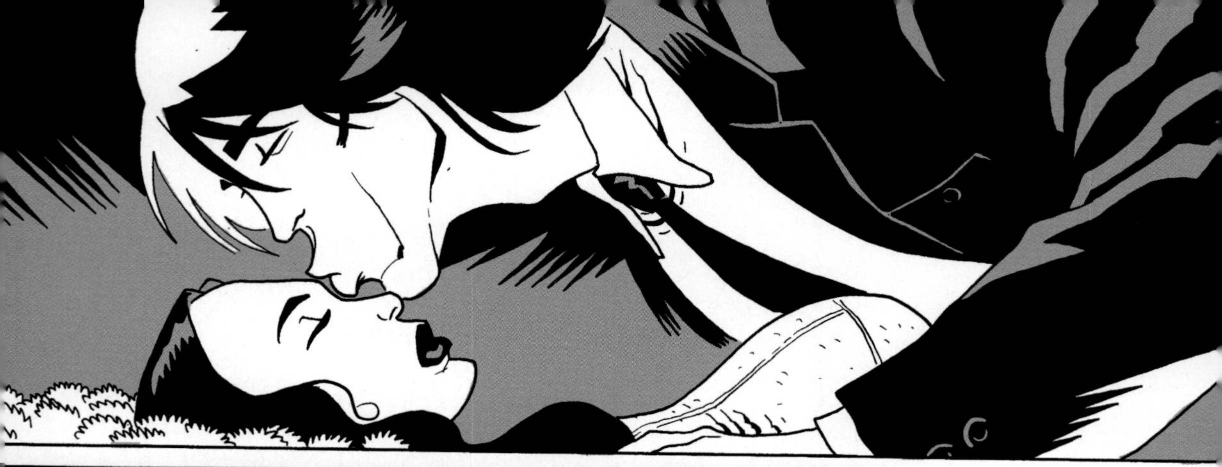

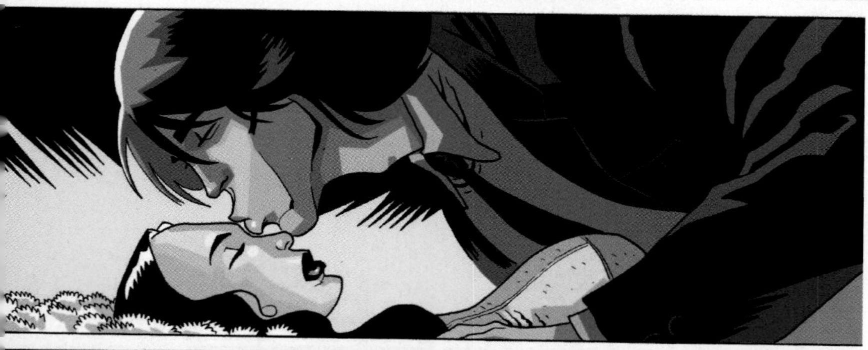

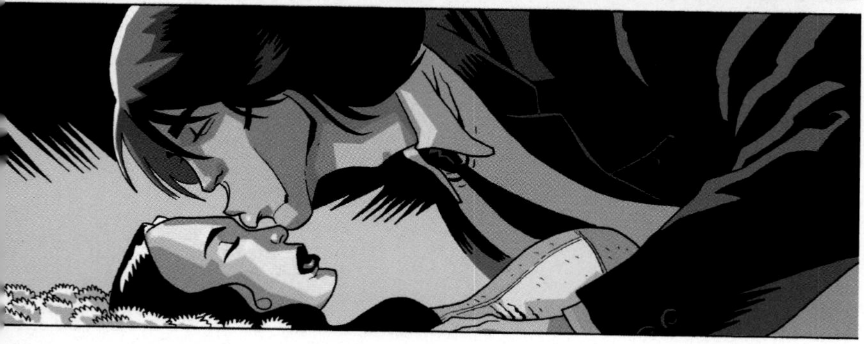

# COLORS

Three different stages of the colors on our book.

First we have the original black and green art.

Second is the first rendering Cris delivered.

Finally we have the final version, with the colors from the palette.

CASANOVA is a comic from another time. That's the whole concept behind its craziness and for all my artistic choices. When I first decided to make it black, white and green, it was a way to make it look like an old comic, with all the production and printing limitations of the past, things that would force creators to make artistic choices in order to achieve what they meant to. Personally, I love the black and green look.

When we decided now it was time to go full color, the concept behind the colors was still the same as before and that's what I had to explain to Cris.

We still want every story arc to have a dominant color and LUXURIA would still be green. That's all I told her before she sent me the first samples, just so we could see what she did right and what was wrong and which way we would go from there.

We are really old school when it comes to comic book art, so we like to make stuff by hand, work in black and white and, if need be, flat colors. Whatever goes outside these borders doesn't really fit with our art style, so we banned all the gradients, airbrushes and smooth, shining areas on the first batch of colors. I wanted it all flat, and of course it's harder to make everything flat, because you have to make decisions when to break one color with the other, how to combine these colors. A smooth transition is always easier, but we're making a comic book and we need all our creativity focused on the graphic aspect of the process.

After we established that, I took her samples and selected some colors she used, mixed some others and created the "CASANOVA PALETTE" for her to use. These 45 colors (and I still think it's too much) were all the colors she could use on the pages.

The last step of the process was choosing the combination of colors, how to use one or the other to enhance the mood of a scene, how to create more drama, how to help the story. Making the foreground pop up a little more, get the focus on the right point of the scene, make clear which panel is the most important one of the page, these kinds of things.

As with everything else about this comic, it's a very difficult process and it takes a lot of back and forth between us and Cris, but in the end it looks great. We are so happy with the results that sometimes we forget there was a time the comic was not in full color.

Gabriel Bá

# CASANOVA PALETTE

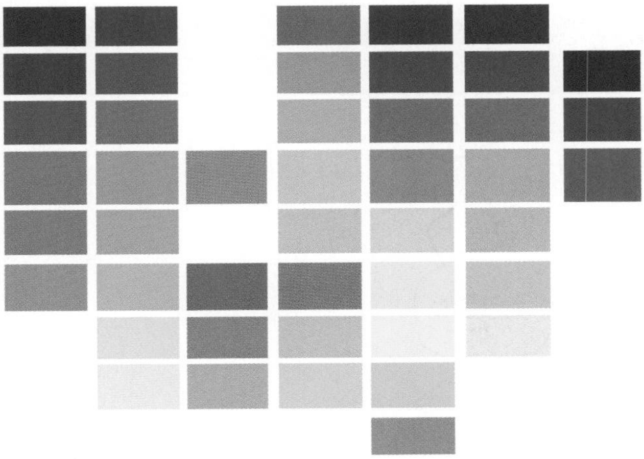

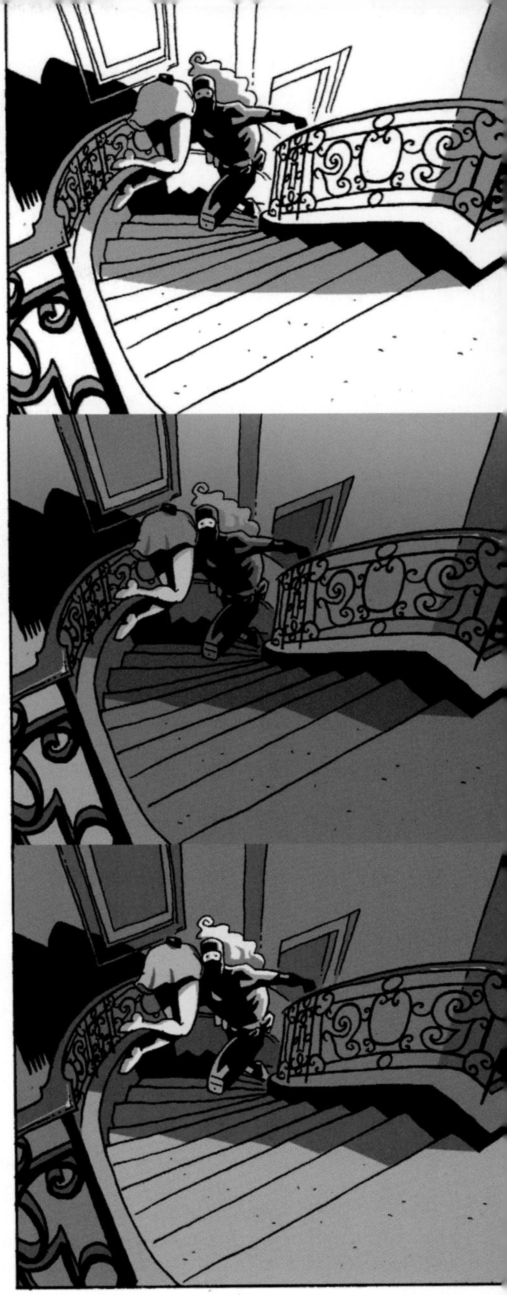

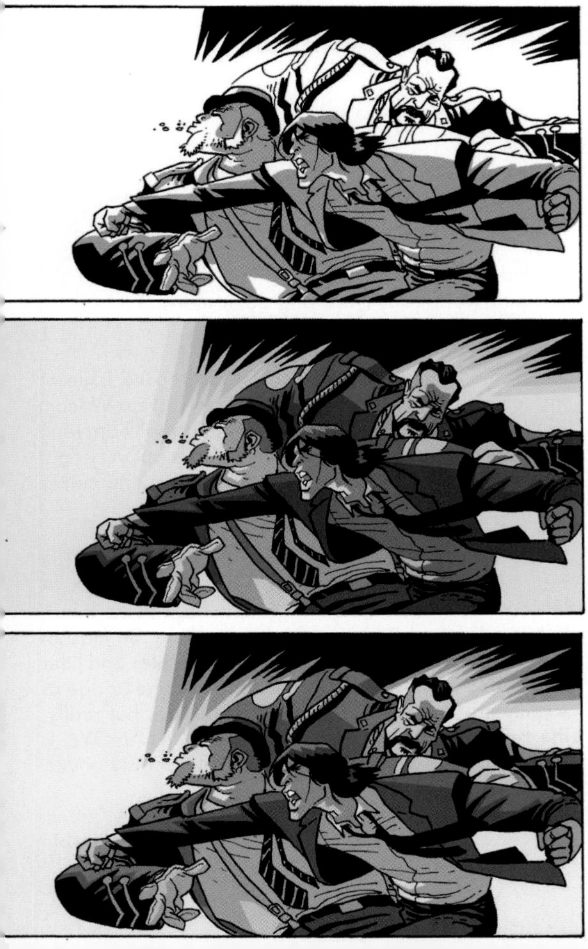

When you first start doing digital colors, you know that you have all the colors you can imagine to work with. After Gabriel set that 45-color palette, I was actually thrilled! It is this kind of thing that forces you to really use your head to color.

In this business, with the short deadlines and pressure, after a while a colorist can start doing combinations and rendering almost automatically, without really thinking about what you're doing to the storytelling, but challenges like these make you grow as a professional, make you start thinking about doing the best work you can, to be a part of an awesome project.

Working with CASANOVA it's been a real learning experience, it made me remember why I got into coloring comics in the first place.

Cris Peter

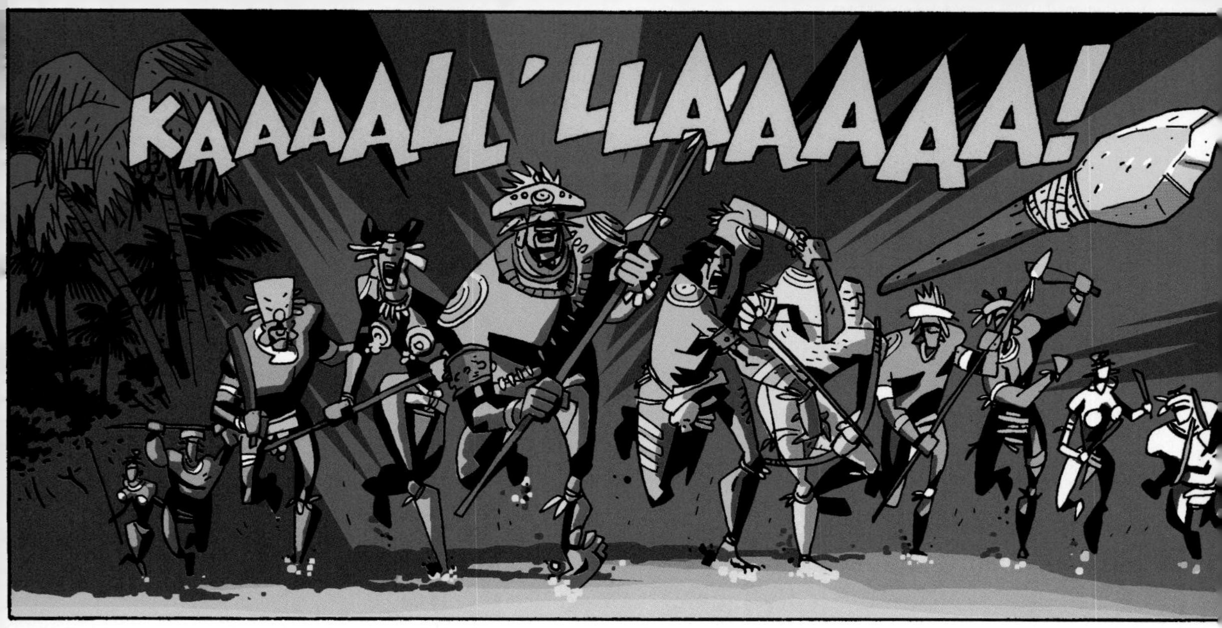
KAAAALL'LLAAAAAA!

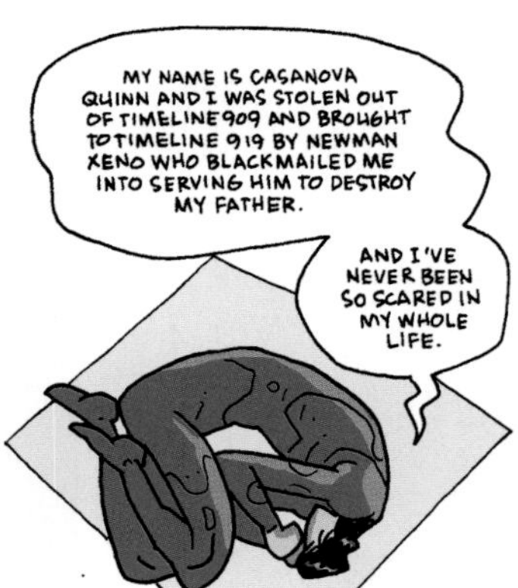
MY NAME IS CASANOVA QUINN AND I WAS STOLEN OUT OF TIMELINE 909 AND BROUGHT TO TIMELINE 919 BY NEWMAN XENO WHO BLACKMAILED ME INTO SERVING HIM TO DESTROY MY FATHER.
AND I'VE NEVER BEEN SO SCARED IN MY WHOLE LIFE.

# LETTERS

Hand-lettering is kind of a weird animal in the digital age. I could go on for days about it, and argue both sides of a digital-vs-analog discussion with passion and zeal. At the end of the day hand-lettering and computer-lettering are just different *tools*, the application is always in the hands of the artist. But real honest-to-gosh hand-lettering has a certain feel to it that can be hard to replace with a font. In my case, that "feel" is comprised of sloppiness, blobby inscrutability, and typos.

But since I started working on CASANOVA I've been refining my process, trying to get faster-- oh boy, lettering by hand is a time consumer of Galactus-ian (comic book reference) proportions-- by using a mishmash of analog and digital tools. By the time I was lettering CASANOVA #4, I was penciling the letters on legal size pieces of bristol board. I'd print the art, blown up by about 115%, in black and white, then use a lightbox to plan the balloons out: where they'll go, how many/how long the lines will be, where their little tails will point. I'd pre-print the boards with very light gray guidelines on my trusty b&w laserjet printer, so I could just move any old where to stick a balloon.

Once I fill up the board with infinitesimal pencil marks, usually about 8 comics pages' worth per board, depending on the script, I shut down the retina-scalding lightbox and ink everything up with Rapidograph pens. I work REALLY small-- I think the blown-up letters are still smaller than most sane people's handwriting-- so the Rapidographs help me keep everything consistent. Then everything gets scanned in to the computer, fiddled with, corrected, and sharpened up, and the pasteup work begins, moving each individual balloon into place over Cris's gorgeous colors.

As of this writing, I'm working on the second issue of the sextastic GULA story-arc, and now I have a Wacom Cintiq tablet as part of my process. I'm actually drawing the letters right on the screen, then I print out very light bluelines and ink those. Saves a ton of time and makes the planning a lot easier.

If all this sounds super-boring, don't worry, it *is*! The real calling of the letterer is to be mostly invisible. A letterer is like a bass player-- great to have in the band, but you don't want him soloing or anything. So most of this stuff is just the web of supports and cables and litter and hobos under a really gorgeous awesome bridge or something. You can check it out if you like, but really, the bridge is the cool part. Although CASANOVA is like the most sexiest, righteousest bridge to work under, let me tell you.

Dustin Harbin

On the right, a page filled with Dustin's letters and balloons, a crazy mash of shapes, words, sounds on a maze only he can get his way around. It's actually really organized visually.

On the top, a close up on some balloons and sound effects that will go on the finalized colored panel right above this text.

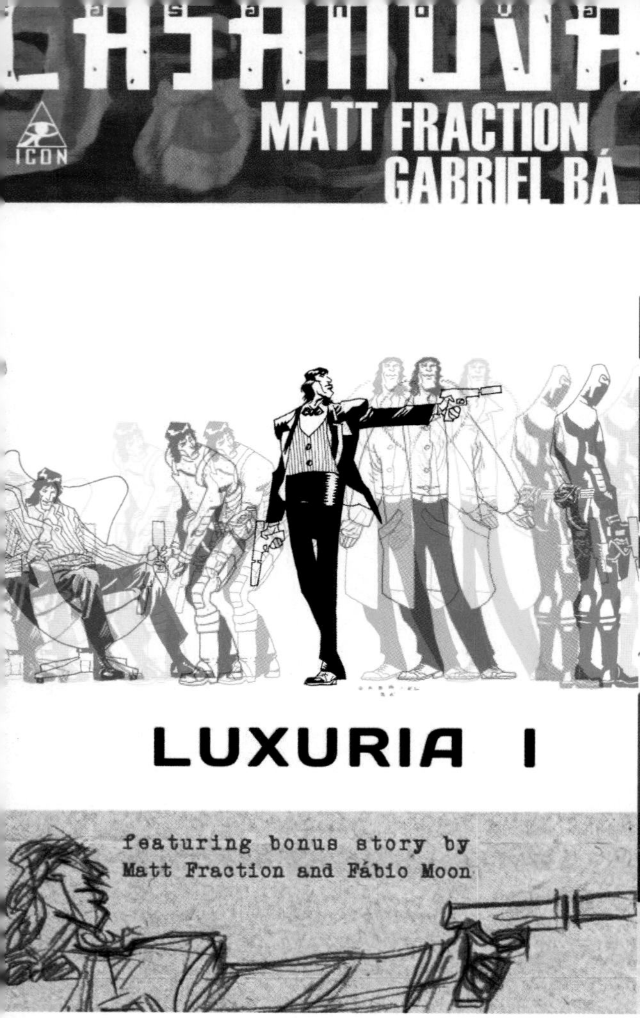
CASANOVA
ICON
MATT FRACTION
GABRIEL BÁ
LUXURIA I
featuring bonus story by
Matt Fraction and Fábio Moon

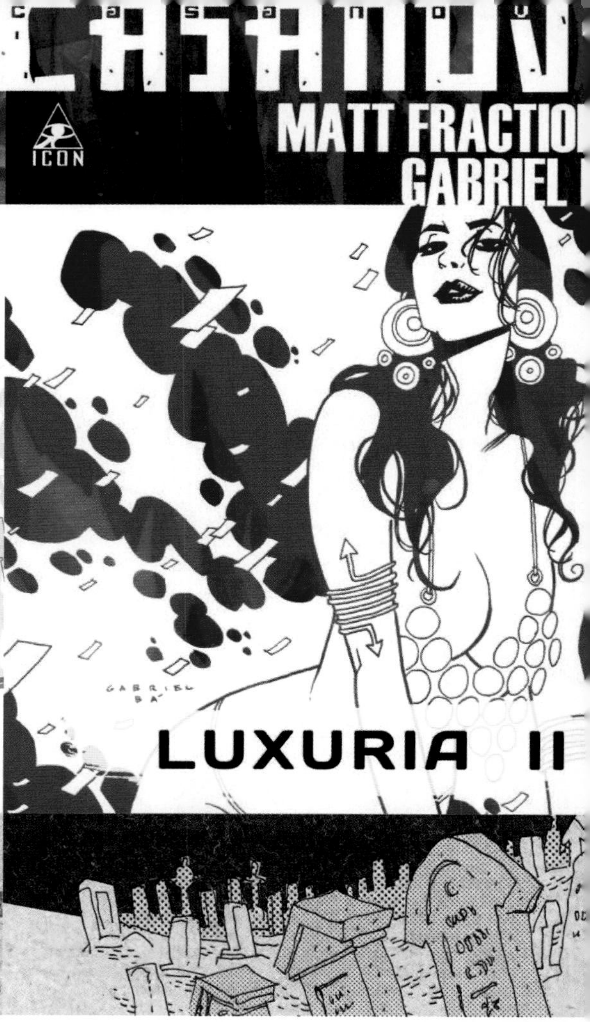
ICON
MATT FRACTIO
LUXURIA II

One of the worst things about making a cover is that it is NOT a comic book page. It has no panels, no storytelling, it's one single image (usually) telling something about the book. Well, one of the best things about making a cover is that it is NOT a comic book page. Actually, when I'm working on a cover, I try to forget about comics entirely. I think about movie posters, fine arts, photography and everything else that is graphic and awesome. Because that's what I want for the covers of CASANOVA: graphic awesomeness! Nothing inside this book is like any other book on the stands, so the covers need to be as unique as the story, as psychedelic as Matt's writing. One thing I learned working on this book is that it has no boundaries, no limits. So why should I restrain the covers?

I really like covers with stripes, different sets of images. They remind me of old pulp magazines or movie posters and I always go back to the "stripe formula" when I start thinking about covers. I also really like to create a set of covers that will work together as a group, that will have a unity, a template so when you put all of them together, you see they belong together. Whenever I work with covers, I try to establish rules or

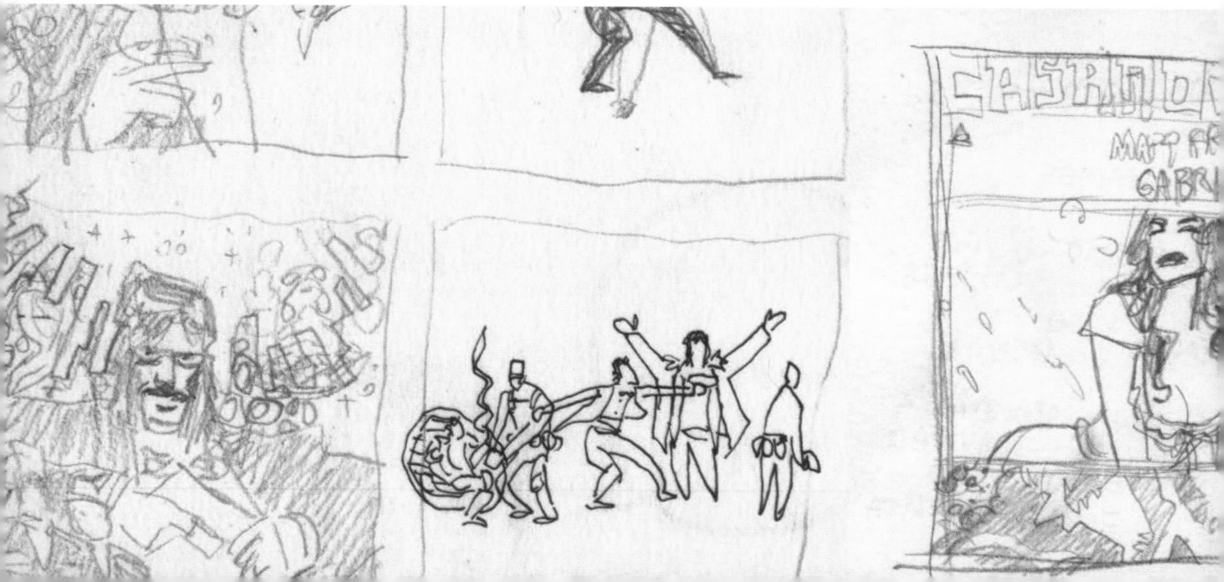

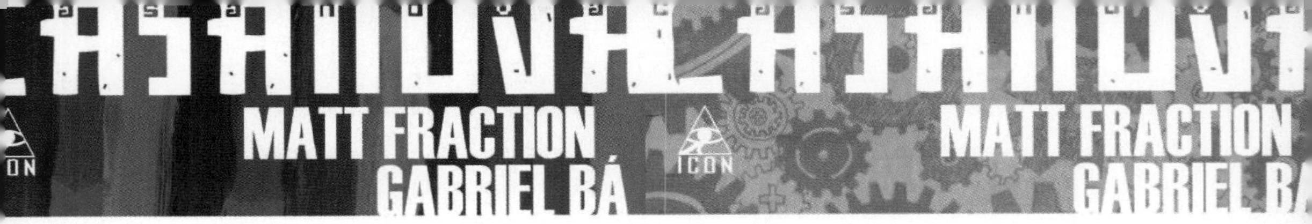
MATT FRACTION
GABRIEL BÁ
ICON
MATT FRACTION

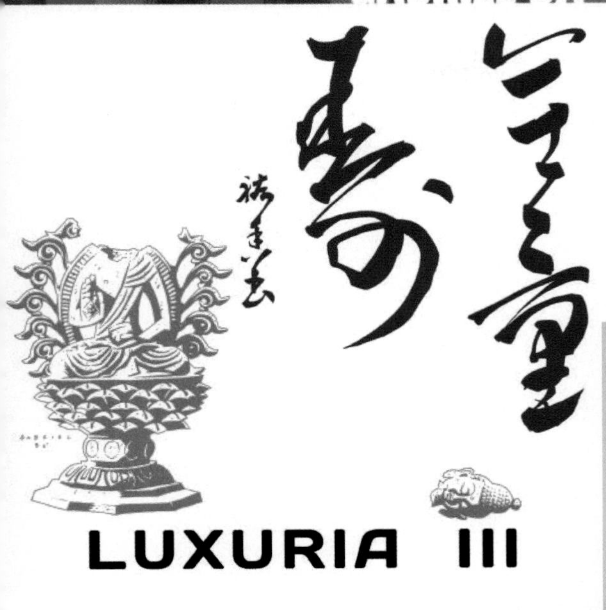
LUXURIA III

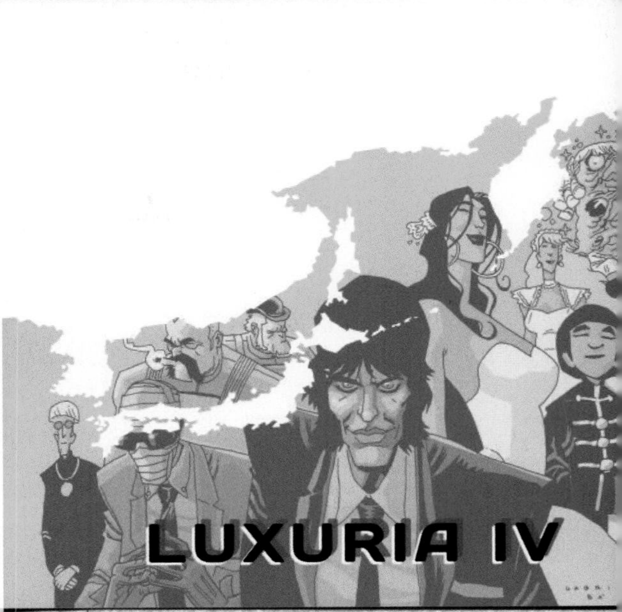
LUXURIA IV

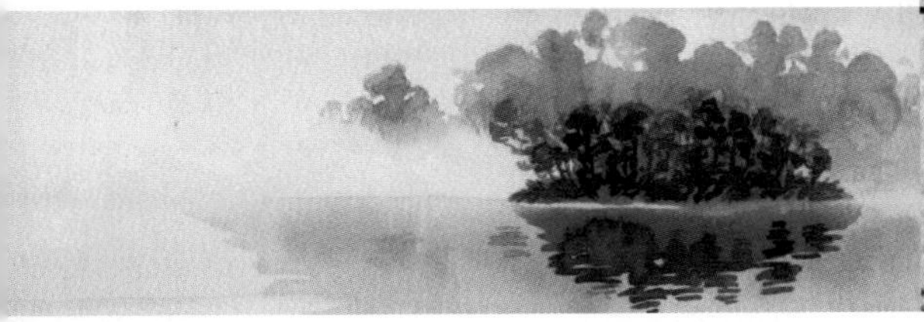

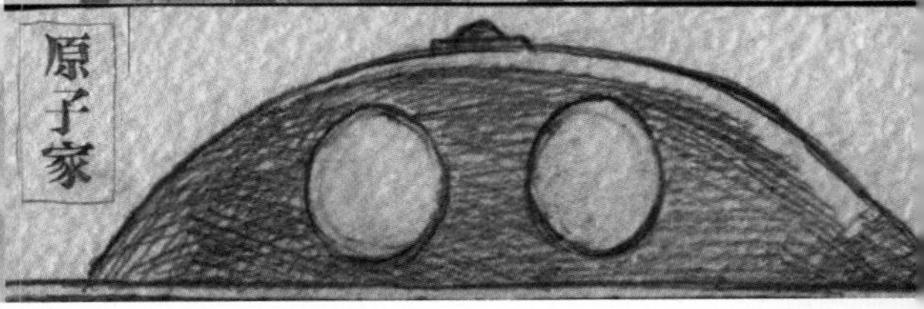
原子家

set parameters to guide my work. This time, I tried to create a pattern that would also allow me to work on a vast range of techniques and use different renderings on our covers.

People usually think covers that follow patterns will become boring over time and that was my challenge for the covers of LUXURIA.

Gabriel Bá

PS: My new challenge is to make the covers of my next arc look better than the ones Fábio is doing for GULA.

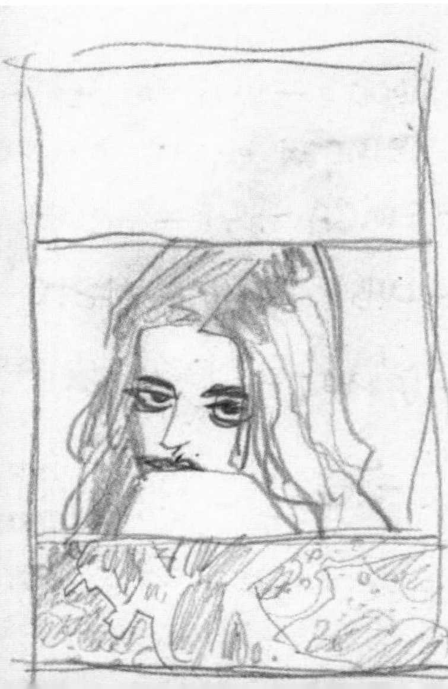

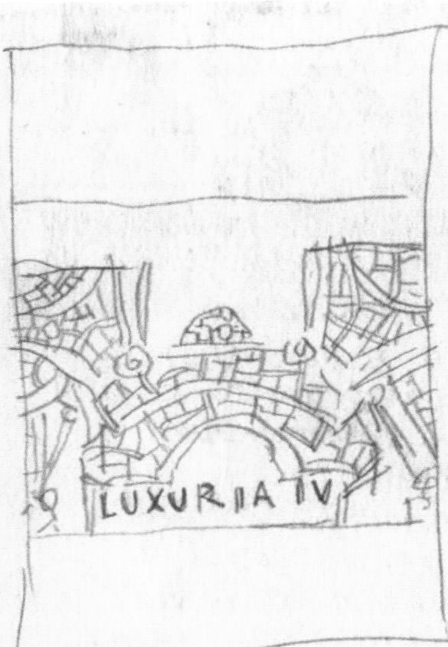
LUXURIA IV

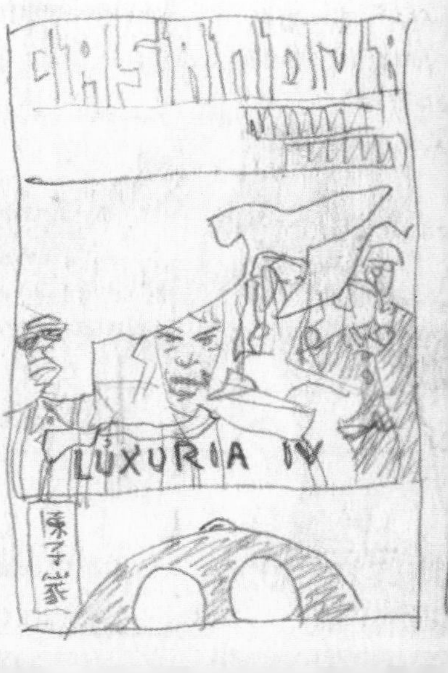
LUXURIA IV

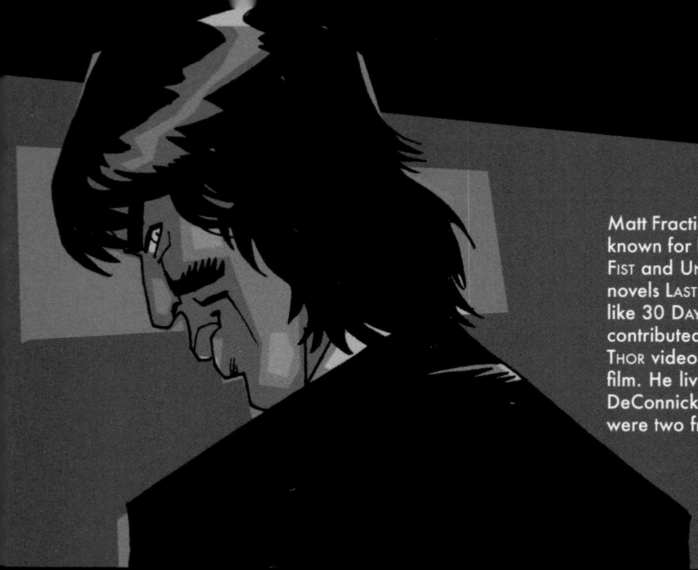

Matt Fraction is an Eisner Award-winning American comic book writer, known for his work on The Invincible Iron Man, Thor, The Immortal Iron Fist and Uncanny X-Men for Marvel Comics. He's written the graphic novels Last of the Independents and The Five Fists of Science, and comics like 30 Days of Night: Bloodsucker Tales and The Order. He's recently contributed to the storylines and dialogue of both the Iron Man 2 and Thor video games for Sega, and was a consultant on the Iron Man 2 film. He lives in Portland, Oregon, with his wife, the writer Kelly Sue DeConnick, and his two children, two dogs, two cats, and frog. There were two frogs but one died.

Gabriel Bá was born in a whole different dimension called São Paulo, Brazil, where he lives until this day. In fact he has an evil twin brother, Fábio Moon, his partner in crime on most of his comics endeavours. He's won awards for both his indie comics and mainstream projects and his work has been published in France, Italy, Spain, Greece, Japan and Germany, as well as in the U.S. and Brazil.

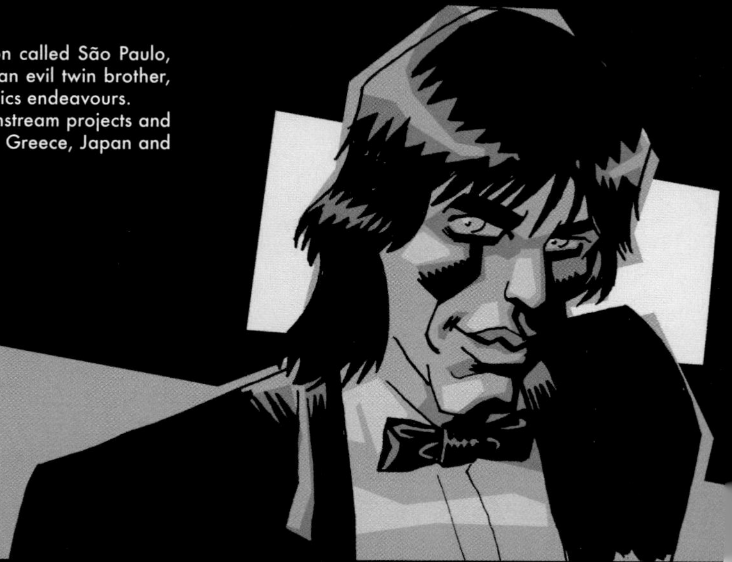

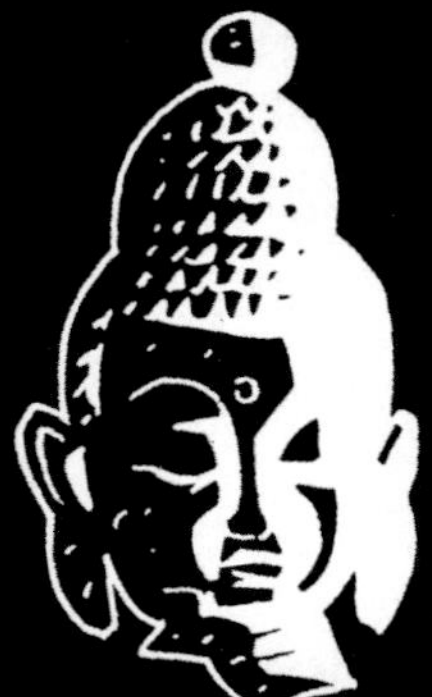

PA-ZOW!